Corporate Governance in Africa

Kerry E. Howell • M. Karim Sorour
Editors

Corporate Governance in Africa

Assessing Implementation and Ethical Perspectives

palgrave
macmillan

Editors
Kerry E. Howell
Plymouth Business School
Plymouth University
Plymouth, United Kingdom

M. Karim Sorour
Newcastle Business School
Northumbria University
Newcastle Upon Tyne, United Kingdom

ISBN 978-1-137-56699-7   ISBN 978-1-137-56700-0 (eBook)
DOI 10.1057/978-1-137-56700-0

Library of Congress Control Number: 2016947271

Printed on acid-free paper

This Palgrave Macmillan imprint is published by Springer Nature
The registered company is Macmillan Publishers Ltd. London

To my partner, Samantha
Kerry E. Howell

To my wife, Mahinour
M. Karim Sorour

Preface

The rationale for developing this project emerged following ten years of research in corporate governance, and specifically cases of corporate governance on the African continent. Deriving specifically from the supervision of a number of PhDs in cases regarding corporate governance in Africa, each of the chapters develops phenomenological studies through critical theory or constructivist perspectives using distinct methodological approaches. General understandings of corporate governance are developed, and ethics and in certain instances related these notions to a specific case or country on the African continent. Two chapters (the ones on Kenya and South Africa) are not based on a PhD, but both provide an ethical perspective regarding corporate governance issues. Chapters 1–3 develop ethical ideas and their relationship with corporate governance, as well as theoretical frameworks concerning shareholdership and stakeholdership. Each of the following chapters uses case studies to help identify relationships between the universal in terms of a global or an occidental perspective regarding corporate governance ethics and codes of conduct in relation to relativist perspectives in the individual states. Through specific case studies, this text provides an opportunity to identify corporate governance and ethical issues in Africa. Indeed, relationships between universal determinants or directives from the international community and relativist local cultural perspectives are assessed. Furthermore, issues regarding globalisation as imposition and the necessity for developing countries to adhere to external governance mechanisms are introduced and analysed. Case studies illustrate what may be considered necessary transformations within specific states if governance procedures are to be transparent and ethical so as to facilitate trust, confidence and inward investment. Good corporate governance can contribute to sustainable economic success as well as enhance credibility and corporate responsibility. Good corporate governance practices may also deter unethical practices that undermine African capability and credibility in the international domain.

The objective of this text is to provide a rigorous, valid and trustworthy study that enables an understanding of experiences regarding what is occurring in each specific context as well as provide some comparison. Each study is qualitative, and transferability rather than generalisation is the main rationale for determining relations between individual African experiences. Obviously, the chapters in the volume do not offer the full findings that can be found in the relevant PhD theses but, rather, attempt to provide a flavour of their essence and act as introductions to each of the larger studies that have been undertaken.

Kerry E. Howell
Newcastle upon Tyne, UK

Contents

1 **Introduction: Notions of Governance, Social Contracts and Ethical Perspectives** 1
Kerry E. Howell

2 **Paradigm of Inquiry: Critical Theory and Constructivism** 29
Kerry E. Howell

3 **Ethical Perspectives on Corporate Governance** 47
Tony Ikechukwu Nwanji

4 **On the Evolution of Corporate Governance Culture in Africa: The Case of the Egyptian Banking Sector** 69
M. Karim Sorour and Ahmed El Sakhawy

5 **Ethical Dimensions of Corporate Governance Practice in Ghana: Developing a Theoretical Perspective** 97
Mark Boadu

6 **Corporate Governance in Nigeria** 131
Umar Abbas Ibrahim

7 **An Examination and Analysis of Bank Corporate Governance Regulation in The Gambia: A Grounded Theory Approach** 159
Sainey Faye

8 **The King Reports on Corporate Governance in South Africa: An *Ubuntu* African Philosophy Analysis** 199
Zenzo L. Dube

9 **The Corporate Governance of the Kenyan Public Sector** 223
D.G. Barako and A.M. Brown

10 **Conclusions** 249
Kerry E. Howell

Index 259

Notes on Contributors

Dulacha Barako is Associate Professor and Head of Academic Division at the Kenya School of Monetary Studies (Central Bank of Kenya). He is a member of the Institute of Public Accountants Australia. He has published several research papers in internationally referred journals.

Mark Boadu holds a PhD in Corporate Governance from Plymouth University, UK, and a Doctoral Fellowship Award from the Institute of Professional Financial Managers, UK. Mark has an MA in Public Administration from the University of Ghana. He is a lecturer in the Department of Management Studies, College of Technology Education, Kumasi University of Education, Winneba - Ghana and lectures in business ethics and corporate social responsibility, public administration, governance and leadership. His research interests are in corporate governance, business ethics and corporate social responsibility and grounded theory research.

Alistair Brown is based at Curtin University, Australia, where he assists with accounting research proposals and theory, and is a member of several professional accounting bodies. He contributes to a number of undergraduate tutorials and regularly acts as an *ad hoc* reviewer for refereed academic journals.

Zenzo L. Dube is a research fellow at the National University of Science and Technology (NUST-IDS) in Zimbabwe. He holds a PhD in Organisational Dynamics (The London Stock Exchange: A New Institutionalist Analysis) from the University of South Wales, United Kingdom. His main publications concern the financial, historical and institutional aspects of the London Stock Exchange, UK markets and corporate governance. Publications include 'Assessing Corporate Governance and the London Stock Exchange: A Historical Analysis'. Corporate Governance and Institutions: A Pan-European Perspective (Ed by Kowalski T and Letza S); Dube Z and Kerry E, 'Assessing Corporate Governance And The London Stock Exchange: A New Institutionalism Analysis' International Journal of Applied Finance For Non-Financial Managers Volume 1); Dube Z, 'The Recent World Recession: A Déjà vu of the South Sea's Turbulent History' in 'The Subprime Crisis and its Impact on Financial and Managerial Environment: An Unequal Repercussion at European Level'. Zenzo is a member of the South African Institute of Financial Markets (SAIFM) and the Institute of Chartered Secretaries and Administrators (ICSAZ). He is currently the country chair (Zimbabwe) and Conference Committee Member for the Global Business and Technology Association (GBATA).

Ahmed El-Sakhawy holds a Bachelor of Commerce in accounting (English section) from Alexandria University, Egypt and is currently a researcher in the Economic and Managerial Studies Department (MRCC) of Arab Academy for Science, Technology and Maritime Transport. Ahmed is also the assistant managing editor of the *Maritime Scientific Research Journal*, edited by the MRCC. His professional interests focus on feasibility studies preparation, teaching accounting and financial management; his research interests include corporate governance and corporate social responsibility. Ahmed holds a MSc in accounting and finance from Alexandria University, Egypt, and is also a Certified Management Accountant (CMA) from Institute of Management Accountants (USA).

Sainey Faye is a senior lecturer and BSc Course Leader in Accounting and Finance at Buckinghamshire Business School, Buckinghamshire

New University, UK. He graduated from the Business Administration programme at the University of Wales in 2004. He received his MSc in Banking and Finance from Cass Business School (City University, London, UK) in 2005. In 2014, he completed his PhD in corporate governance. He is a fellow with the Higher Education Academy. His research interests include finance, banking and corporate governance, and he has consulted for a number of companies on finance and governance.

Kerry E. Howell holds the Chair of Governance at the Plymouth University Graduate School of Management. Through his studies, Howell has generated scholarly expertise in areas relating to governance, ethics and methodology, and written research texts with Nova Science Press, Palgrave Macmillan and Sage. Howell has produced numerous refereed journal articles and managed funded research projects for various public and private sector institutions. He is currently Chair of the Public Administration Committee (PAC), member of the Joint University Committee (JUC) and British Academy of Management (BAM) Research Committee. Howell is also a Jean Monnet Associate and has acted as chair of the practitioner committee for the University Association for Contemporary European Studies (UACES). Howell teaches corporate governance and ethics, philosophy of research, and methodology. He is also programme leader for the Graduate School of Management Professional Doctorate Programme and Post Graduate Certificate in Research Methodology.

Umar Abbas Ibrahim holds a PhD in Business and Management and a Post Graduate Certificate in Research Methodology from the University of Plymouth, UK. He has an MBA (Finance) from the University of Wales, UK and an MSc in Urban Land Appraisal from the University of Reading, UK. He recently retired from the services of the Federal Capital Development Authority (FCDA) as Director of Special Duties. Currently, he is a Management Consultant based in Abuja. His research interests are in Corporate Governance, Leadership, Business Strategy and Grounded Theory.

M. Karim Sorour is Senior Lecturer in Accounting and Financial Management and the PhD programme leader at the Faculty of Business and Law, Northumbria University, UK. He has more than thirteen years' experience in the fields of consultancy, research and executive training. His research interests include corporate governance, corporate social responsibility and management accounting, with an emphasis on developing countries. Karim holds a PhD in Corporate Governance from the University of Plymouth. He is a member of the Risk, Responsibility, Ethics and Governance Research Interest group at Newcastle Business School and a certified member of the Institute of Management Accountants (USA). Karim is an editor of *Cogent Business and Management Journal* and a steering committee member of the BAFA - Accounting & Finance in Emerging Economies (AFEE) research interest group.

Tony Ike Nwanji is Associate Professor of Accounting and Dean of the College of Business and Social Sciences at Landmark University, Nigeria. Before joining Landmark, Nwanji spent a year as Visiting Professor of Accounting at Covenant University and Associate Professor in Corporate Governance, as well as Senior Lecturer in Accounting and Finance at numerous universities and colleges in the UK. He was educated in the UK and holds a PhD in Corporate Governance and Business Ethics; Nwanji's research interests include corporate governance, business ethics, corporate social responsibility and transformational leadership.

List of Figures

Fig. 4.1	Bank compliance level for various disclosure requirements	90
Fig. 6.1	The development of corporate governance for banks in Nigeria	139
Fig. 6.2	A model integrating the core categories with the subcategories	146
Fig. 7.1	The human factor model	184

List of Tables

Table 4.1	Corporate governance disclosures made by banks in Egypt	90
Table 6.1	Summary of open categories and their properties	144
Table 7.1	Share of GDP and work force per sector in The Gambia	162
Table 7.2	Employment by size of organisation	162
Table 7.3	Key points in the ADB profile of Gambian governance	167
Table 7.4	Legislation affecting corporate governance and regulation	170
Table 7.5	Proposed ethical values and principles and expected behaviour	180
Table 9.1	Summary of events surrounding the emergence of ICPAK	230
Table 9.2	Kenya's ministries and departments	233
Table 9.3	County governments of Kenya	235
Table 9.4	Audit Opinions by OAGK	236

1

Introduction: Notions of Governance, Social Contracts and Ethical Perspectives

Kerry E. Howell

Introduction

This text provides an original opportunity to identify and assess implementation and ethical issues relating to corporate governance in Africa. Through specific case studies regarding corporate governance in individual African states and relationships with generic determinants, advice and direction from the international community, this text provides an ethical assessment of issues regarding globalization as an imposition and the necessity of developing countries to adhere to external governance mechanisms. In addition, through the case studies the text will illustrate what may be considered necessary transformations within specific states if governance procedures are to be transparent and ethical so as to facilitate trust, confidence and inward investment. There is recognition that corporate governance contributes to sustainable economic success as well as enhanced credibility and corporate responsibility (Armstrong 2003); each a necessary variable when attracting funding from both regional and foreign investors. 'Good' corporate governance practices are also perceived as

K.E. Howell (✉)
Graduate School of Management, Plymouth University, Plymouth, UK

K.E. Howell, M.K. Sorour (eds.), *Corporate Governance in Africa*,
DOI 10.1057/978-1-137-56700-0_1

means of deterring unethical and corrupt practices which may undermine African capability and credibility in the international domain. 'Good' corporate governance may also ensure market discipline and transparency (Armstrong 2003). Indeed, 'standardization of corporate governance … across many different countries may … seem like a sound approach' (Letza 2015, p. 191). However, because of cultural and historical differences such an approach has largely been resisted. That said, it is not unusual for developing and 'transition economies to adopt with little modification the established codes and regulations of developed countries' (ibid). Indeed, local cultures and traditions exist in individual countries and this text identifies relationships between universal and relativist perspectives of corporate governance in Africa. In addition, rationales for acting through self-interest (egoism) and/or the common interest (altruism) underpin the ways agents behave when dealing with moral dilemmas and regulation.

In this study a number of different countries are assessed and analysed through specific paradigms of inquiry and methodological approaches. Critical theory and constructivism provide paradigms of inquiry, leading to research programmes that challenge universal perspectives of corporate governance in relation to the needs of separate states and the contradictions that arise when local cultures are not taken into consideration. Phenomenological and qualitative research enables understanding of specific environments and situations through identifying human activity and agency. Indeed such research allows transferability of findings through the amalgamation of similarities and difference in relation to each of the African states analysed. All of the countries identified in the study have been influenced by colonization which has impacted on cultural attitudes and evolving business environments. Fligstein and Choo (2005) argued that corporate governance involved a reflection of political and socio-economic upheavals and struggles in a given environment rather than efficiency and agency relations between stakeholders and boards.

Africa consists of 53 countries and can roughly be divided into three areas which include the 'Arab-speaking countries in North Africa (the Maghreb zone), the French-speaking countries of central and western Africa (the Franc or Francophone zone), and the English-speaking countries of southern, eastern, and western Africa (the commonwealth states or Anglophone zone)' (Roussouw 2005, p. 95). Roussouw (2005) provides an overview of African reports regarding corporate governance and a number of PhDs have dealt with specific African states (Sorour 2011; Boadu 2013; Ibrahim 2013; Faye 2014) as well as ethics and corporate governance (Howell and Letza 2000; Nwanji 2006). Chapter 2 concentrates on the paradigm of inquiries (constructivism and critical theory) that underpin the methodologies utilized by the case studies identified in this text. Chapter 3 deals with the notion of corporate governance in a universal context and identifies how ethical perspectives and theoretical frameworks inform practice.

The rest of this chapter discusses the notion of governance and how this is developed through contractual arrangements between individuals and states. Through a discussion of the social contract the necessary underpinnings of ethical perspectives for different governance procedures can be identified. To give a full comprehension of corporate governance this text provides a discussion of governance in general and illustrates how corporate governance as a framework of rules and regulations incorporates a social construction. The text also outlines the relationships between levels of governance relating to global, regional and national activities as well as how corporate governance is embedded in the difficulties and dichotomies that arise between these dimensions. This assessment provides the basis for our understanding of ethics and individual behaviour in both universal and relativist contexts. Notions of 'good' governance based on different ethical perspectives are also identified and explored. Aristotle contended that the 'good' state and the 'good' individual could be created through education and rational thought. Ultimate good involved the individual and the state pursuing virtue through the golden mean. Political science should ensure that the right things are taught in the state to allow the individual the opportunity to distinguish the golden mean and become a rational thinking entity, i.e. to find the self (Aristotle 2001). Plato (1997) identified education, understanding and thought as the only means of attaining the 'good' state. Power remains exclusively in the hands of those that are properly capable of wielding it; these were the philosopher kings who would rule by superior virtue and rationale. 'Good' can be considered 'as being such as to satisfy the requirements or interests of the wants of the kind in question' (Brown 1986, p. 132). However, this indicates that no substantive or objective universal moral position exists when identifying what can be termed good. For some notion of 'good' governance to exist some form of external standards are required; consequently, some structure with identified rules and regulations is necessary (ibid). Bourdieu argued that 'if one admits that the subject emerges in the tension between the individual and the universality, then it is obvious that the individual needs a mediation, and thereby an authority, in order to progress on this path' (cited in Zizek 2014, p. 183). Some form of authority is required to provide notions of good governance and the rules and regulations premised on these conceptualisations and interpretations.

Developing Notions of Governance: Social Contracts

Governance is a nebulous term and may be used to identify and describe patterns of rules and regulations that emerge when a nation-state depends on other institutions to provide control, direction and consistency. At the international and European or transnational level global and regional governance refers to the patterns of rules and regulations that provide guidance and assistance for nation-states. In addition, 'corporate governance refers to patterns of rules within businesses—that is, to the systems, institutions and norms by which corporations are directed and controlled' (Bevir 2009, p. 3). In a general context governance involves the development of social structures and co-ordination of these structures through contract, consensus and obligation. Governance involves individual behaviour in terms of levels of participation in developing and administrating procedures. 'Governance … means creating an effective political framework conducive to private economic action—stable regimes, the rule of law, efficient state administration adapted to the roles that governments can actually perform, and a strong civil society independent of the state' (Hirst 2006, p. 14). Political frameworks have historically relied on nation-states implementing top-down procedures with limited reference to international, regional, local and/or community based governance. However, in the modern world, governance is required at the international level or beyond national boundaries, e.g. regulation of world trade, financial markets and accounting procedures. Linked closely to these areas is the concept of corporate governance which is 'a watchword (for) those who wish to improve the accountability and transparency of the actions of management' (ibid, p. 17). Multiple levels and ideas of governance reflect a shift beyond the notion of sovereign nation-states as the main disseminators of rules and regulations. Through notions of the social contract or civil constitution the development of political communities became structures that defined decisions and political affairs and through these political communities the notion of governance expanded to numerous levels and domains. In general, the idea of the social contract has been used to 'explain and defend the state' as an immutable sovereign institution and expected residual of political power (Hampton 1998, p. 380). However, constructivist perspectives also identify the social contract as underpinning notions of governance but argue that 'authoritative political societies are human creations' (Hampton 1998, p. 382). Governance is linked with leadership and ethics as it identifies the relationship between the individual and the community (the governance of society is shaped by contractual arrangements at multiple levels).

There is a clear relationship between governance, morality and the social contract as well as ethical perspectives relating to human existence and social development. 'Philosophers such as … Hobbes, Locke, Rousseau and Kant have argued that human beings would find life in a state of nature … so difficult that they would agree (either with one another or prospective ruler) to the creation of political institutions that they believe would improve their lot' (Hampton 1998, p. 380). This would necessitate a contractual agreement that required individuals to 'join others in acting in ways that each, together with others, can reasonably and freely subscribe to as a moral common standard' (Diggs 1982, p. 104).

In a state of nature social restraints are removed and all are continually open to a violation of person and possessions. As Hobbes famously indicated, in a state of nature human existence would be 'solitary, poore, nasty, brutish and short' (Hobbes 1651/1990, p. 62). However, it may be correct 'that a society of perfectly consistent prudent egoists would invent institutions for mutual insurance' but this does not mean that morality arises from 'calculated self-interest' alone (Midgley 1993b, p. 4). Other human qualities exist which arise directly in relation to the claims of others and people act through altruistic notions such as a sense of 'justice', 'friendship', 'compassion' and 'generosity'. Such qualities exist and are respected and 'honoured in most human societies' (ibid., p. 5). Egoists can be seen as individuals who put their self-interest before and above others in all contexts. One behaves egoistically if the pursuit of one's own good conflicts with others in situations where the failure to restrain such pursuits is morally reprehensible and the 'proportion of behaviour that is egoistic exceeds a given measure, typically the average' (Baier 1993, p. 197). However, one may argue that egoism and the pursuit of self-interest is a means of developing the common good and 'if each pursues her own interest as she conceives of it, then the interest of everyone is promoted' (Baier 1993, p. 200). For example, in a state of nature humans necessarily distrust one another. My thoughts or instincts tell me that others are deceitful and will be a threat; others think the same and consequently perceive me as a threat. In this way, humans act egoistically through the rational anticipation of danger, which renders each individual a potential threat. The formation of the common good through the pursuit of unfettered self-interest will only occur if there is no conflict between competing interests or some form of arbiter or sovereign emerges. As interests will always conflict some form of coordination of activities that minimises individuals interfering with one another is required. Consequently, there is a level of egoism in the development of the social contract which ultimately works in the common interest.

Hobbes (1651/1990, Chaps. 14 and 15) outlines his directives for the realisation of a social contract:

- Bring about peace and co-operation whenever this is possible.
- Each individual should lay down the right of self-protection and transfer rights of protection to a third party (a ruling entity).
- Both individuals and the third party should keep covenants, promises and honour agreements.

Because peace and cooperation benefit everyone, individual and social survival would be enhanced if this state of affairs were achieved. However, when peace is not possible there are no limits on individuals when they need to defend themselves. Each human being has liberty to use his or her own power 'for the preservation … of his own Life and … of doing anything, which in his own Judgement and Reason, hee shall conceive to be the aptest means thereunto' (Hobbes 1651/1990, p. 89). However, to ensure peace individuals can 'lay down this right to all things; and be contented with so much liberty against other men, as he would allow other men against himselfe' (Hobbes 1651/1990, p. 64). Hobbes identifies two ways by which one's rights may be given up: either 'renounced' so anyone benefits; or 'transference' whereby someone specific is the recipient of the right and that this transference involves a covenant with a specific individual. This third directive is only binding if promises and contracts are upheld. The one with which the covenant or contract is undertaken 'should … performe all he promises (or) procure his own certain ruine' (Hobbes 1651/1990, p. 79). This is the basis of justice and morality in the state of nature because pre-agreement there is no right and wrong; morality is based upon this covenant and once the rights have been transferred injustice involves the breaking of the covenant. Only then can the concept of humanity come into being because to be or act as a human, predictability is necessary and obligation, regulation and responsibility render individuals predictable. Once the covenant is made the subject has no rights unless the covenant becomes invalid; only a unified single power can overcome the anarchy of wills and fashion a state of unity. The sovereign is the regulator of customs, common law, taxation, property and inheritance and all are subsumed under the decision or will of the sovereign. Governance is based on a covenant and predictability is the necessary outcome of regulatory procedure. In general Hobbes's 'state of nature is not a semi-historical myth lodged in the past; it is an ever-present abyss which we skirt daily, and thankfully unwisely forget … Civil society … is a precarious construction depending on a correct disposition of human wills' (Minogue 1986, p. 60).

Locke (1690/1971) also considered that there must have been a time when people lived in a state of nature where existence proved intolerable because all were a law unto themselves and, consequently, were disorderly and unpredictable. The weak were unprotected and the strong perpetually feared their rivals. However, in a state of nature the punishment of offenders may be undertaken through the 'duty of self-preservation' which includes the 'right to exact reparations', whereas the right to exact punishment as a non-victim derives from the law that enables the preservation of humanity (the preservation of God's creatures) (Hampsher-Monk 1992, p. 83). That is, human beings that renounce reason or the God given rationale of existence through the unjust violation or murder of another have 'declared war against all mankind, and therefore may be destroyed as a Lion or Tiger, one of those wild savage beasts with whom Men can have no Society nor Security' (Locke 1690/1971, 11, pp. 8–9). In other words, there is a pre-political law of nature which emphasises that 'all men are naturally in that State, and remain so, till by their own consents they make themselves members of some political society (Locke 1690/1971, 15, p. 11). However, if humanity is 'absolute lord' and free in a state of nature, why give up this liberty and be subjected to the rule of others? Locke (1690/1971) argued that even though the state of nature provided such rights these were 'uncertain and constantly exposed to the invasion of others; for all being kings as much as he, every man his equal and … no strict observer of equity and justice the enjoyment of property he has in this state is very unsafe and very insecure … full of fears and continuous dangers' (Locke 1690/1971, 123, p. 73) Humans congregate together, develop political societies and entrust civil rulers with authority. Locke (1690/1971) argued that authority was never absolute and humanity should be under no other legislative power than that established by consent, nor be constrained by any law, rule or regulation enacted by a legislator in which the peoples trust or sovereignty had not been endowed. Freedom was not a state where all did as they wished but a regulated state (made by the legislative authority). Rather than the Hobbesian covenant, consent was the basis of social governance and control. The sovereign could be expelled when trust was betrayed and governance according to settlement was abandoned for 'inconstant, uncertain, unknown and arbitrary government … Whenever the legislators endeavour to take away or destroy the property of the people, or reduce them to slavery under arbitrary power, they put themselves into a state of war with the people, who are thereupon absolved from any further obedience' (Cranston 1986, p. 76). In addition, Hume (1748/1971) argued that because each human was equal in strength and mental capabilities 'till cultivated by education … voluntarily for the sake of peace and order, abandoned their native liberty and received laws from their native and companion' (p. 148). Locke propagated a concept of natural rights which included life, liberty and property. Enforcement of these rights necessitated a mode of governance through institutions, e.g. a representative assembly to authorise taxation and regulation as well as an independent judiciary to ensure liberty and adherence to rules and regulations. Through his contract Locke attempts to set the limits of liberty: in political society liberty stops where it injures another's liberty. Liberty in political society is regulated and its limitation illustrates how much freedom we have as well as what we should strive to achieve. Liberty involves a moral dimension in the rules and regulations that curtail freedom and determines a social structure and human capacity for the development of trust. Furthermore, the limits of liberty also provide the basis for accountability and responsible activity.

Conversely, Rousseau considered that humanity had been corrupted by society and propagated an idea of 'natural man' who would ensure his notion of the 'social contract'. Rousseau argued that unhappiness and conflict were formed through civilization and the formation of the social self; in a natural state humanity is 'attuned only to the disposition received from nature, not to the taste he could not yet have acquired', so arguments regarding envy or greed for possessions would be minimal (Rousseau 1755/1984, p. 780). Rousseau disagrees with the social contracts identified by Hobbes and Locke and considered that 'man is born free, and is everywhere in chains (and) those who think themselves the masters of others are indeed greater slaves than they' (Rousseau 1762/1988, p. 49); whereby he denies existing authority. The contract defended and protected all with the force of the goods of each. Even though unified with all, the individual remained free and was guided and legislated by him or herself alone. However, Rousseau's dilemma was that if the individual contracts to an association and creates a 'moral and collective body composed of as many members as the assembly contains votes' how can the individual be guided by him or herself? Rousseau argued that through an act of unity a common identity is formed; a 'general will' which incorporated the moral collective. Not the sum total of all individual wills, nor a majority decision; the 'general will' is only actualised when it aims at the common good and is supported by all members with goodwill (there is a moral dimension to the decision). That is, even though decisions may not be best for certain individual members they are accepted for all in common; decisions are deemed to be accepted by all and reflected the common good. 'The greater harmony that reigns in public assemblies, the more … that public opinion reaches unanimity the more the general will is dominant' (Rousseau 1762/1988, p. 151).

Rather than a quantitative means of governance we are presented with a qualitative model which may be represented through common cohesion in times of crisis. The 'general will' must emanate from and apply to all. Indeed, the 'general will' is different from the will of all; the latter is the sum total of all particular selfish wills and the former indivisible because it reflects the unity of the general will. 'The constant will of all the members of the state is the general will; it is through it that they are citizens and free' (Rousseau 1762/1988, p. 153). For Rousseau the starting point is not self-interest but a definitive common interest reflected through the 'general will'.

Kant (1784/1995) argued that through the *unsocial sociability* of individual humans social order is created. 'Nature should thus be thanked for fostering social incompatibility, enviously competitive vanity, and insatiable desires for possessions or even power … The greatest problem for the human species, the solution of which nature compels him to seek, is that of attaining a civil society which can administer justice universally' (ibid., p. 45). Nature identifies an ultimate problem for humanity, the creation and formulation of the just society or a 'perfectly just civil constitution': only through a solution to this dilemma 'will nature accomplish its other intentions with our species' (ibid., p. 46). The 'just civil constitution' is the last and most difficult problem that humanity has to resolve.

For Kant the purposeless state of savagery stunted the development of our natural capacities. Eventually, barbarism forced humans to leave this state so their natural capacities may be further developed in a 'just civil constitution'. Indeed, because the natural capacities of states may be stunted, in exactly the same way they too are also forced to quit barbarism and enter a 'just civil constitution'. Armament production and preparations for war as well as the destruction actual wars bring about hinder the development of individual states. However, these evils have some benefit for they compel humanity to seek out perpetual peace and provide a 'cosmopolitan system of general political security' (Kant 1784/1995, p. 49). 'Perpetual peace is *guaranteed* by no less authority than the great artist *nature* herself (*natura daedala rerum*)' (Kant 1784/1995, page number). As a mechanism for promoting direction, nature 'visibly exhibits the purposive plan of producing concord among men, even against their will and by means of their discord' (Kant 1795/1995, p. 108). In this context, nature is considered purposive as the 'history of the human race as a whole can be regarded as the realisation of a hidden plan of nature to bring about an internally—and for this purpose also externally—perfect political constitution as the only state within which all natural capacities of mankind can be developed completely' (Kant 1784/1995, p. 50). Initially we develop a social contract between individuals and consequently one between nation-states or an international civil constitution.

The social contract or civil constitution is a mechanism for 'identifying the requirements of impartiality or mutual advantage, which are the grounds of obligation' and provide the basis for moral existence, which requires 'a willingness and capacity to look for shared solutions' through social interaction and discourse (Midgley 1993a, p. 12). Morality emerges through social existence and our ability to discuss and determine what morality should entail. In the next section we will explore different modus operandi for ensuring a moral existence. Through the development of contractual obligation and consent, rules and regulations involve notions relating to trust, accountability and responsibility. Indeed, the moral basis of a social contract argues for and facilitates governance procedures at all levels of society.

Identifying Ethical Perspectives

In this section we overview ethical perspectives that may be used to assess corporate governance procedures at the international/global, regional and national levels. Ethical perspectives involve value-judgements regarding what is good and/or what is right and, as with a descriptive judgement, a value-judgement is universalisable if it can be applied in similar and relevant situations. A value-judgement can be universalised if it shares a feature of a descriptive judgement; that is, conveys or delivers descriptive meaning. Consequently, if something is described as red, for example, anything else that is red is red. In the same way, if something is described as a 'good *X* (we are) committed to calling any *X* like it good' (Hare 1965, p. 15). Ideas of universal morality relate to an ethical perspective that should apply to the activities of everyone. All individuals in a given situation/scenario regardless of nationality, race, culture and so on should adhere to a given general or universal ethical rule. This is slightly different to moral absolutism which considers that certain activities are right or wrong. For example to lie or kill is wrong and immoral no matter what the rationale for undertaking such an activity.

Deontologists would argue that a person must refrain from doing what is known to be wrong, which may be seen as refraining from flouting rules, breaking laws, over-stepping limitations or undermining norms. Unlike teleology (a consequentialist approach) for deontologists it is not the consequences of lies that make them wrong but the fact that lies are wrong in themselves; lies are wrong because of what they are even if they can predict good consequences. Deontological constraints are usually 'negatively formulated', e.g. don't lie or harm the innocent, and can be substituted with their positive formulas, such as tell the truth or assist those in need; however, the positive formulas do not automatically become equivalents. For example, lying and failing to tell the truth are not the same type of acts. Acts that are deemed wrong are what deontologists are interested in, so they may see lying as wrong but say nothing about failing to make the truth known. Consequently, lying is wrong, while withholding the truth is permissible, even though someone may be harmed through the information being withheld. This is because withholding a truth is not lying. 'Lying is wrong, while withholding the truth which another needs is perfectly permissible … because withholding the truth is not lying' (Fried 1978, pp. 9–10). This creates a problem for governance as deontology may comprise the moral basis for withholding information from the public or stakeholders that may be harmful to society, the company or stakeholders themselves.

Kant (1785/1987) provided a deontological position when he argued that duty and obligation should bind humanity. Indeed, the only thing that 'can possibly be conceived in the world … which can be called 'good' without qualification (is) a Goodwill' (Kant 1785/1987, p. 17). Fundamentally, goodwill is not dependent on results but by virtue of being good. Goodwill is fostered by human beings acting rationally in accordance with the principles laid down by the *categorical imperative.* A categorical imperative is one that a fully rational agent would follow, and Kant includes three formulas. First, act only on a maxim or principle that through your will you would have as a universal law of nature. Secondly, act in such a way as to treat people as means and not only ends. Finally, only do something if you are prepared for everyone else to be able to do it as well. Goodwill will then be developed through individuals acting rationally in accordance with these principles. Morality is derived from individuals acting in an ethical manner through precise procedures; through moral agency trust emerges and governance procedures are realised. 'To have moral worth an action must be done from duty … *not from the purpose to be attained from it … Duty is the necessity of acting from respect for the law*' (Kant 1785/1987, pp. 24–25). Eventually Kant (1785/1987) considered that there was only one categorical imperative: '*Act only on the maxim whereby thou canst at the same time will that it should become a universal law*', as well as '*Act as if the maxim of thy action were to become by the will a Universal Law of Nature*' (p. 49).

The Enlightenment emphasised rationality, and Kant argued that each individual had the power of autonomy, consequently each had the right and responsibility to be self-governing, and dignity was inalienable (treat others as ends not means). Self-governance through the categorical imperative provides the civil constitution and perpetual peace. Kant (1785/1987) argued that moral norms cannot be based on empiricism. Experience identifies different types of conduct and negates the possibility of constructing an over-arching morality (a universal law). Moral standards should never be subject to necessity; they are universal and absolute. Indeed, through this stance Kant (1785/1987) challenges consequentialist notions of expedient lying and making false promises when the ends justify the means.

Utilitarianism is based on the notions of consequentialism, welfarism and the felicitous calculus or the sum of the good enabled by the outcome. 'An action … may be said to be comfortable to the principle of utility … when the tendency it has is to augment the happiness of the community is greater than any it has to diminish it' (Bentham 1789, 5, p. 35). Welfarism is related to consequentialism in that choices that are made must be 'judged by the utilities it generates' (Sen 2001, p. 59).

Indeed, the choices made by agents should be added together to provide an aggregated merit. 'Injustice consists of the aggregate loss of utility compared with what could have been achieved' (Sen 2001, p. 59). 'The creed which accepts the foundation of morals, Utility, or the Greatest Happiness Principle, holds that actions are right in proportion as they tend to promote happiness, wrong as they tend to promote the reverse of happiness' (Mill 1861/1986, p. 257). Consequently, individuals should adhere to the pursuit of an overriding common good (for the majority) and adhere to governance structures that enable such a state of affairs.

Moral nihilism understands that nothing is intrinsically immoral or moral; for example lying in itself is fundamentally neither right nor wrong. Moral relativism develops this notion and considers that morality is determined through the judgements of individuals/communities that are culturally bound. Objective absolute and universal moralities do not exist and we ought to recognise difference and tolerate behaviour of others different to ours. Meta-ethical relativists argue that issues such as right/wrong or good/bad are not informed by universal truths but are relative to groups, practices and cultures. Individual and group interpretations of what is good or bad are determined by traditions, customs and practices of specific cultures.

When considering distinctions between relativist and universal positions we may revisit the *Histories* of Herodotus in which the King of Persia (Darius) asks the Greeks what it would take for them to eat their dead. He was explicitly answered with their immediate revulsion. In the same context Darius enquired of the Callatiae (a tribe who ate their ancestors) what it would take for them to burn their dead. Again he was faced with the same response. 'For if one were to offer men to choose out of all the customs in the world such as seemed to them the best, they would examine the whole number, and end by preferring their own; so convinced are they that their own usages far surpass those of all others' (Herodotus 440BC/2013; Bk 3, pp. 67–160). In addition, in the platonic dialogue *Theaetetus* the idea of relativism is discussed and ideas relating to Protagoras (an Athenian Sophist) are identified. Protagoras argued that 'truth and falsity are dependent upon individual impressions' that 'man is the measure of all things' and 'as each thing appears to me, so it is for me, and as it appears to you, so it is for you' (Plato 1997, p. 169). However, if it be true that humanity is the measure of all things then this statement is refuted by this very truth; humanity as the measure of all things is a form of universal. This issue involves the notion and authority of truth and whether we can claim absolute knowledge. Socrates considered that ultimate authority does exist, that there is an ultimate arbiter external to humanity, whereas Protagoras took the relativist stance and argued that each human possessed their own truth. This relationship between relativism, universalism and absolutism is central to the definition of ontology, or what knowledge consists of, and epistemological relationships between subject and object. These ideas are discussed in more detail in Chap. 2 where we relate these notions to the relationship between subject and object and the extent to which an external reality may be realised in relation to critical theory and constructivist paradigms of inquiry.

In the modern technological globalised world we are continually confronted with each other's perspectives, cultures and customs and continue to exclaim regularly that it would be unthinkable to accept all of these distinctions as we would our own. However, there is a difference to our present situation than that faced by Darius. Today most individuals realise that people exist with customs very different from our own. Through globalisation we each possess knowledge of other customs (knowledge that in the past was quite rare). Consequently, should we now accept them as unthinkable? This said occidental societies have interfered in the concerns of developing countries without understanding and in certain contexts inflicted greater harm on any moral discrepancy they wished to dissipate. However, 'it cannot be the consequence of the nature of morality itself that no society ought ever interfere with another, or that one society confronted with the practices of another ought, if rational to react with acceptance' (Williams 1972, p. 39).

What we may argue is that a 'relatively fixed background is a necessary starting point' from which we construct a complex way of life or existence (Midgley 1993b, p. 78). Indeed, it is worth noting that as modern human beings we are not exempt from the bonds of rituals, custom and symbols. However, why are the demands of custom so binding? Why are people prepared to die for certain rituals (burial rights) or symbols (details of clothing)? Evidently, such symbols, rituals and customs carry meaning or values. Once we get over our initial surprise we usually ask what lies beneath the ritual, symbol or custom. Hence, when we look closer at the differences between the Greeks and the Callatiae we see that a 'common respect for their dead' underlies both of their symbols and rituals (Midgley 1993a, p. 80). A shared social/common value is necessary if we are to live with other people. Of course, diversity exists but if we are to communicate we have to assume there is an adequate similarity in basic structures and underlying values. Here there is an assumption that we inhabit a single world and that this world is coherent and understandable; assumptions that are necessary for both science and morality in terms of social existence and governance. In Herodotus' example we can identify the similarities between cultural values (in that each respect the dead) and differences in how this is achieved (eating or burning). The symbolic and ritualistic means of undertaking such respect has grown out of each culture because of different environments, backgrounds, lives and values. Furthermore, once the rituals and symbols are chosen they affect the meaning that underlies them. In this context, we can see that there is a communal aspect to morality and a serious core of truth to the idea of relativism. 'Law is the king o'er all' (Herodotus 440BC/2013; Bk 3), and what may initially seem ethically contradictory can provide evidence of similarity and cohesion.

The ability to undertake business in an ethical way underpins a generic element of corporate governance; the problem is what may be perceived as ethical in one context may not be perceived as such in another. It would be difficult to construct a completely universal, absolutist or global approach to corporate governance. However, many of the occidental structures that have been developed do not consider local culture and the need to provide flexibility. Through providing a general overview of ethical perspectives and corporate governance, as well as distinct case studies relating to developing economies in Africa, relationships between relativist and universal moral perspectives are assessed and analysed.

Ultimately, whether developed through egoistical or altruistic motives, or as a mechanism to ensure 'natural man' and/or the just civil constitution, individuals transfer authority to a political community for protection, which can be entered into at different levels of social existence, e.g. local, regional, national, global or corporate. What is clear is the existence of explicit relationships between individual constructions of political communities and social structures which identify governance procedures and linkages with ethics. Governance involves a means of providing a structure by which rules and regulations are formed in a manner accepted by the community, and the social contract provides a moral basis for this. North (1984) argued that 'institutions consist of a set … of moral, ethical behavioural norms which define the contours … that constrain the way in which rules and regulations are specified' (p. 8). However, what form of virtue, morality or ethic should underpin corporate governance in the twenty-first century? The next section will build on the ethical perspectives above and identify theoretical frameworks which can inform corporate governance procedures/reforms and explore these notions in relation to globalization and the levels of governance that this nebulous phenomenon has materialised.

Levels of Governance in a Globalized World

Governance institutions have been developed through moral and ethical perspectives based on the social contract and civil constitution, e.g. devolution, individual states, the League of Nations, the United Nations and a united Europe. Kant (1784/1995, 1795/1995) perceived forms of governance through individual and state cohesion as well as the formation of a world civil constitution and international regulatory bodies and structures. This identified the shift to an international dimension for governance and a dichotomy of authority between those regulations based in individual states/cultures and those identified at the international level. In a globalised technological world there exist a number of different interpretations of governance, and it has effectively emerged as an umbrella term for a variety of phenomena, such as public management, policy networks, economic coordination, corporate governance as well as themes relating to the EU and international arenas. Furthermore, specific governance arrangements exist which relate to hierarchies, markets, networks and communities, each of which provides direction for societies and economies.

A primary notion for understanding the global dimension relates to issues of market governance regarding Adam Smith's *invisible hand* and resource allocation. The former employs self-interest and the individual actions of entrepreneurs and consumers, while the latter relies on overarching policy to ensure an effective market structure. Market governance relies on networks, which involve a number of actors, and include interest groups and policy-making institutions such as parliaments, the Commission in the EU or the International Monetary Fund (IMF) in the international environment (Giddens 1999; Habermas 2006; Hay and Marsh 2000; Held et al. 1999). Globalization has primarily involved neo-liberal perspectives, which considered that the state should be subordinate to the market. Neo-liberalism argued that all would benefit through globalisation and free trade. However, multi-national companies have been engaged in global mergers and have become 'centres of economic and financial power' as well as proponents of a '*laissez-faire* globalist ideology'. Through extensions in economic power their political capability is extended at the 'expense of nation-states that once balanced their private economic power with public purposes and national stabilisation policies'. Indeed the success of multi-nationals in the economic domain is taken as substantiating their perspective 'that global *laissez-faire* is the optimal way to organise a modern economy' (Kuttner 2001, p. 147).

Habermas (2006) argued that globalisation incorporated a free market ideology, which through the dissipation of national sovereignty aimed to dismantle national economic policies and welfare systems. This form of globalisation is interpreted as the outcome of self-interest, market power, efficiency drives and profit maximisation (global capitalism). A general argument in favour of globalised unregulated free trade is that it will lead to a general rise in living standards. However, experience illustrated that by opening up trade and financial markets investors have made extensive profits but many developing countries have seen a marked fall in living standards. According to neo-liberal theory, for globalisation to work best, state intervention should be excluded and markets deregulated.

Conversely, the opposite variant involves political governance 'guided by the idea that politics should take precedence over the logic of the market' (Habermas 2006, p. 83). The anti-globalisation movement proposes governance 'based on resistance to the social decline of the actual or potential losers of structural change and the disempowerment of the democratic state and its citizens' (Habermas 2006, p. 81). Habermas (2006) further argued that 'politics will succeed in catching up with globalized markets only if it becomes possible to create an infrastructure capable of sustaining a global domestic politics without uncoupling it from processes of legitimation … political power depends on communicative processes which first authorise the use of power … at the cost of displacing a different regulatory mechanism' (pp. 83–84). Rather than market governance which pursues deregulation and disempowerment of community, a communicative governance process should be the means of developing binding decisions. Community governance reverts to issues such as Rousseau's general will and involves compromise between authority and market models of governance. Governance can benefit from two-way decision-making procedures as well as interaction between levels in terms of learning or lesson-drawing (learning from other states and or levels of governance procedure) through the exchange of ideas, experiences and information (Rose 1991). In this context, governance needs to support local and sub-national and regional policies. Governance involves interaction between international and supranational institutions, the state, civil society, local communities and individuals. Governance transcends and encompasses the state. The state is made up of public and political institutions and the private sector (industry, manufacturing, services). Furthermore, the private sector is part of civil society which encompasses companies, individuals and groups. What type of market governance, involves a moral question that effect individuals and socio-economic environments. Arguments relate to self-interest and the common good, or egoism and altruism, as well as relativism and universal principles; in the next section we will give a more detailed assessment of these ethical perspectives and identify their relationship with corporate governance and theoretical frameworks.

Corporate Governance: Ethical Perspective and Theoretical Frameworks

Smith (1776/1985) purports an egoistic basis to his main argument; that is, if individuals were allowed to promote their own good or self-interest 'unimpeded by legal or moral restraint to protect the good of others [it] would at the same time be the most efficient promotion of the common-good' (Baier 1993, p. 200). The theme of exchange in Smith

(1776/1985) involves 'self-regarding agency'. 'It is not from the benevolence of the butcher that we expect our dinner but from his regard for his own self-interest' (Smith 1776/1985, p. 119). Through interpretations of the 'invisible hand' it is normally considered that Smith identified a laissez-faire attitude and unregulated free market perspective. The main point made by Smith (1776/1985) was that 'if exchange between two parties is voluntary, it will not take place unless both believe they will benefit … (and) that process that emerge from voluntary transactions … in a free market … could coordinate the activity of millions … each seeking his own interest in such a way to make everyone better off' (Friedman and Friedman 1980, p. 13). However, Smith 1776/1985 recognised the need for governance and considered that a sovereign entity has three functions or duties: first the duty of protection in terms of external threats; second ensuring and exacting justice within the community; and third maintaining public institutions that are 'good' for society in general (Smith 1776/1985).

Smith (1759/2009) also emphasises 'other-regarding agency' and the sympathetic impartial spectator. Humanity displays certain principles that have an altruistic nature; provision for others that does not rely on self-interest alone (Smith 1759/2009). Subsequently, these principles guide human actions, and out of such social relations emerges the concept of moral conscience, i.e. the impartial spectator. The impartial spectator incorporates our inner person and the means by which we judge ourselves and others (1759/2009). Smith identifies four types of impartial spectators: individual conscience; imagined moral agents observing one's motives and actions; communal law; and ultimately God. This provides an attainable ethical theory where benevolence is the activity of the gods and not imperfect human beings (ibid.). Ethical corporate governance structures incorporate aspects of the 'impartial spectator' that helps to ensure that individuals and companies adhere to socio-legal requirements and allow them to compete in the international domain. Indeed, Wilson (1989) links the 'impartial spectator' with the conscience of board members who should perceive the company as their community. Based on contractual relations and problems regarding global variables in relation to economic governance the late twentieth and early twenty-first centuries have seen increases in international or global corporate governance reform. Most countries require companies that operate within their jurisdiction to add to both the wealth and social cohesion of their socio-economic structures. Problems regarding corporate governance structures in the international domain led to a number of inquiries and reports designed to improve international corporate governance (The Greenbury Report 1995; The Cadbury Report 1992; The Hampel Report 1998; The Combined Code on Corporate Governance UK 1999). However, because of the numerous variables involved and magnitude of such a study this text contends that these reports have been carried out without taking into consideration relative cultural and historical interpretations. Consequently, by definition there is a lack of understanding regarding local or relativist issues when dealing with the formation on international corporate governance agreements. In the main, debates regarding objectives for corporate governance are based on two basic models: the traditional Anglo-Saxon model of corporate governance which advocates the protection of shareholder interests; and the German model which considers that corporations should be managed and governed in the interests of stakeholder groups in general, e.g. shareholders, employees, management, creditors, customers, suppliers.

The Anglo-American model of corporate governance aims at the maximisation of shareholder wealth (Friedman and Friedman 1980; Friedman 1970). Alternatively, there are those who consider that corporate governance involves further responsibility and should take other stakeholders into consideration (Freeman 1994; Galbraith 1979, 1994; Giddens 1998; Hutton 1995, 1997). Stigler (1976) considered that Smith's concept of the invisible hand placed the notion of self-interest and competition at the core of the market and economic theory. Friedman and Friedman (1980) argued that the invisible hand provided the '*possibility of cooperation without coercion*' where minimal state intervention leads to greater public welfare. This underpins a neo-classical view of markets, where governance should be minimal and, where necessary, related to the maximisation of shareholder wealth. Fundamentally, companies should maximise profits for the shareholders, which (through trickle-down economics) would eventually translate into greater wealth for the wider society and provide the realisation of the 'wealth of nations'.

Forster and Brown (1986) argued that Smith (1759/2009) explained the basis of stakeholder theory and why companies should be morally bound to consider and prioritise all stakeholders. Morality for Smith was underpinned by '*justice and beneficence*' and '*commutative justice*' (Forster and Brown 2013). Indeed, the contractual relationship identified in commutative justice would oblige companies to share company profitability with stakeholders in general. Proponents of stakeholder theory further developed the idea that organisations have moral obligations to stakeholder groups as well as shareholders (Freeman 1984). This hypothesis underlies the assumption that institutions, as well as individuals, possess moral status and should therefore act in a morally responsible manner. Evan and Freeman (1993) considered that acting in a morally responsible manner entailed two significant principles.

The first principle involved harming the rights of others and is premised on *deontological ethical reasoning*. The second incorporated being responsible for the effects or outcomes (telos) of company activity and individual actions and is based on *teleological ethical reasoning*. The debate regarding the shareholder model intensified when Friedman (1970, p. 7) claimed, 'there is one and only one social responsibility of business—to use its resources to engage in activities designed to increase its profits as long as it stays within the rules of the game'. This formulation identified three aspects of the market economy: private ownership, competition and profit maximisation.

Profit maximisation is the offspring of a market system governed by the price mechanism. Implicit in this model is the belief that individual entrepreneur's profit maximisation improves the overall economic welfare of society (Smith 1776/1985). The stakeholder model attempted to derive, describe and prescribe alternatives for corporate governance that included multiple interests. Stakeholder theory incorporated the executive power model, which claimed that the purpose of a corporation is the maximisation of corporate wealth. However, this intensified the problem with directors acting in their own self-interest, as they support policies that lead to the protection of their positions and powers in the company instead of creating shareholder wealth (Hutton 1995; Kay and Silberston 1995).

In Africa such theoretical and practical perspectives regarding corporate governance are evident in the number of national reports that have been produced regarding corporate governance reforms. This edited text overviews these reports and assesses the extent to which corporate governance codes have been implemented in specific African states. In addition, the case studies explore ethical issues in individual states and how the relationship between moral perspectives and corporate governance are perceived.

Conclusions

This chapter commenced with a discussion regarding the social contract which provided a foundational overview for the notion of governance and ethical perspectives in general. We then developed an understanding of how different ethical perspectives can inform social existence and provide the basis for specific notions of governance (particularly corporate governance and theoretical perspectives regarding shareholdership and stakeholdership). This text will assess these issues in relation to the African experience and how individual states have dealt with the pursuit of corporate governance in an ethical and practical context, by way of case studies. Many researchers consider that corporate governance is socially constructed and varies according to the institutional environment where it is embedded (Letza and Sun 2002; Aguilera and Jackson 2003; Letza et al. 2004; Kirkbride et al. 2005; Mason et al. 2007; Ardalan 2007; Letza et al. 2008; Sorour 2011; Sorour and Howell 2013). Flinstead and Freeland (1995) suggest that 'corporate governance structures are based on political factors (the role of the state and business), institutional factors (social organization and elites) and evolutionary factors (level of industrialization and institutionalization of the process)' (Letza 2015). Indeed, a definitive set of best practices are difficult to identify and what is imperative are legitimate stable institutions that prevent intensive rent seeking by governments and other market activists (Fligstein and Choo 2005). As such, this text explores case studies in African corporate governance to identify distinctions regarding ethical perspectives. The next chapter identifies the paradigms of inquiry that underpin the ontological and epistemological positions which directed the utilisation of the phenomenological and qualitative methodologies the authors adhered to whilst undertaking their research. In Chap. 3 Nwanji provides an in-depth understanding of ethical perspectives in relation to the relative and universal positions identified above. Chapter 4 deals with North Africa, where Sorour and El Sakhawy investigate the evolution of corporate governance culture in the Egyptian Banking Sector. Boadu, in Chap. 5, then undertakes a study of Ghana and notes that the nature of the Ghanaian business environment allows traditional cultural values to permeate governance practice but points out that these practices fall short of promoting ethical, responsible and transparent corporate governance. In Chap. 6 Ibrahim continues the West African theme and explores non-economic variables to provide an understanding of corporate governance activities in banks in Nigeria and identifies why these banks continue to fail despite ethically based reforms. In Chap. 7 Faye concentrates on another West African country and investigates corporate governance in the Gambia where he identifies that ethical codes and regulations are not currently part of the banking system's regulatory framework. Consequently, financial institutions do not have to comply with specific corporate governance rules and regulations and therefore requirements are internally generated or imposed upon them by their parent company. In Chap. 8 Dube concentrates on South Africa and analyses corporate governance and the King Reports from an African socio-economic, ethical and cultural perspective. Chapter 9 identifies issues in East Africa, where Barako and Brown develop a comprehension of the Office of the Auditor General of Kenya, regarding corporate governance and ethical issues in the Kenyan public sector, and focus on specific state attempts at constructing corporate governance principles. Each chapter provides an ethical perspective and adheres to a specific methodology related to phenomenological philosophical positions as well as critical theory and constructivist paradigms of inquiry; an overview of each of these paradigms will be covered in Chap. 10.

References

Aguilera, R. V., & Jackson, G. (2003). The cross national diversity of corporate governance: Dimensions and determinants. *Academy of Management Review, 28*(3), 447–465.

Ardalan, K. (2007). Governance: A paradimatic look. *International Journal of Social Economics, 32*(2), 506–524.
Aristotle. (2001). Nicomachean ethics. In R. McKeon (Ed.), *The basic works of Aristotle*. Toronto: Random House.
Armstrong, P. (2003). *Status report on corporate governance reform in Africa*. Johannesburg: Pan-African Consultative Forum on Corporate Governance.
Baier, K. (1993). Egoism. In P. Singer (Ed.), *A companion to ethics* (pp. 197–204). Oxford: Blackwell.
Bentham, J. (1789). An introduction to the principles of morals and legislation. In M. Warnock (Ed.), *Utilitarianism* (pp. 33–77). Glasgow: Fontana.
Bevir, M. (2009). *Key concepts in Governance*. London: Sage.
Boadu, M. (2013). *Ethical dimensions of corporate governance in Ghana: Building a theoretical perspective*. PhD Thesis, University of Plymouth Business School.
Brown, A. (1986). *Modern political philosophy: Theories of the just society*. Middlesex: Penguin.
The Cadbury Report. (1992). http://www.egci.org
The Combined Code on Corporate Governance UK. (1999). *The Department of Trade and Industry (DTI)*. http://www.egci.org
Cranston, M. (1986). John Locke and government by consent. In D. Thomson (Ed.), *Political ideas* (pp. 53–80). Middlesex: Penguin.
Diggs, B. J. (1982). Utilitarianism and contractarianism. In H. B. Miller & W. H. Williams (Eds.), *The limits of utilitarianism* (pp. 101–114). Minneapolis: University of Minnesota Press.
Evan, W. M., & Freeman, R. E. (1993). A stakeholder theory of modern corporation: Kantian capitalism. In T. Beauchamp & N. Bowie (Eds.), *Ethical theory and business*. The Modern Corporation: Englewood Cliffs, NJ.
Fligstein, N., & Choo, J. (2005). Law and corporate governance. *Annual Review of Law and Social Science, 1*, 61–84.
Flinstead, N., & Freeland, R. (1995). Theoretical and comparative perspectives on corporate organizations. *Annual Review of Sociology, 21*, 21–43.
Forster, W., & Brown, J. (2013). CSR and stakeholder theory: A tale of Adam Smith. *Journal of Business Ethics, 112*, 301–312.
Freeman, R. E. (1984). Strategic management: A stakeholder theory. *Journal of Management Studies, 39*(1), 1–21.
Freeman, R. E. (1994). The politics of stakeholder theory: Some future directions. *Business Ethics Quarterly, 4*(4), 409–422.
Fried, C. (1978). *Right and wrong*. Cambridge, MA: Harvard University Press.

Friedman, M. (1970, September 30). The social responsibility of business is to increase its profits. *The New York Time Magazine*.
Friedman, M., & Friedman, R. (1980). *Freedom to choose*. London: Secker & Warburg.
Galbraith, J. K. (1979). *The new industrial state*. Harmondsworth: Penguin.
Galbraith, J. K. (1994). *The Good Society considered: The economic dimension*. Annual Lecture for the *Journal of Law and Society*, Cardiff Law School.
Giddens, A. (1998). *The third way: The renewal of social democracy*. Polity. Cambridge, UK
Giddens, A. (1999). *Runaway world*. UK: Profile Books. Cambridge, UK
The Greenbury Report. (1995). http://www.egci.org
Habermas, J. (2006). Euroskeptism, market Europe, or a Europe of world citizens. In C. Cronin & M. Pensky (Ed. & Trans.), *Time of transition* (pp. 73–88). Cambridge, UK: Polity.
The Hampel Report. (1998). http://www.egci.org
Hampsher-Monk, I. (1992). *A history of modern political thought*. Oxford: Blackwell.
Hampton, J. (1998). Contract and consent. In R. E. Goodwin & P. Pettit (Eds.), *A companion to contemporary political philosophy* (pp. 379–93). Malden, MA: Blackwell.
Hare, R. M. (1965). *Freedom and reason*. Oxford: Oxford University Press.
Hay, C., & Marsh, D. (Eds.). (2000). *Demystifying globalization*. Polsis, University of Birmingham UK. Cambridge, UK
Held, D. D., McGrew, A. G., Goldblatt, D., & Perraton, J. (Eds.). (1999). *Global transformations*. Cambridge, UK: Polity.
Herodotus. (440BC/2013). *Histories* (P. Cartledge, Ed.). London: Penguin Classics.
Hirst, P. (2006). Democracy and governance. In J. Pierre (Ed.), *Debating governance: Authority, steering and democracy* (pp. 13–35). Oxford: Oxford University Press.
Hobbes, T. (1651/1990). *Leviathan* (R. Tuck, Ed.). Cambridge: Cambridge University Press.
Howell, K. E., & Letza, S. (2000). Virtue, virtu, categorical imperative and the civic constitution: Defining corporate governance. *Journal of Interdisciplinary Economics, 11*(1), 95–100.
Hume, D. (1748/1971). Of the original contract. In E. Barker (Ed.), *Social contract: Essays by Locke, Hume and Rousseau*. Oxford, UK: Oxford University Press.
Hutton, W. (1995). *The state we're in*. London: Cape.

Hutton, W. (1997). *The state to come*. London: Vintage.

Ibrahim, A. U. (2013). *Investigating the effects of corporate governce of banks in Nigeria: A grounded theory approach*. PhD Thesis, University of Plymouth Business School.

Kant, I. (1784/1995). Idea for a universal history with a cosmopolitan purpose. In: H. Reiss (Ed.), *Political writings* (pp. 41–53). Cambridge UK: Cambridge University Press.

Kant, I. (1785/1987). *Fundamental principles of the metaphysic of morals*. New York: Prometheus.

Kant, I. (1795/1995). Perpetual peace a philosophical sketch. In H. Reiss (Ed.), *Political writings* (pp. 93–130). Cambridge, UK: Cambridge University Press.

Kay, J., & Silberston, A. (1995). Corporate governance. *National Institute Economic Review, 84*, 84–97.

Kirkbride, J., Letza, S., & Sun, X. (2005). Corporate governance: Towards a theory of regulatory shift. *European Journal of Law and Economics, 20*(1), 57–70.

Kuttner, R. (2001). The role of governments in the global economy. In W. Hutton & A. Giddens (Eds.), *On the edge: Living with global capitalism* (pp. 130–146). London: Vintage.

Letza, S. (2015). Corporate governance: Towards a new foundation for both developed and transition economies. In J. Holscher & T. Horst (Eds.), *Palgrave dictionary of emerging markets and transition economies*. Basingstoke, UK: Palgrave Macmillan.

Letza, S., Kirkbride, J., Sun, X., & Smallman, C. (2008). Corporate governance theorising: Limits, Critics and Alternatives. *International Journal of Law and Management, 50*(1), 17–32.

Letza, S., & Sun, X. (2002). Corporate governance: Paradigms, dilemmas and beyond. *Poznan University of Economics Review, 2*(1), 43–59.

Letza, S., Sun, X., & Kirkbride, J. (2004). Shareholding versus stakeholding: A critical review of corporate governance. *Corporate Governance: An International Review, 12*(3), 242–268.

Locke, J. (1690/1971). An essay concerning the true original extent and end of civil government. In E. Barker (Ed.), *Social contract: Essays by Locke, Hume and Rousseau*. Oxford: Oxford University Press.

Mason, C. Kirkbride, J., & Bryde, D. (2007). From stakeholders to institutions: The changing face of enterprise governance theory. *Management Decision, 45*(2), 284–301.

Midgley, M. (1993a). *Can't we make moral judgements?* New York: St. Martin's.

Midgley, M. (1993b). The origin of ethics. In P. Singer (Ed.), *A companion to ethics* (pp. 3–13). Oxford: Blackwell.
Mill, J. S. (1861). Utilitarianism. In M. Warnock (Ed.), *Utilitarianism* (pp. 251–321) (1986). Glasgow: Fontana Press.
Minogue, K. R. (1986). Thomas Hobbes and the philosophy of absolutism. In D. Thomson (Ed.), *Political ideas* (pp. 53–66). Middlesex: Penguin.
North, D. C. (1984). *Institutions, institutional change and economic performance.* Cambridge UK: Cambridge University Press.
Nwanji, I. T. (2006). *Ethical implications of corporate governance on banks in Nigeria: A grounded theory approach.* PhD Thesis, Anglia Ruskin University Business School.
Plato (1997). Republic in Plato: complete works. (Ed) Cooper, J. M. 971-1223. Indiana: Hackett Publishers.
Rousseau, J. J. (1755/1984). *A discourse on inequality* (M. Cranston, Ed.). London: Penguin.
Rousseau, J. J. (1762/1988). *The social contract* (M. Cranston, Ed.). London: Penguin.
Roussouw, G. J. (2005). Business ethics and corporate governance in Africa. *Business and Society, 44*(1), 94–106.
Sen, A. (2001). *Development as freedom.* Oxford: Oxford University Press.
Smith, A. (1759/2009). *The theory of moral sentiments.* Middlesex: Penguin Classics.
Smith, A. (1776/1985). *An inquiry into the nature and causes of the wealth of nations.* Middlesex: Penguin Classics.
Sorour, M. K. (2011) An explanation and analysis of the evolving bank corporate governance practices in Egypt: A grounded theory approach. PhD Thesis University of Plymouth Business School, UK
Sorour, M. K., & Howell, K. E. (2013). A grounded theory analysis of corporate governance in Egyptian banking. *Qualitative Research Journal, 13*(3), 289–316.
Stigler, G. (1976). The successes and failures of Professor Smith. *Journal of Political Economy, 84*(6), 1199–1213.
Williams, B. (1972). *Morality: An introduction to ethics.* Cambridge: Cambridge University Press.
Wilson, J. Q. (1989). *Bureacracy: What government agencies do and why they do it.* New York: Basic Books.
Zizek, S. (2014). *Trouble in paradise: From the end of history to the end of capitalism.* London: Penguin.

2

Paradigm of Inquiry: Critical Theory and Constructivism

Kerry E. Howell

Introduction

Understanding phenomena, continual inquiry and search for truth identify central rationales for human existence. Indeed, the very necessity of continual inquiry and searching for understanding provides indication of our limitations; the world we attempt to comprehend is opaque and our inquiries involve uncertainty and limited clarity. 'Even the self is in many respects unknown and alien to itself; we are often confused and dismayed by our ignorance of our own motives and actions (Dillon 1997, p. 9). Both world and self 'transcend us'; as we inquire we seek to 'overcome the world's otherness and our own self-estrangement' (ibid.). Phenomenology concentrates on how we understand the world through experience, identifies social engagement and how this develops our understanding and worldviews. Phenomenology focuses on the way we experience certain events and how meaning is created through these experiences rather than the events themselves. 'Phenomenology concentrates on the life-world

K.E. Howell (✉)
Graduate School of Management, Plymouth University, Plymouth, UK

K.E. Howell, M.K. Sorour (eds.), *Corporate Governance in Africa*,
DOI 10.1057/978-1-137-56700-0_2

and uncovering … what may be considered … trivial elements of human existence when developing interpretations and understanding human experience' (Howell 2013, p. 56). 'Consciousness and world are not separate entities but a holistic construction of lived experience … Through our personal histories, culture, language and environment individuals are provided with an understanding of the world' (ibid.). In addition, we are also representations of others: 'my own person is object for another and is therefore that other's representation, and yet … I should exist even without the other representing me in his mind' (Kant 1788/1997, p. 6). The other whose object I am is not an absolute subject, but a knowing entity, 'therefore if he … did not exist' or any other person exist other than myself 'this would still by no means be the elimination of the subject in whose representation alone all objects exist' (ibid.). Hegel (1807/1977) identified the naïve mind's emergent comprehension of external reality. 'Mind becomes aware of itself through subjective and objective self-consciousness. Subjective awareness of self is not enough … self needs an objective recognition of its own consciousness to provide an understanding of its own reality' (Howell 2013, p. 8). Even though notions of reality become nebulous when assessed in terms of the relationship between subject and object one thing we can surely depend on is the notion of 'facts'. Surely a fact is a fact and either something exists, something has happened or something has been done that is known about or knowable? However, this is incorrect; for example 'every actual thing is inexhaustible and … every fact is subject to unlimited *interpretation* and *re-interpretation*. If one desires to grasp a fact in a determinate way, he will have to construct it. All facts are already theories' (Jaspers 1995, p. 67).

In an attempt to deal with notions of subject/object, reality, knowledge and interpretations of facts this chapter identifies and overviews the two main phenomenological paradigms of inquiry utilised in this text: critical theory and constructivism (each of which builds on the Kantian and Hegelian perspective and critiques the notion of unmitigated external reality and objectivity within the social sciences). Indeed, because of the ethical/normative, interpretive and qualitative dimensions to the studies developed in this text we concentrate on these two paradigms of inquiry and illustrate how they underpin methodological approaches and challenge corporate governance procedures in Africa in relation to international/global perspectives. The aim of inquiry for critical theory involves social transformation and emancipation through critique, whereas, for constructivism, even though a normative dimension exists, the main objective involves understanding through reconstruction. Each paradigm of inquiry provides a means of challenging accepted perspectives regarding universal and relative dimensions of cultural and ethical dilemmas when assessing corporate governance in Africa. During the past couple of decades there has been an extension in work that provides guidance for delivering research studies and projects in a phenomenological context (critical theory and constructivism). This has led to a distinct shift in social science through critiques and interpretations of data and phenomena from non-positivist ontological and epistemological perspectives.

Changing Perspectives in Social Science: Critical Theory and Constructivism

Through identification and synthesis of phenomenological perspectives the hegemony of positivist paradigms of inquiry has been challenged (Guba 1990; Guba and Lincoln 1985; Guba and Lincoln 1989; Heron and Reason 1997; Howell 2013; Lincoln and Guba 2000). For positivism an external world exists which focuses on empirical occurrences and 'concentrates on the precise nature and rules of events' (Howell 2013, p. 2). At the other extreme, Kant (1781/1992) stated that 'all objects of any experience possible to us are nothing but appearances that are mere representations which … have no independent existence outside our thoughts' (p. 519). Fundamentally, paradigm shifts in the research process have increasingly made it apparent that methodologies no longer needed to be bound by a concrete set of rules but are 'interwoven with and emerge from the nature of particular disciplines … and … perspectives' (Lincoln and Guba 2000, p. 164).

This transformation in position/perspective rests on re-assessments of relationships between subject and object and the extent to which an external reality exists beyond the subjective mind. The problem regarding the notion of reality and the relationship between humanity and external phenomena was crystallised in ancient Greece (see Chap. 1, for a discussion regarding man as the measure of everything) and continued through the Enlightenment to modern times. For modernists, who abjure to certain Enlightenment notions/ideas regarding scientific method and positivism, an external reality exists that human beings may partially apprehend through approximation methods that eliminate human bias and contamination. Through identifying a distinction between subject and object and elevating the object domain, 'what can be known' can only be discovered in the objective realm. 'True knowledge is limited to objects and their relationships that exist between the realm of time and space. Human consciousness, which is subjective, is not accessible to science and thus not truly knowledge' (Polkinghorne 1989, p. 23).

Objective understandings of truth and reality can be perceived either as the outcome of rational thought and/or results of observation or outcome of experience. Each, however, requires engagement with the external world in terms of experience and observation. Realists' considerations that external reality exists *out there* may also relate to foundationalist thinking which considers that even though we are able to experience or observe phenomena these are transcendent of humanity and beyond direct comprehension. Foundationalists consider that an ultimate criterion for testing whether a phenomenon is true (or not) is required, whereas non-foundationalists argue that no such ultimate criterion actually exists and we can only rely on those available or agreed at a certain time. 'Foundational criteria are discovered; nonfoundational criteria are negotiated … most realists are foundationalists and many nonfoundationalists … are relativists' (Lincoln and Guba 2000, p. 176). Recent paradigms of inquiry such as critical theory and constructivism build on the problems and discrepancies identified through these arguments, which provides the basis for ontological and epistemological transformation. Critical theorists and constructivists 'take their primary field of interest to be precisely the subjective and intersubjective social knowledge and the active construction and co-creation of such knowledge by human beings that is produced by human consciousness' (ibid., pp. 176–177). Certain critical theorists lean toward a foundationalist perspective of an external reality. However, rather than identify knowledge as external to humanity, it is instead found through oppression in historical and social structures. Marxist dialectics provide an example of such a process whereby social transformation from one type of society may be identified and predicted through economic variables and determinism. 'Knowers are not portrayed as separate from some objective reality, but may be cast as unaware actors in such historical realities (false consciousness) or aware of historical forms of oppression but unable or unwilling … to alter specific conditions in this historical moment (divided consciousness)' (ibid., p. 177). Subsequently, for critical theory the basis of ontology and epistemology involves a duality of the self in relation to the other (history and society) and a critique of the other to raise understanding and consciousness of oppression with the objective of liberation. Validity for critical theory involves the extent of social transformation in relation to levels of equity and social justice.

Constructivists lean toward the non-foundational perspective and argue that no universal standards exist by which one may measure the validity of knowledge or truth. Validity of knowledge arises through negotiated understandings of what knowledge may encompass. Agreement regarding knowledge emanates from dialogues that move beyond objectivity and subjectivity toward an unfixed 'communicative and pragmatic' means of identifying knowledge (Rorty 1979/2009). Fundamentally, democratic communal discourse and narratives with normative dimensions regarding human improvement and flourishing define and determine the validity of knowledge. For constructivists validity rotates around issues relating to authenticity, ethic-centred criteria, relational criteria and community centred perspectives.

Control for critical theory involves intersubjective intellectual notions that are transformative. These could develop new constructions which then return to the community; for constructivists control is shared between researcher and research participants. Critical theorists understand and propagate the need for research participants (community members) to take control of present and future events. Constructivists encourage research participants to co-construct and nominate questions, areas for inquiry and modes of dissemination of findings in developing research projects. For critical theory and constructivism 'control is a means of fostering emancipation, democracy and community empowerment, and of redressing power imbalances such as those who were previously marginalized now achieve voice' (Lincoln and Guba 2000, p. 175); or as Heron and Reason (1997) expressed it, the development and continuation of 'human flourishing'.

Voice for both critical theorists and constructivists involves levels of subjective interaction between researcher and participants; however, for the constructivist paradigm, participant voices occasionally predominate and reflexivity is an important element of analysis. 'Reflexivity forces us to come to terms not only with our choice of research problem and with those with whom we engage in the research process, but with our separate distinct selves and with the multiple identities that represent the fluid self in the research setting' (Alcoff and Potter 1993). There is a demand that we interrogate ourselves in the research process and undertake a 'continuing mode of self-analysis and political awareness' (Hertz 1997, p. viii). 'Reflexivity incorporates an iterative interactive dialogue about past experience in relation to present perspective and future possibilities … Researchers should be aware of their own self-interest and social standing as these will direct the research process … the core of reflexivity incorporates reflection of interpretation and … self-analysis of the person undertaking interpretation' (Howell 2013, p. 187).

The axiological position or nature of knowledge involves historical or institutional insights for critical theory and consensus building through individual reconstructions for constructivism. For both critical theory and constructivism the axiological position involves a 'propositional, transactional knowing (that) is instrumentally valuable as a means to social emancipation, which as an end in itself, is intrinsically valuable' (Lincoln and Guba 2000, p. 172). Indeed, the critical theory and constructivist approaches are commensurable with each other when dealing emancipatory issues. For example, 'positivism and post-positivism are clearly commensurable. In the same vein, elements of … critical theory (and) constructivism … fit comfortably together' (ibid., p. 174).

Action for both critical theory and constructivist paradigms is an intrinsic element; action for critical theory incorporates emancipation, empowerment and the possible; social transformation in terms of equity and justice is the telos. Constructivism is more hands on as the formulation involves political activity and necessitates training for developing such activity within the research process; as with validity the inquiry is normally incomplete without some form of activity or action on the part of those participants involved with the research. Positivists and post-positivists would consider such action or activity as subjective and biased which would ultimately undermine research results. However, critical theorists incorporate levels of social action in terms of dealing with inequitable practice to social radicalization and revolution. Action is an intrinisic element for both critical theory and constructivism; for critical theory action incorporates emancipation, empowerment and social transformation in terms of equity and justice. Constuctivism adheres to similar ideals but involves political activity at the grassroots levels and developimg training programmes within the research process. Constructivist action transforms from a position of developing understanding of phenomenon to one where previously non-utilised findings underpin or create strategies for social action through commitment to political and ethical perspectives. Because of an emphasis on normative ethical critique, critical theory and constructivist paradigms of inquiry change the dynamics of research and undermine the dividing line between morality and science. We shall now look at the paradigms in more detail and identify how they have provided ontological, epistemological and methodological bases for the studies undertaken in this text.

Critical Theory

Critical theory rejected positivism and attempted to build 'social theories that were philosophically informed and of practical political significance' (Alvesson and Skoldberg 2009, p. 145). The idea of the objective observer was challenged and 'specific methodological rules for acquiring knowledge' disputed (ibid.). Knowledge development in this paradigm recognises the opaqueness of common-sense perceptions because (as with Plato's allegory of the cave) what we observe may not correspond with reality. Most individuals are 'half-awake or dreaming'; to know means to 'penetrate through the surface in order to arrive at the roots, and … strive critically and actively in order to approach truth ever more closely' (Fromm 1997, p. 33). Critical theory introduced the notion of emancipation as the rationale for knowledge development and provided an awareness of material conditions as the basis of understanding. Indeed, as a means of identifying what knowledge incorporated, critical theory considers that it resides within the structure and dynamics of social existence.

A critique of the dominant role of capitalism played a central role in the development of critical theory for the first generation of critical theorists, namely Theodor Adorno (1903–1969), Erich Fromm (1900–1980), Max Horkheimer (1895–1973) and Herbert Marcuse (1898–1979). The critical theory paradigm involves the 'ideological orientation of … inquiry' in terms of neo-Marxism, feminism, determinism as well as variants of critical theory itself (Guba 1990). However, these ideologically orientated perspectives are grouped together to illustrate their unified criticism of positivist value free epistemology. Fundamentally, nothing observed is as it really is, everything is understood and interpreted through the prism of values. If values are inevitably part of the analysis and interpretation, then questions regarding *whose values dominate* arise, and a political dimension to the research ensues. This indicates a certain level of difficulty in defining critical theory, which incorporates a number of different perspectives. However, one may consider that the following central tenets may be included in a basic definition: criticisms of occidental complacency, an understanding that individual assumptions are influenced by social and historical forces and are a challenge to ruling ideas and elites, and a facilitation of equality and liberty. Through these three central tenets it is possible to synthesise points of agreement and determine the basis for a paradigm of inquiry with a specific ontology, epistemology and overall methodological approach.

Through this synthesis critical theory exposes positions of power between institutions, groups and individuals as well as the role of agency in social affairs. In addition, critical theory identifies the rules, regulations and norms that prevent people from taking control of their own lives; the means by which they are eliminated from decision-making and consequently controlled. Through making clear the relationships between power and control, agency may be extended and human emancipation realised. Of course, individuals are never completely free from the social and historical structures which they both construct and from which they emanate. Through shaping consciousness, power dominates human beings in social settings. Individual critical theorists disagree, but one may argue that power constitutes the foundation of social existence in that it constructs social and economic relations; that is power is the basis of all political, social and organisational relationships. In addition, Horkheimer (1972) considered that the opposition between the individual and social structures should be absolved and the relationship between objectivity and subjectivity embraced. The main idea for critical theory was the formulation of social theory based on philosophical positions and empirical studies (Howell 2013).

The second generation of critical theorists congregated around ideas propagated by Habermas (2004). He reorganised the theoretical perspective through 'moving it from a paradigm of the isolated subject to one of inter-subjectivity and from a paradigm of consciousness to one of language and communication. Habermas (2004) identified the need for a fundamental paradigm shift. Understandings of theory needed to be moved from intellectual situations in which the ends justify the means, or instrumentalism, to one where communicative rationality took centre stage. Post-positivist pursuits of objectivity that ignored the worldviews, values and norms through which the world is structured failed to comprehend social phenomena fully' (Howell 2013, p. 83). Habermas (2004) introduced a fundamental distinction between strategic and communicative rationality in order to address the theoretical failure of the first generation of critical theorists (Pensky 1999).

Habermas (2004) identified and criticised the ideological assumptions on which science or positivistic knowledge depended. Fundamentally, the second generation provided an ideal regarding communication which is enabled through rational subjects completely independent of domination and error-inducing interest. Three functions provide mediation between theory and practice: first, critical theorems which aim at true statements; second, organisation of the enlightenment processes aiming at authentic insights; and third, appropriate strategies for developing prudent decisions (Habermas 2004). Habermas raised the epistemological discussion to a new level when he identified critical knowledge as based on principles that differentiated it either from the natural sciences or the humanities through orientations toward self-reflection and emancipation. Adorno and Horkheimer (1997) considered that the modern era illustrated a shift from the liberation of the Enlightenment toward enslavement. Indeed, the Enlightenment equated with positivism, because for 'the Enlightenment, that which does not reduce to numbers, and ultimately to the one, becomes illusion; modern positivism writes it off as literature' (p. 7). 'Under the levelling domination of abstraction (which makes everything in nature repeatable) and of industry (for which abstraction ordains repetition) the free themselves finally came to form that "herd", which Hegel has declared to be the result of Enlightenment' (ibid., p. 13).

A critical theory perspective asserts that influential groups define what knowledge entails; it is developed in relation to historical change and incorporates normative or ethical challenges to the existing state of affairs. Habermas (2004) related social science to human interaction based on ethical considerations. Changes in society have brought about human rights, and social science should not be defined in terms of its accumulated stock of knowledge but its commitment to normative perspectives and ethical principles. Society is in a state of flux so theories cannot be determined through correspondence to a present state of affairs because social mobilisation may prove the existing state of affairs unjust. Furthermore, because social scientists participate in the research process, their judgements are part of interpretations underpinning knowledge and/or theoretical frameworks. Indeed, Habermas edges toward a constructivist perspective where theory is no different from everyday life and grounded in individual activity and communities. The third generation challenged the approach of the first and second generations but supported the critical re-examination of the first generation's understanding of critical theory undertaken by Habermas (Pensky 1999). Honneth (1995) emphasises the importance of conceptual reformulation, the mediation of the present state of our knowledge and the positive impact of practising shared values in group dynamics. For critical theory, subjective humans develop knowledge and understanding in historical and cultural contexts (Howell 2013).

A general perspective of critical theory ontology involves an understanding that reality is shaped through social and historical processes: 'historical realism'. An example of this would be the nation-state in terms of its changing role within international relations and the issues this raised for ideas such as sovereignty and democratic accountability. As the role of the nation-state changes, so does our understanding of it, which has implications for our interpretation of reality in terms of the role of the state, the nation and sovereignty. Indeed, international institutions have implications for changes regarding these issues and provide the impetus for theoretical change as well as empirical outcomes. States are now required to adhere to international laws and economic edicts if they are to participate actively in the international order, and this raises issues for ideas such as sovereignty and democratic accountability. Globalisation can undermine the sovereignty of the nation-state and provide frameworks for improvement while at the same time detract from individual cultures and leave local economies to the problems that rampant free-trade may engender. As the role of the nation-state changes, so does our understanding of it, which has implications for our interpretation of reality in terms of the role of the state, the nation and sovereignty. This has implications for global variables in terms of corporate governance as an international phenomenon in relation to the individual states in Africa and how sovereignty in these contexts are also challenged, deconstructed and side-lined. Indeed, international institutions have implications for changes regarding these issues and provide the impetus for theoretical change as well as identifying empirical or practical outcomes in terms of governance procedures (Howell 2004).

The epistemological aspect of the critical theory paradigm considers that findings and theoretical perspectives are developed because the investigator and investigated are linked through historical values, which through subjectivity influence the inquiries. This leads toward a specific methodology, which identifies a dialogic and dialectical approach. Dialogue and discourse are required between researchers and the researched; interaction between past and present is also required. Indeed, because of the historical nature of transformation, for this methodological approach structures change and mutate through agency and actions. Reality or truth is developed by human beings in historical and cultural circumstances while agency and historical values influence the analysis. In general critical theory provides a specific understanding of reality in that it is shaped by 'social, political, cultural, economic and gender values crystallize(d) over time' (Guba and Lincoln 1994, p. 105).

Constructivism

Constructivism is linked with critical theory and seeks to understand how humans interpret or construct knowledge in social, linguistic and historical contexts (Schwandt 2000). 'We are all constructivists if we believe that the mind is active in the construction of knowledge' (ibid., p. 197). Berger and Luckman (1966) argued that realities are created through experiences, relationships with self and others as well as social interaction; consequently knowledge accumulation and understanding are derived through social interaction. Gergen (1994) considered that research and analysis have little meaning until interpretations arise 'from a process of negotiating meaning in the community' (p. 119). Constructivism also criticises the positivist notion that it is possible for theoretical and observational languages to be independent and that the collection of facts must be independent of the theoretical statements. However, 'philosophers of science now uniformly believe that facts are facts only in some theoretical framework'. Consequently, the means by which reality can be discovered is undermined and may only exist through 'a mental framework' or 'construct for thinking about it' (Guba 1990, p. 25). Fundamentally, interpretation for constructivism is shaped by the researchers' experiences, views and background (Cresswell 2013; Burr 2010; Howell and Annasingh 2013). In a perspective context all claims of knowledge and the evaluation of these claims 'take place within a conceptual framework through which the world is defined and explained' (Schwandt 2000, p. 197). Through perspectivism the idea of a positivist naïve realism ontology is critiqued and the notion that reality can be directly apprehended in an unmediated way challenged (ibid.). Constructivism incorporates 'relativist realism' where realities are constructed through shared understandings and interpretations of social and cultural factors (Guba and Lincoln 1989). Reality depends on constructions which 'are not more or less true in any absolute sense but simply more or less informed or more sophisticated. Constructions are alterable, as are their associated realities' (Guba and Lincoln 1994, p. 111).

The epistemology of constructivism is similar to a critical theory epistemology where knowledge is developed between the interaction of researchers and respondents. However, constructivism is different from critical theory because it creates and develops findings as the investigation process goes along. The results are created through consensus and individual constructions as well as those of the researcher (Howell 2013; Howell and Annasingh 2013). Constructivism understands reality as locally constructed and based on shared experiences and, because groups/individuals are changeable, identifies 'relativist realism' or a 'relative ontology'. Epistemologically, constructivism is similar to critical theory except that the results of the study are created through consensus and individual constructions, including the constructions of the investigator. Constructivism and critical theory are closely linked and each attempts to unveil the ideological perspectives relating to knowledge generation and accumulation. Methods used to organise and analyse data and identify cause and effect are not epistemologically free from interference: they are 'contextual' and intersubjective in terms of assumptions, beliefs and culture. Longino (1993a) argued that contextual and intersubjective assumptions and beliefs encompass 'the vehicles by which social values and ideologies are expressed in inquiry and become subtly inscribed in theories, hypotheses and models defining research programs' (p. 263). Consequently, if research programmes accept contextual and intersubjectivity they can then critique these background assumptions. Longino (1993b) outlined a set of criteria that would allow a transformation of critical discourse. Such criteria incorporated standards of evaluation that were accepted and shared, acknowledgement and inclusion of community responses to criticism and equality regarding intellectual authority.

In addition, Longino (1993a) considered that it was evident that experimentation and observation were not undertaken by completely autonomous objective researchers: research is contextual, intersubjective and incorporates background assumptions. These background assumptions need a critique and a comprehension that objectivity necessitates social interaction and that knowledge development is a social activity (Howell 2013). A critique of basic assumptions enables the identification and challenge of values and interests that can otherwise be perceived as necessary or natural elements of phenomena and which encapsulate the norm (ibid.). In line with notions identified by critical theory Longino (1993b) argued that critique should be central to the research process and include a community's reaction to criticism and individual/social toleration of this criticism. In addition, standards of evaluation need to be transparent as well as having intellectual authority. For constructivism practical issues are interwoven with a more generic conceptualisation through intersubjectivity. Overall, knowledge development or construction is carried out through a continual conversation or dialogue with history. The object is social knowledge as an aspect of the human world; that is inhabited by people and made by people through historical processes and in cultural environments (Berger 1967). Objectivity is impossible because each of us through necessity 'must encounter the world from some perspective … No human being can step outside of their humanity and view the world from no position at all, which is what the idea of objectivity suggests (Burr 2010, p. 152). Consequently, those who have undertaken certain studies reported in this text have immersed themselves in the African cultures studied and provided insights regarding cultural perspectives within these states. Objectivity for each of the studies is perceived as problematic and methodological approaches inductive.

Conclusion

Critical theory and constructivism involve interpretive perspectives which emphasise understanding and elevate the relationship (epistemology) or interaction between interpreter (researcher) and the phenomenon under investigation. Emphasis is placed on the interconnection between patterns rather than cause and effect. Reality, truth or knowledge accumulation involves interpretation through wide ranging imaginative analyses and allows for multiple meanings, realities and uncertainty. Values and facts are intrinsically linked and knowledge or truth is dialectical or changeable and provisional. As social life evolves into different environments/epochs so too does the reality that provides an understanding of this transformation.

Critical theory and constructivist paradigms of inquiry involve ideas relating to the empowerment of individuals and groups; they challenge injustice in social relations and pursue improvement for social existence. For more traditional or positivist approaches the objectives for the research project involve knowledge accumulation, attempts at description and explanation. Critical theory and constructivism promote transformation, conscious emancipation and political activity as the basic rationales for undertaking research. Accumulation of knowledge is not the central objective and political activity and social transformation incorporate the driving force. Reflexivity or self-consciousness is a central mechanism. Ideological perspectives that penetrate accepted norms are made explicit in relation to self-conscious subjectivity, intersubjectivity, normative morality and epistemological precepts. Fundamentally, subjective preconceptions in terms of epistemological and political positions are incorporated within the research process.

Central to both constructivism and critical theory is the connection with everyday life in the interest of abolishing social injustice. However, one of the main concerns for critical theory involved investigating the ultimate source or foundation of social domination in relation to the market mechanism. It may be argued that intervention in the economy abolished the capitalist tension between the 'relations of production' and the 'material productive forces of society', which according to traditional critical theory constituted the primary contradiction within capitalism. The market (as an 'unconscious' mechanism for the distribution of goods) and private property had been replaced by regulation and social ownership of the means of production. However, contrary to the economic determinism of naïve Marxism, this did not lead to revolution but, as pointed out by Hayek (1944/1999), fascism and totalitarianism. Indeed, this posed the problem of how to account for the apparent persistence of domination in the absence of the contradiction that, according to traditional critical theory, was the very source. This text explores domination in an international or global context between developed and developing countries and in such a way that a critical theory approach enables an analysis in terms of relative and universal positions regarding this evolving relationship.

Both constructivism and critical theory are underpinned by a phenomenological philosophical position (understanding through experience) and operationalized through methodological approaches such as grounded theory, phenomenological hermeneutics and constructivist ethnography (these are explained further in individual chapters). For example, 'grounded theory builds theory through data collection and analysis in relation to pre-existing theory and practice. Grounded theory suggests that there is an over-emphasis on quantitative research and wishes to demote the idea that the discovery of relevant concepts and hypotheses are a priori to research' (Howell 2013, p. 131). Grounded theory considers that theory is derived from data and cannot be divorced from the process by which it is developed. Subsequently, most hypotheses and concepts are generated through the data and worked out in relation to this during the course of the research (Glaser and Strauss 1967). The studies presented here each identify either critical theory or constructivist paradigms of inquiry and in most instances grounded theory is the preferred methodological approach.

Each supplies a critique of the existing state of affairs in relation to the universal perspectives identified by global forces as well as relativist positions and deficiencies in specific African states. This structure provides a framework for undertaking analysis and developing a valid indication of activities and concerns in the formation of African corporate governance. Each paradigm of inquiry offers rich understandings of the corporate governance phenomenon. Such paradigms are normally 'inductive qualitative (and) allow the researcher to identify the main concern of a group of subjects and the behaviours they use to resolve their main concern'. Underpinned with historical/relativist ontologies, critical theory and constructivist methodologies can offer a deep understanding of socially constructed phenomena (Guba and Lincoln 1994).

References

Adorno, T. W., & Horkheimer, M. (1997). *Dialectic of enlightenment*. London and New York: Verso.

Alcoff, I., & Potter, E. (Eds.). (1993). *Feminist epistemologies*. New York: Routledge.

Alvesson, M., & Skoldberg, K. (2009). *Refelexive methodology*. London: Sage.

Berger, P. L., & Luckman, T. (1966). *The social construction of reality*. New York: Anchor.

Burr, V. (2010). *Social constructionism*. Sussex, UK and New York: Routledge.

Cresswell, J. W. (2013). *Qualitative inquiry and research design*. London: Sage.
Dillon, M. C. (1997). *Merleau-Ponty's ontology*. Evanston, IL: Northwestern University.
Fromm, E. T. (1997). *To have or to be?* New York: Continuum.
Gergen, K. J. (1994). *Realities and relationships: Soundings in social construction*. Cambridge, MA: Harvard University Press.
Glaser, B., & Strauss, A. (1967). *The discovery of grounded theory*. New York: Alpine.
Guba, E. G. (1990). The alternative paradigm dialogue. In E. Guba (Ed.), *The paradigm dialogue*. Thousand Oaks, CA: Sage.
Guba, E. G., & Lincoln, Y. S. (1985). *Naturalistic inquiry*. London: Sage.
Guba, E. G., & Lincoln, Y. S. (1989). *Fourth generation evaluation*. London: Sage.
Guba, E. G., & Lincoln, Y. S. (1994). Competing paradigms in qualitative research. In N. Denzin & Y. S. Lincoln (Eds.), *Handbook of qualitative research* (pp. 105–117). Thousand Oaks, CA: Sage.
Habermas, J. (2004). *Theory and practice*. Cambridge, UK: Polity and Blackwell.
Hayek, F. A. (1944/1999). *The road to Serfdom*. London: Routledge.
Hegel, G. W. F. (1807/1977). *Phenomenology of spirit* (A. V. Miller, Trans., Foreword: J. N. Finlay). London: Clarendon.
Heron, J., & Reason, P. (1997). A participatory inquiry paradigm. *Qualitative Inquiry, 3*, 274–294.
Hertz, R. (Ed.). (1997). *Reflexivity and voice*. Thousand Oaks, CA: Sage.
Honneth, A. (1995). *The struggle for recognition*. Cambridge: MIT Press.
Horkheimer, M. (1972). *Critical theory: Selected essays*. New York: Continuum.
Howell, K. E. (2004). *Europeanization, European integration and financial services: Developing theoretical frameworks and synthesising methodological approaches*. Basingstoke, UK: Palgrave Macmillan.
Howell, K. E. (2013). *An introduction to the philosophy of methodology*. London: Sage.
Howell, K. E., & Annasingh, F. (2013). Knowledge generation and sharing in UK universities: A tale of two cultures. *International Journal of Information Management, 33*(1), 32–39.
Jaspers, K. (1995). *Philosophy of existence*. Philadelphia: University of Pennsylvania.
Kant, I. (1781/1992). *Critique of pure reason* (N. K. Smith, Trans.). Basingstoke, UK: Palgrave Macmillan.

Kant, I. (1788/1997). *Critique of practical reason*. Cambridge, UK: Cambridge University Press.

Lincoln, Y. S., & Guba, E. G. (2000). Paradigmatic controversies, contradictions and emerging confluences. In N. K. Denzin & Y. S. Lincoln (Eds.), *Handbook of qualitative research* (pp. 163–188). Thousand Oaks, CA: Sage.

Longino, H. (1993a). Essential tensions—phase two: Feminist, philosophical and social studies of science. In L. M. Antony & C. E. Witt (Eds.), *A mind of one's own: Feminist essays on reason and objectivity* (pp. 257–272). Boulder, CO: Westview.

Longino, H. (1993b). Subjects, power and knowledge: Descriptions and prescriptions in Feminist Philosophies of Science. In L. Alcott & E. Potter (Eds.), *Feminist epistemologies* (pp. 101–120). New York: Routledge.

Pensky, M. (1999). Truth and interest: On Habermas's 'Afterword' to Nietzsche's Theory of Knowledge. In B. E. Babich (Ed.), *Nietzsche's Epistemological Writings and the Philosophy of Science. Boston studies in the philosophy of science* (pp. 265–273). Dordrecht: Kluwer.

Polkinghorne, D. E. (1989). Changing conversations about human science. In S. Kvale (Ed.), *Issues of validity in qualitative research* (pp. 13–46). Lund: Studentlitteratur.

Rorty, R. (1979/2009). *Philosophy and the mirror of nature*. Princeton and Oxford: Princeton University Press.

Schwandt, T. A. (2000). Three epistemological stances for qualitative inquiry: Interpretivism, hermeneutics and social constructionism. In N. K. Denzin & Y. Lincoln (Eds.), *Handbook of qualitative research* (pp. 85–106). Thousand Oaks, CA: Sage.

3

Ethical Perspectives on Corporate Governance

Tony Ikechukwu Nwanji

Introduction

The motivation for identifying and using ethical perspectives in decision-making regarding corporate governance has been growing in importance over the last 25 years. In the UK for example there have been four important and influential reports termed Corporate Governance Codes published in the 1990s: Cadbury Report (1992), Greenbury Committee (1995), Hampel Committee Report (1998) and Turnbull Committee Report (1999) (Letza 2015, p. 190). Indeed, these reports laid the foundations of corporate governance for the UK as well as other developed and developing economies. Following the collapse of Enron and WorldCom in 2001, corporate governance gained a much higher profile and was further developed through the Myners Report (2001), Derek Higgs Report (2003), Smith Report (2003), Myners Review (2004), Walker Review

T.I. Nwanji (✉)
Department of Accounting and Finance, College of Business
and Social Sciences, Landmark University, Kwara, Nigeria

K.E. Howell, M.K. Sorour (eds.), *Corporate Governance in Africa*,
DOI 10.1057/978-1-137-56700-0_3

(2009) and a revised Combined Code (2012) (ibid.). During the twenty-first century we have witnessed a growing number of research projects and literature on both the general areas of corporate governance and different mechanisms, including directors' remuneration, accountability, non-executive directors (NEDs) and audit committees.

In this chapter both deontological and teleological ethical perspectives as well as shareholder and stakeholder theoretical frameworks will be used to consider issues regarding corporate governance procedures identified by the reports, reviews and codes identified. Deontological or duty-based ethics and teleological or utilitarian ethics are general perspectives that can help to explain the moral behaviours of those responsible for managing the affairs of an organisation. These ethical perspectives and theoretical frameworks were briefly discussed and applied to corporate governance issues in Chap. 1. In this chapter we will consider the relationship between these areas and identify how they may provide insight into considerations for notions of 'good' corporate governance.

Much research has been conducted in the area of Corporate Social Responsibility (CSR) and business ethics. Indeed, the starting point for these studies could be seen as Friedman (1970) who claimed that the modern corporation has no social responsibility to the public in general, only fiduciary duties to its owners (shareholders). However, in opposition to this extreme position, stakeholder theory advocates ethical and moral duties of corporations to all stakeholders as well as the interests of shareholders.

The financial meltdown in 2008 increased the debate regarding ethical perspectives of corporate governance. In Africa, the financial meltdown hit emerging economies in Egypt, Ghana, Nigeria, the Gambia, Kenya and South Africa. Indeed, as well as the business sector in particular, society in general called for a more focused assessment of corporate governance (one that took ethical perspectives into consideration). This chapter, therefore, assesses ethical perspectives regarding corporate governance and regulations globally while the rest of the text (the following chapters) deals with the identified individual African countries.

Corporate Governance: A Definition

Corporate governance has been defined as 'the manner in which organisations, particularly limited companies, are managed and the nature of accountability of the managers to the owners' (Cadbury Report 1992, para. 2.5). According to Letza (2015), 'if management is about running the corporation, then governance is about ensuring that the corporation is run properly' (Letza 2015, p. 191). The Cadbury Report (1992) described corporate governance as 'the system by which companies are directed and controlled. Boards of directors are responsible for the governance of their enterprises. The shareholders' role in governance is to appoint the directors and auditors and to satisfy themselves that an appropriate governance structure is in place in the organisation' (para. 2.5). Corporate governance also involves guiding management through company affairs and issues that lead to the achievement of specific objectives (Friedman 1970). The Hampel Committee Report (1998) stated that 'corporate governance must contribute both to business prosperity and accountability'.

Corporate governance practices can be defined as the way the management of a firm can influence stakeholders, including owners/shareholders, creditors, employees, governments and other stakeholders. Parkinson (1994) argued that corporate governance incorporated the process of supervision and control which intended to ensure that the company's management act in the interests of shareholders. Ticker (1984) stated that 'the governance role is not concerned with the running of the business of the company *per se*, but with giving overall direction to the enterprise, with overseeing and controlling the executive actions of management and with satisfying legitimate expectations of accountability and regulation by interests beyond the corporate boundaries' (cited in Solomon and Solomon 2004, p. 13). This chapter takes into consideration ethical and theoretical perspectives of corporate governance and applies deontology and teleology to decision-making processes and investigates whether the governing actions/behaviour of boards of directors and their companies are ethical.

Initially I will outline the theoretical perspectives on corporate governance regarding deontological and teleological ethical approaches. I investigate whether there is a trade-off between business ethics and corporate objectives, which are underpinned by an understanding of deontological and teleological ethical approaches to the decision-making of boards of directors. In addition, the global discussion on ethical perspectives on corporate governance has resulted in a growing number of research inquiries. Consequently, the following sections consider what corporate governance entails and assess global corporate governance as well as major changes in research and practices. Corporate governance is essential to the success of long-term development in developing, transition and emerging-market economies. The quality of a country's governance institutions—of which those of corporate governance now constitutes an integral part—matters greatly for development as a whole (OECD 2003).

What Is Corporate Governance?

Corporate governance comprises private and public institutions (both formal and informal) which together govern the relationship between the people who manage corporations (corporate insiders) and those who invest resources. These institutions notably include a country's corporate laws, securities laws, accounting rules, generally accepted business practices and prevailing business ethics. The issue of corporate governance has centred on shareholder vs stakeholder approaches and which of the two models is most effective or efficient for governing corporations. Influences such as the globalisation of capital markets, increases in institutional investors and greater shareholder activism have added to the growing importance of corporate governance issues (Oman et al. 2003; Mills 1998; Fera 1997). The idea that companies should behave in a responsible way grew in importance following scandals such as the Maxwell Corporation pensions, Polly Peck, BCCI, Barings Bank and the Paddington rail accident in the UK in the 1990s as well as the collapse of Enron, WorldCom and the accountancy firm, Andersen. Indeed following these incidents there has been increasing research on the kinds of behaviour that might constitute corporate social responsibility and the extent to which such activities are legally permissible.

The Global Debate on Corporate Governance

A global perspective regarding corporate governance and ethics requires an assessment of the transformations in related research and practices. Oman et al. (2003) stated that:

> Corporate governance is necessary for the success of long-term development in developing, transition and emerging-market economies ... In all countries, and for all segments of a country's population, including the poor, the ability to move from relationship-based to predominantly rules-based institutions of corporate, as well as public, governance is essential. (p. 6)

The OECD Report (2003) indicated that corporate governance was essential for the success of long-term development in transitional and emerging-market economies. The quality of a country's governance institutions—of which those of corporate governance now constitute an integral part—matters greatly for development as a whole (ibid.).

Corporate Governance in the UK: Assessments of the development of regulations based on the Corporate Governance Code result from different corporate governance reports; these include the Cadbury report (1992), the Turnbull Committee Report (1999) (Internal Control and Financial Reporting), the Myners Report (2001) (Institutional Investment in the UK), the Derek Higgs Report (2003) (Role and Effectiveness of Non-Executive Directors and their Responsibilities in Corporate Governance Practices), the Smith Report (2003) (Audit Committees and Combined Code Guidance), the Myners Review (2004) (Principles for Institutional Investment Decision-Making), the Walker Review (2009) (Response to the Financial Crisis) and a revised Combined Code (2012) (Letza 2015).

Corporate Governance in the European Union: Assessment of corporate governance regulations and practices in the EU were based on the shareholder and stakeholder models of corporate governance. In some European countries, the stakeholder model predominates, which imposes explicit obligations to consult with other groups, e.g. the German stakeholder model of corporate governance where companies have to appoint a supervisory board that encompasses employee and bank representatives.

Corporate Governance in the USA: Changes in corporate governance regulations and the creation of the Sarbanes-Oxley Act (SOX) (2002) resulted from the collapse of Enron. SOX was passed with the expectation that it would restore investor confidence and underwrite the integrity of the financial information of non-US companies and businesses that had dealings in the USA. In addition, there were further financial crises relating to WorldCom and major corporate failures and unethical practices resulting from the financial meltdown during 2008.

The OECD Principle of Corporate Governance: OECD aspects of corporate governance cover five major areas:

- The rights of the shareholders;
- The equitable treatment of shareholders;
- The role of outside stakeholders in corporate governance;
- Adequate disclosure and transparency;
- The responsibilities of the board.

The OECD (1999) principle of corporate governance, like the UK/US Codes, is based on shareholder theory and the price mechanism, which states that shareholders are the owners of the company, who benefit from the business's profits and bear risks through losses and expropriation. In many developing, transition and emerging-economies the effects of the expropriation problem are severely exacerbated through the behaviour of powerful vested interest groups that are entrenched in highly concentrated oligopolistic structures of local political and economic powers. Particularly damaging is the extent to which the behaviour of such powerful local groups (closely tied to foreign investors in some countries) serves to weaken or undermine healthy competition and the proper functioning of markets—which are indispensable for a country to achieve reasonably sustained productivity growth—as well as to weaken or undermine the development and consolidation of democratic political institutions.

Corporate Governance in the Developing World: Following the banking and financial meltdown of 2008 the inadequacies of corporate governance systems in guiding the board in managing the affairs of the firm to deliver performances that meet the needs of its shareholdership/stakeholdership were once again highlighted. Corporate governance in developing, transitional and emerging-market economies should provide the shareholder with the right to earn profits and, through the institution's corporate governance (along with those of market competition and government regulation), ensure that corporations collectively serve the best interests of shareholders and stakeholders (Nwanji and Howell 2004, 2005). The significant move in many countries—developing and emerging economies—to privatise formerly state-owned corporations, reduce anti-competitive market regulations, liberalise trade and investment policies, and attract foreign investors is having a positive impact. However, these moves may not be sufficient to create the kind of dynamic and interactive processes of long-term productivity growth and political and economic-policy reforms which these countries need to achieve and sustain continued growth and strengthen political democracy and modernisation of the state. For these countries, institutions of corporate governance that work efficiently to complement and reinforce the (still weak) competitive market mechanism and (fledgling) democratic political institutions are becoming increasingly necessary.

As globalization enhances the strength of the market and nullifies the influence of national and sub-national governments, corporate governance has incrementally grown in importance. In many developing and emerging-market economies two other phenomena further amplify the increased importance of corporate governance. First, (a positive phenomenon) is the sea change many of these countries have undertaken in recent years to move to more market-friendly policy regimes. Second, (a negative phenomenon) is the continued pervasiveness of concentrated oligopolistic local power structures—structures that are highly conducive to insider-dealing and unethical activity by those who exercise power in both the private and public sectors.

Ethical Perspectives on Corporate Governance

This section builds on the discussion outlined in Chap. 1 in terms of deontology and the extent to which this can be applied to shareholder or stakeholder models of corporate governance. 'Ethics' refers to the normative appraisal of the actions and character of individuals and social groups. It is often used interchangeably with morality and refers to obligations and duties that govern individual action. However, there are grounds for holding that morality in this sense is a peculiarly modern institution and that the term 'ethics' should be understood more widely (Williams 1985). Ethics is the study of human moral conduct or the rules of conduct recognised as appropriate to a particular profession or area of life. It relates to moral principles or conscience. There are those who hold that ethics derives from a universal natural law (Kant 1973; Sherwin 1983; Singer 1993, 1998).

Deontological ethics indicates that the most important aspect of how we ought to live is governed by moral rules that should not be broken, even when breaking these rules may have advantageous consequences. Deontology is based on the action that is taking place (means) and the morality of this action. Deontologists maintain that an action is good or bad or right or wrong and identified by the act itself. The deontological ethical approach has its foundations in the works of Immanuel Kant (1724–1804) who argued that we should '*impose on ourselves the demand that all our actions should be rational in form*' (Burns 2000, p. 28).

Deontology stipulates that duties must be observed irrespective of their consequences: legitimate rights must be respected and wrong action is prohibited. Deontologists believe that there is no clear specifiable relation between doing right and doing well (in the consequentialists' sense, such as producing a good outcome). As Fried (1978) identified '*goodness of the ultimate consequences does not guarantee the rightness of the actions that produced them. The two realms are not only distinct for the deontologist, but the right is before the good*' (p. 9). This suggests that people only have the ability to do what is morally right. Kant's categorical imperative states that 'an action is moral only if you can make your reason for acting as a rule that everyone can follow' (Dienhart 2000). If this aspect of the categorical imperative were applied to child labour, the legislation/rules that are in place in the developed Western world could be seen as universal to all children. Child labour would therefore not be ethical. However, the fact that children need to work in less developed countries illustrates that it is difficult to universalise this position and that a relative teleological perspective is necessary. Differences in culture between developed countries and less developed countries illustrate that it is difficult to separate the roles of individuals in the family.

Deontological ethical theory regards the action itself as the object of moral evaluation (Kant 1785, 1973, 1995, 2000; Donagan 1977; Davis 1980). To hold a deontological position is to deny consequentialism, that is utilitarianism or a teleological view, and claim that moral reasons are grounded in certain duties. Utilitarianism allows the welfare of an individual to be overridden if this leads to the maximisation of happiness or preference satisfaction. Deontological ethics solve some problems associated with consequentialist ethics such as utilitarianism. According to deontology, all persons have certain obligations and these obligations are non-negotiable; they cannot be bought-off or disposed of, and different kinds of inalienable rights form the basis of these obligations (Kaptein and Wempe 2002). Davis (1980) argued that 'deontological … ethics tell us that the most important aspects of how we ought to live are governed by morals that ought not to be broken, even when breaking them might have better consequence' (p. 205).

Teleological Ethical Theory

According to consequential ethics, 'the moral content of an action is determined by the real and expected consequences of that action' (Kaptein and Wempe 2002, p. 54). An action is morally good if its implications or outcomes are desirable and bad if they are not. Consequentialist ethics employs a certain standard (the purpose or outcomes) against which the consequences of an action are judged. Kaptein and Wempe (2002) stated that:

> one or more of such outcomes are chosen as a standard for judging the moral content of actions, and the outcomes that function in teleological theories are not moral in themselves, they become morally charged in their use as a standard for the moral content of actions. (p. 55)

Consequentialism has no answer to the concepts of rights, obligations and justice. However, this is the focal point in a duty-based ethics. According to this theory, an action is morally right if it honours a given obligation (which does not depend on the consequence of the action). Such a theory entitles certain people or groups to rights or a claim to justice. Cargile (1998, p. 66) analyses the views of two consequentialists (G.E.M. Anscombe and Jonathan Bennett) regarding the consequences of a given action. For Anscombe, it is wrong to procure the judicial execution of an innocent person whatever the consequences. However, Bennett argued that in certain cases it is not wrong to take such an action. Anscombe was concerned with the idea that it is morally wrong to find an innocent individual guilty whereas Bennett considered that if the outcome of finding such a person guilty benefited society or the community then it is not wrong to take such action. Consequentialists see the relation between values and agents as instrumental: agents are required to determine a designated value for whatever actions they promote. Opponents of consequentialism see the relation between values and agents as non-instrumental: agents are required or at least allowed to let their actions exemplify a designated value, even if the realisation is less than that expected.

Teleology identifies and explains human activities by reference to ends, aims, goals, objectives and purposes. It recognises that the same physical acts can be undertaken for very different purposes and that their proper interpretation requires knowing what the purpose entails. Purposes are essential for evaluating goodness. Teleologist ethics states that the moral content of an action is determined by the real and expected consequences or outcomes of that action (Machiavelli 1980, 1986; Singer 1998). They also regard the nature of an action and the intentions as morally relevant (Bowie 1991, 1997; Beauchamp and Bowie 1997).

The various teleological ethical perspectives differ not only on exactly what the '*correct consequences*' are but also on how people balance the various possible consequences. After all, few choices are unequivocally positive and this means it is necessary to determine how to arrive at the correct balance of good and bad in what we do. It should be said that merely being concerned with the consequences of an action does not make a person a consequentialist—the main factor is, rather, basing the morality of that action on the consequences instead of on something else. The key questions which teleological theory asks include:

- What will be the consequences of this action?
- What will be the consequences of inaction?
- How do I weigh the harm against the benefits of this action?

What will be the consequences of this action? The outcome of an action is judged good or bad by reference to the end to which the action is aimed. Teleological moral judgement is based on the outcomes of a certain action. If these outcomes are desirable, then the action in question is morally right; if the outcomes of the action are not desirable, then the action is morally wrong.

What will be the consequences of inaction? Moral judgement for teleology is based on intended outcomes. The aims or the goals of a certain action are important, not why an action is undertaken in the first place; it is the results or end goals that are important for the teleologist. Teleology is the science of ends.

How do I weigh the harm of an action against the benefits of this action? This is realised in the utilitarian rule of the 'the greatest happiness' where action is judged beneficial if the outcome leads to happiness for the majority of people affected by the action. It is judged harmful if the action or decision leads to the unhappiness of the majority, or if it results in more harm and less pleasure to those at which the action is aimed.

Deontological and Teleological Perspectives

The essential difference between *deontological and teleological perspectives* lies in the role that is attributed to the consequences of the action under review. The fact that an action's consequences do not determine its moral character does not imply that deontologists do not take consequences of actions into consideration. An action that violates a moral obligation is immoral. However, acting through moral obligations does not necessarily mean that such actions are always morally right. In a sense, the consequences of a given action could very well be factored into the obligation itself (Kaptein and Wempe 2002). However, a deontologist would not go as far as committing to a specific, major consequence. The principles are based on the action taken and not the outcome of such action. For example, keeping a promise is important because it is a moral duty, and not because of the consequences (Rawls 1971; Anscombe 1958; Donagan 1977; Davis 1980; Scheffler 1982).

Kaptein and Wempe (2002) argued that significant differences between variations of deontological perspectives concern the foundation of the above principles, and how they are identified. Three types of deontological positions can be distinguished. The first holds that duties are *God-given*; the second that they are based on common sense; while the third holds that they are founded on a social contract. The basis for deontological theories can be sought in God's commandments. We can see from the above that the rightness or wrongness of an action can be sought, like the action itself. Therefore, some deontological theories appeal to a kind of social contract as the foundation for the principles that are endorsed (social contract theories are identified and discussed in Chap. 1). Most religions of revelation rely on a kind of deontology. The rules are '*God-given*' and communicated in the *Bible* for example. Also, it is our obligation to follow these revelations because it is the will of God. How do we determine whether an action is morally right or wrong? Immanuel Kant's view is that this can be obtained from rational arguments and what he labelled the '*Golden Rule*', or we can follow our '*voice of consent*'. By grounding principles in a social contract, we presume the implicit consent of all parties involved. Therefore, the obligatory principles thus lie in mutual consent to the conditions of the contract.

Business Ethics and Corporate Governance

There are increasingly research projects dealing with the interface between business ethics and corporate governance issues. However, many researchers on business ethics propose it is the integrity and commitment of the board rather than compliance that is at the root of accountability and relationships between corporate ethics and corporate objectives, both at board level and amongst other organisational members. When dealing with business ethics decisions, the company reviews its goals, methods and motives and considers the potential consequences of its actions. Each of the company's multiple goals and methods is matched with one or more consequences. The question that boards of directors must ask when taking business ethics decisions is: What are the consequences of using a particular method for reaching a specific goal? (Chryssides and Kaler

1993). Indeed when faced with moral decisions that affect the affairs of the company, boards should consider '*a set of principles prescribing a behaviour code that explains what is good and right or bad and wrong: it may even outline moral duty and obligations generally*' (p. 51). Teleology or consequentialism can be applied to the shareholder and stakeholder models of corporate governance. The view that the moral worth of an action is determined by the consequences of the action rather than the action itself can be used to illustrate the consequences of the action of corporate boards when meeting the business objectives of the firm and the interests of its shareholders, while at the same time taking into consideration the effect of such decisions on the needs of the firm's stakeholders.

Shareholder Theories of Corporate Governance

This section considers the shareholder model of corporate governance. It explains the theoretical and empirical debate on the shareholder theory of corporate governance. It provides critiques of the Anglo-American system of corporate governance and asks whether corporate boards can justify their business objectives of focusing on maximising shareholder wealth. It asks if short-term profit objectives by corporate boards benefit the shareholders and the long-term goals of the corporation. It discusses the four competing models of corporate governance systems, which are the principal-agent or finance model, the myopic market model, the executive model and the stakeholder model (Nwanji and Howell 2007).

It could be argued that shareholder theory is central to 'capitalism', which can be defined as an economic system combining the private ownership of productive enterprises with competition and the pursuit of profit. The advantage of this formulation is that it picks out the three aspects that are generally accepted as defining features of the system. These are private ownership, competition and the profit motive. In theory, in an ideal capitalist system there should be minimal government intervention in the running of the economy. In a post-war scenario this started to become explicit in the 1980s when capitalist countries such as the UK and certain EU members started selling their state-controlled organisations to the private sector. Indeed this created millions of shareholders and wealth which convinced many developing countries to follow suit. However, in practice for most capitalist countries there is often a great deal of government intervention in the running of the economy and it is certainly always more than minimal. Most importantly, there is macro-economic management through government manipulation of interest rates, tax rates, public expenditure and public borrowing. Also, there is frequently a more direct kind of government economic intervention through the offering of tax incentives, subsidies, state aids for ailing industries, government rescue packages for bankrupt businesses and, in many cases, a degree of state ownership of business. In the 1980s, we saw a decline in this kind of direct intervention with a strong trend towards policies of *deregulation* and *privatisation* in many capitalist countries—most notably in the UK and the USA. Nonetheless, direct intervention by governments remains a considerable feature of capitalist economies. In any case, the kind of indirect intervention represented by government macro-economic management remains essentially intact and seems to be a permanent part of any modern capitalist economy (Chryssides and Kaler 1993).

The above paragraphs introduced the capitalist system to understand the link between shareholder theory and capitalist countries, as it can be argued that the shareholder model is more distinctly linked with a free-market capitalist economy. However, it may be argued that in the modern global business environment boards of directors and management should look beyond the interests of shareholders alone and take into consideration the interests of other stakeholders of the organisation. There are also issues of business ethics and the unethical behaviours of those who control organisations, which can affect the long-term shareholders' value as the cases of Enron, WorldCom and other corporate failures have illustrated.

An Analytical Approach to Stakeholder Theory

Freeman (1984) proposed a framework which fits three levels of stakeholder analysis—the rational, process and transactional. The first concerns how the company as a whole fits into its larger environment, or the rational level. The second concerns how the business relates to its environment as a matter of standard operating procedures and routine management processes, or the process level. The third concerns how the business executes actual transactions, e.g. deals or contracts with those individuals who have a stake in the company, or the transactional level. These three levels of analysis are connected, and one can argue that for any successful business the three levels will fit together in a coherently organised pattern. These three levels can be further explained in the following way.

At the rational level, an understanding of who are the stakeholders of the corporation and what their perceived stakes are is necessary. The rational level must depict the nature of the relationship between the company and its stakeholder groups. Freeman (1984) uses a generic stakeholder map as a starting point. It is also possible to prepare a stakeholder map around one major strategic issue, which is prepared by identifying specific stakeholders based on the stakeholder route. Furthermore, the issues important for the specific stakeholder groups are identified and analysed. Freeman also used a two-dimensional grid as an analytical device to depict an organisation's stakeholders. The first dimension categorises stakeholders by interest or stake and the second dimension is based on power. Freeman makes the grid more realistic by improving on the classical stakeholder grid to prepare an existing world stakeholder grid.

Elias and Cavana (2003, p. 4) claim that at the process level 'it is necessary to understand how the organisation either implicitly or explicitly manages its relationships with its stakeholders, and whether these processes fit with the normal stakeholder map of the organisation. Moreover, existing strategic processes that work reasonably well could be enriched with a concern for multiple stakeholders'. At the transactional level, we must understand the set of transactions or bargains among the organisation and its stakeholders and deduce whether these negotiations fit with the stakeholder map and the organisational processes for stakeholders. According to Freeman successful transactions with interested parties are built on an understanding of the legitimacy of the stakeholders' interests and having processes to surface their concerns routinely (Elias and Cavana 2003). Stakeholders are those groups and individuals who can affect and are affected by the achievement of an organisation's purpose/

objectives. How can we construct a stakeholder map of an organisation? What are the problems in constructing such a map? The Hampel Committee Report (1998) in its final report stated that:

> Corporate governance must contribute both to business prosperity and accountability. It was claimed that in the UK more attention has been concentrated on the accountability to the detriment of the prosperity. Therefore, to redress the balance we can say that the purpose of those responsible for corporate governance is to safeguard the interests of shareholders and to protect and promote the interests of other stakeholders such as employees, customers, suppliers, government and the communities where the companies operate. (Para. 15)

Metcalfe (1998) argued that a 'stakeholder is entitled to consideration in some ways similar to shareholders. Stakeholders may thus include employees, customers, shareholders, suppliers, the state, the local community, society, and bankers' (p. 12). Elias et al. (2000) also pointed out that another interesting characteristic of the stakeholder concept is that the dynamics of stakeholders, the mix of stakeholders that is, may change over time (Nwanji and Howell 2005). New stakeholders may join and wish to be included in any considerations, while others may drop out through no longer being involved with the company. Fundamentally, stakeholder management is increasingly a key factor in improving business performance. Management needs to build relationships with very different stakeholders (shareholders, employees, customers, society, etc.), act more transparently, provide opportunities for dialogue, involvement or participation, and be accountable to all stakeholders. Consequently, managers need to mobilise the sense of responsibility of all the relevant stakeholders, create the best organisational context for involvement, organise and manage that involvement and participation, consider all the stakeholder arguments and manage the constantly shifting balance between the interests of stakeholders (pp. 225–226). Donaldson and Preston (1995) suggest that research on stakeholders has proceeded along three often confused lines. First, there is instrumental stakeholder theory, which assumes that if managers want to maximise the objective function of their firms, then they must consider stakeholder interests. Second, there is descriptive research about how managers, firms and stakeholders interact. Third, there is a normative sense of stakeholder theory that prescribes what managers ought to do. To this framework we can add a fourth dimension, the metaphorical use of stakeholder, which depicts the idea as a figure in a broader narrative about corporate life. The first two senses of stakeholders can be called the *analytical approach* to stakeholder theory while the third and fourth senses can be called the *narrative approach* to stakeholder theory. Phillips (2003) suggests that:

> Organisations in the early twenty-first century are confronted with a unique set of moral issues requiring moral theory ... and that stakeholder theory is a strong candidate for such a theory of organisational ethics. Therefore, an amended principle of fair play—the principle of stakeholder fairness—provides a valid source of moral obligations among stakeholders that has been therefore missing in the literature on stakeholder theory. (pp. 5–6)

Conclusion

This chapter has outlined and discussed ethical and theoretical perspectives (deontological, teleological, shareholdership and stakeholdership) regarding corporate governance. Discussions on ethical perspectives regarding corporate governance has resulted in a growing number of research publications, and this chapter has assessed the ethical issues and the conduct of those who manage the affairs of corporations (directors' duties and responsibilities towards their stakeholders). As stated, in corporate governance procedures and documentation, boards of directors have many responsibilities, some statutory and others based on trust. Directors have to be clear about their personal responsibilities toward others. Accountability is central for corporate governance but in its traditional sense it has always exercised the minds of directors in the context of the profit and loss accounts, the balance sheet and shareholders' interests. Deontological and teleological perspectives allow researchers to investigate whether there is a trade-off between moral and corporate objectives. In this context empirical investigations may concentrate on:

- What ethical issues may/could influence directors?
- How should directors deal with the ethical issues in governance practice?
- What is the difference between directors' mind-sets and reality?
- What might influence/cause this discrepancy and how may this be dealt with?
- These issues provide the basis research questions which include:
- Should corporations take into consideration deontological and/or teleological considerations in realising their business objectives?
- *More specifically*, is the purpose of a corporation ethical?
- Is the governing action/behaviour ethical?
- Does an increased emphasis on business ethics affect enterprise?

In the twenty-first century the success of the world economy depends on the capitalist and shareholder/stakeholder systems, which are based on trust and the credibility of the financial markets. Therefore, 'good' and effective corporate governance is needed to achieve long-term business objectives of the corporation and its shareholders. There may also be the need to introduce a 'global–corporate governance' system that comprises both the Anglo-American systems (the shareholdership model) and the German stakeholder systems (stakeholdership model), as both models argue for the long-term interests of the corporation and its stakeholders (including the shareholders). Overall, while the stakeholder model of corporate governance seems to be the best way of achieving the business objective of the company, critics of stakeholdership have argued that without meeting the shareholders' interests through profit maximisation the company may not meet the needs of other stakeholders.

References

Anscombe, G. E. M. (1958). Modern moral philosophy. *Philosophy*, *33*, 1–19. (Reprinted in *Ethics*, pp. 186–210, by J. Thomson & G. Dworkin (Eds.), 1968, New York: Harper & Row).

Beauchamp, T., & Bowie, N. (1997). Ethical theory and business practice. In T. Beauchamp & N. Bowie (Eds.), *Ethical theory and business*. Prentice Hall: Upper Saddle River, NJ.

Bowie, N. (1991). Business ethics as a discipline: The search for legitimacy. In R. Freeman (Ed.), *Business ethics: The state of the art*. Oxford: Oxford University Press.

Bowie, N. (1997). New directions in corporate social responsibility. In T. Beauchamp & N. Bowie (Eds.), *Ethical theory and business*. Prentice Hall: Upper Saddle River, NJ.

Burns, R. (2000). Enlightenment. In R. Burns & H. Raymond-Pickard (Eds.), *Philosophies of history*. Oxford: Blackwell.

Cadbury Report. (1992). *The Cadbury Committee report*. European Corporate Governance Institute. http://www.ecgi.org/codes/documents/cadbury.pdf_br

Cargile, J. (1998). 'On Consequentialism' Ethical Theory 2: Theories about how we should live. In J. Rachels (Ed.), *Oxford readings in philosophy* (pp. 64–75). Oxford: Oxford University Press.

Chryssides, G. D., & Kaler, J. H. (1993). *An introduction to business ethics*. London: International Thomson Business Press.

Combined Code. (2012). *Compliance with the UK Corporate Governance Code*. UK: Financial Services Commission.

Davis, N. (1980). The priority of avoiding harm. In B. Steinbock (Ed.), *Killing and letting die* (pp. 172–214). Englewood Cliffs, NJ: Prentice Hall.

Derek Higgs Report. (2003). *Review of the role and effectiveness of Non-executive Directors (NEDs) and their responsibilities in corporate governance practice*.

Dienhart, W. J. (2000). *Business, institutions, and ethics: A text with cases and readings*. Oxford: Oxford University Press.

Donagan, A. (1977). *The theory of morality*. Chicago: University of Chicago Press.

Donaldson, T., & Preston, L. (1995). The Stakeholder theory of the corporation: Concepts, evidence and implications. *Academy of Management Review, 20*(1), 65–91.

Elias, A. A., & Cavana, R. Y. (2003). *Stakeholder analysis for systems thinking and modelling*. School of Business and Public Management, Victoria University of Wellington: New Zealand.

Elias, A. A., Cavana, R. Y., & Jackson, L. S. (2000). *Linking stakeholder literature and system dynamics: Opportunities for research* (pp. 174–179). Proceedings of the International Conference on Systems Thinking in Management, Geelong, Australia.

Fera, N. (1997). Using shareholder value to evaluate strategic choices. *Management Accounting (USA), 79*, 47.

Freeman, E. (1984). *Strategic management: A stakeholder approach*. Boston, MA: Pitman Press.

Fried, C. (1978). *Right and Wrong*. Cambridge, Mass: Harvard University Press.
Friedman, M. (1970, September 13). The social responsibility of business is to increase its profits. *The New York Times Magazine*.
Greenbury Committee. (1995). *Directors' Remuneration: Final Report of a Study Group on Directors' Remuneration*. July 1995 CBI UK.
Hampel Committee Report. (1998). *Corporate Governance Code UK for the DTI*. London. http://www.dti.gov.uk
Kant, I. (1973). *Immanuel Kant's Critique of Pure Reason* (N. K. Smith, Trans.). London: Macmillan.
Kant, I. (1785/1997). *Groundwork of the metaphysics of morals* (M. Gregor, Ed., p. 31). Cambridge University Press.
Kant, I. (1995). Political writings. In H. Reiss (Ed.), *Cambridge texts in history of political thought* (H. B. Nisbet, Trans.). Cambridge University Press.
Kant, I. (2000). Progress in history. In R. Burns & H. Raymond-Pickard (Eds.), *Philosophies of history*. Oxford: Blackwell.
Kaptein, M., & Wempe, J. (2002). *The balanced company: A theory of corporate integrity*. Oxford: Oxford University Press.
Machiavelli, N. (1980). *The discourses*. Pelican Classics.
Machiavelli, N. (1986). *The prince* (Vol. XV, p. 91). Harmondswork: Penguin.
Metcalfe, C. E. (1998). The Stakeholder Corporation; An Article in Volume 7, No. 1 (January), 30–35
Mill, S. R. (1998). *The dynamics of shareholder value*. Lechlade: Mars Business.
Myners' Report. (2001). *Myners Report on Institutional Investment*. London: HM Treasury.
Myners Review. (2004). *Myners principles for institutional investment decision-making: review of progress*. UK: HM Treasury.
Nwanji, T. I., & Howell, E. K. (2004). *Ethical perspectives on corporate governance: Developing substantive theory*. UK: Earlybrave Publication.
Nwanji, T.I., & Howell, K. E. (2005). The stakeholder theory in the modern global business environment. *International Journal of Applied Institutional Governance, 1*(1), 1–12. www.managementjournals.com.
Nwanji, T. I., & Howell, K. E. (2007). Shareholdership versus stakeholdership. *Journal of Corporate Ownership and Control, 5*(1), 9–23. ISSN: 1727–9232.
OECD. (2004). *OECD Principles of Corporate Governance*. Paris: OECD. http://www.oecd.org/social/poverty/28658158.pdf_br
OECD. (1999). *Corporate governance principles: OECD—Organisation for Economic Co-operation and Development*. OECD Steering Group on Corporate Governance. www.cecd.com

Oman, C., Fries, S., & Buiter, W. (2003). *OECD report on corporate governance in developing, transition and emerging–market economies*. http://www.oecd.org/dev

Parkinson, J. E. (1994). *Corporate power and responsibility*. Oxford: Oxford University Press.

Phillips, R. (2003). *Stakeholder theory and organisational ethics* (p. 16). San Francisco, CA: Berrett-Koehler. http://managementjournals.com/ig/

Rawls, J. (1971). *A theory of justice*. Cambridge, MA: Harvard University Press.

Sarbanes-Oxley Act. (2002, October 16). *The US influence, supplement: New York Stock Exchange and NASDAQ proposed listed company corporate governance rules*. Governance Rules.

Scheffler, S. (1982). *The rejection of consequentialism*. Oxford: Oxford University Press.

Sherwin, D. (1983). *The Ethical Roots of Business System*. Harvard Business Review Harvard Business School (November-December).

Singer, P. (1993). A companion to ethics. In *Blackwell companions to philosophy: Blackwell reference*. Oxford: Blackwell.

Singer, P. (1998). *Practical ethics* (2nd ed.). Cambridge University Press.

Smith Report. (2003). *Audit Committees Combined Code Guidance. A Report and Proposed Guidance by an FRC Appointed Group*. Financial Reporting Council. Retrieved From (http://en.wikipedia.org/wiki/Review_of_the_role_and_effectiveness_of_non-executive_directors_br) (www.frc.org.uk/publication).

Solomon, J. (2004). *Corporate governance and accountability*. Chichester: John Wiley. http://www.barnesandnoble.com/w/corporate-governance-and-accountability-jill-solomon/1119390211?ean=9780470843659_br

Ticker, R. I. (1984). *Corporate governance: Practices, procedures and powers in Turnbull Report (2005), Internal control and risk management: Developing roles of internal audit*. http://en.wikipediaorg/wiki/Review_of_the_role_and_effectiveness_of_non-executive_directors_br

Turnbull Committee Report. (1999). *The Internal Control: Guidance for Directors on the Combined Code*. The Institute of Chartered Accountants in England and Wales, ICAEW: London.

Walker Review. (2009). *Review of UK Corporate Governance in the Banking Industry*. UK: HM Treasury.

Williams, B. (1985). Ethics and the limits of philosophy. In O. Williams & T. Bottomore (Eds.), *Dictionary of twentieth-century social thought* (pp. 202–204). London: Blackwell.

4

On the Evolution of Corporate Governance Culture in Africa: The Case of the Egyptian Banking Sector

M. Karim Sorour and Ahmed El Sakhawy

Introduction

There is no doubt that corporate governance failure was cited as a major contributor to the financial crisis of 2008 (Kirkpatrick 2009; Dermine 2013). Countries around the globe were urged to review their banks' corporate governance systems and introduce changes and developments to address the deficits exposed by the financial crisis. For instance, the UK has responded by initiating 'the biggest reforms to the banking sector in a generation: to make banks more resilient to shocks, easier to fix when they get into difficulties, and to reduce the severity of future financial crises' (UK Government 2015). Here, a major lesson from the financial crisis was that there is no 'one size fits all or a magical recipe as far as good corporate governance is concerned' (Buchs 2009, p. 1). Thus,

M.K. Sorour (✉)
Newcastle Business School, Northumbria University, Newcastle upon Tyne, UK

A. El Sakhawy
Economic and Managerial Studies Department (MRCC), Arab Academy for Science, Technology and Maritime Transport, Latakia, Syria

K.E. Howell, M.K. Sorour (eds.), *Corporate Governance in Africa*,
DOI 10.1057/978-1-137-56700-0_4

effective reform should deal with corporate governance as a socially constructed phenomenon because of 'the temporary, transient and emergent patterns of corporate governance on a historical and contextual basis in a given society' (Ardalan 2007, p. 511). Indeed, this particular approach is deemed suitable in the context of developing countries due to their unique institutional contexts that makes it difficult to follow unconditionally Western corporate governance systems (Rwegasira 2000).

Egypt is the second biggest African economy in terms of GDP (purchasing power parity) and 28th in comparison to the rest of the World (CIA 2015). Its banking sector plays an important role in the economy fulfilling approximately 85 % of businesses financing requirements (El-said 2009). Therefore, banks were seen as a main vehicle for corporate governance reform in Egypt. The Egyptian Corporate Governance Codes (2005, 2011) have assigned banks a principal role to promote corporate governance culture, which can help in attracting more foreign direct investment. Additionally, in response to bank failures related to weak corporate governance, the Central Bank of Egypt (CBE) initiated corporate governance reform more than a decade ago in an attempt to create a corporate governance culture in the banking sector (CBE 2009). Indeed, this is not only important for the safety and soundness of the banking sector, but also for the promotion of corporate governance in other sectors of the economy. Following a relativist approach, this chapter discusses the corporate governance reform process and culture creation within the Egyptian banking sector (EBS) as identified by Sorour (2011). Moreover, as significant changes have taken place both in Egypt and its banking sector during the last few years, this chapter extends Sorour's (2011) study by analysing the corporate governance disclosures of 38 banks, thus identifying the level of maturity of the respective corporate governance culture.

Background to Corporate Governance Reform in Egypt

Egypt began undertaking corporate governance reforms in the early 2000s as part of a wider economic restructuring. Since then many reforms have been implemented to bring about changes and create a corporate governance culture in the Egyptian business environment, which would signify 'a mode of behaviour of the principal players ... that must reflect a deep and abiding commitment to governance ... which comes naturally' (Dey 2001, p. 4).

According to Sorour (2014) the evolution of corporate governance in Egypt was underpinned by four pillars. The first pillar was the role of international organisations in corporate governance reform, such as the World Bank and the International Monetary Fund (IMF) through the series of country assessment reports known as the observance of standards and codes (ROSC) in 2001, 2004 and 2009. It is worth noting that, to an extent, the recommendation of these reports formed the basis for corporate governance reform in Egypt. For example, this included the Egyptian stock exchange introducing new listing rules in 2002, reforming company law, and upgrading the accounting and auditing standards. The second pillar was the creation of the Egyptian Institute of Directors (EIOD) which has an important role not only in raising awareness and enhancing corporate governance competencies, but also in drafting the first Egyptian Code of Corporate Governance issued in 2005 (ECOCG 2005). The third pillar involved broad legal and regulatory reforms and in particular the capital market law and company's law number 159. The fourth pillar was the corporate governance reform in the EBS. As mentioned earlier, the EBS is one of the most influential sectors in the business environment; as such the two Egyptian Codes of Corporate Governance 2005 (ECOCG 2005; 2011) tasked the banking sector with the promotion of the corporate governance concept amongst its wide base of corporate clients. Therefore, corporate governance reform in the EBS has emerged not only as part of the banking sector reform (CBE 2009) but also as part of a wider reform process that aims to build a corporate governance culture in the Egyptian business environment. Indeed, this is not a trouble free task.

Corporate Governance Reform and Culture Creation in the EBS

The reform of corporate governance was part of a wider reform process underway in Egypt; during the 2000s the business environment began to comprehend this situation, especially after agreeing to an Arabic equivalent of corporate governance or *Hawakamat Al-Sharikat* (World Bank 2015). That said, EBS corporate governance reform was initiated to tackle a number of corporate governance weaknesses which contributed to the late 1990s' bank failures and the hefty non-performing loans (NPL) bill (CBE 2009). Notably, weak corporate governance facilitated inappropriate lending and investment decisions (Oldham and Benaddi 2005). As Kalhoefer and Salem (2008, p. 5) put it, 'loans were given based on intentionally overvalued assets to fit the collateral base of each bank and disregarding the future cash flows of the borrowers'. Weak corporate governance was more evident in state-owned banks where credit decisions were influenced by cronyism and favouritism rather than the mere commercial aspects, with board members playing a pivotal role in such malpractices (Mohieldin and Nasr 2007). Other reasons for the CBE to tackle weak corporate governance included the practices of state-owned banks in financing mega-projects based on their political rather than commercial merit. Further corporate governance weaknesses in state owned banks included distorted incentive systems, poor management, weak internal governance, lack of performance incentives, overstaffing and inadequate risk management (Mohieldin and Nasr 2007), while in private banks the motive for corporate governance reform was more related to strengthening risk management practices to protect shareholders and depositors. On the other hand, Kalhoefer and Salem (2008) indicated that the weak supervision of the CBE during this time would also be added to the list of troubles that led to the NPL problem. Furthermore, El-Shazly (2001, p. 16) has indicated that during this period transparency and disclosure levels were also inadequate and that banks' publications of their financial statements was only made at the end of the year and, even when published, were of limited use. This was also substantiated by the global assessment of bank disclosure practices report, which classified the EBS as one of the most opaque banking systems around the world (Huang 2006, p. 12). Therefore, within the banking sector, failures created an immense pressure on the regulator to address weak corporate governance to avoid the exacerbation of the NPL problem and thus protect shareholders and depositors and the overall health of the banking sector. Of note was the very high expectation that the banking sector would lead the promotion of the corporate governance concept in the business environment. These pressures formed an impetus to introduce/create a corporate governance culture within the banking sector in Egypt. Despite its clear importance, the corporate governance of banks has not received much attention in the literature except for Sorour (2011) who utilised a grounded theory approach to develop a substantive theory on corporate governance reform in the EBS. This study was underpinned by a combination of social constructivism and interpretivist paradigms subscribing to a relativist ontology and an objectivist epistemology (although they often refer to the same paradigm, see Guba and Lincoln 1989, which followed Schwandt 1998 who recognised them as two paradigms). This study adopts Strauss and Corbin's (1990, 1998) grounded theory approach. The data collected for this study were analysed using grounded theory methods. This included the processes of data reduction, concepts discovery and categories development. These categories were integrated into the substantive theory (Howell 2000) (see Sorour 2011).

Drivers of Corporate Governance Culture Creation in the EBS

Many entities played an effective role in bringing about corporate governance reform and the creation of a corporate governance culture in the banking sector. This included independent parties who had no direct interest with banks as well as governmental bodies. Essentially, these entities pursued the corporate governance agenda for different reasons, as discussed in the following sections.

Pressure by Independent Entities

Independent groups are those who do not have any business interest or connection with banks. These include the regulator, external audit firms and international organizations such as the World Bank and the Basel Committee on Banking Supervision (BCBS). Both the CBE and the external auditors should be independent according to the banking law 88/2003, which states that the CBE is 'a public legal person, directly subject to the president of the republic' (Article1:1). Similarly, the same law requires that auditors must be independent and prohibits the auditor or any of his or her family to be engaged in any transaction that would impair their independence. Various participants from the banking field have agreed that the CBE, auditors and international organisations have influence on the corporate governance of the EBS. This signifies that these bodies exert certain types of pressure. The CBE as the regulator has the authority to issue and enforce corporate governance related regulations. As such the CBE is exerting coercive pressures on the banking sector. The CBE can punish or delist any non-complying bank by the powers entitled to it by law as follows:

> The CBE shall take the means with which it ensures the realization of its objectives and discharge of its functions. It shall, in particular, have the following powers … supervising the units of the banking sector … the bank may undertake any tasks or take any measures required for applying … credit, and banking policies, as well as for guaranteeing the soundness of bank credit. (Law88, 2003, Article 6: 5–6)

The CBE also exerts a normative pressure through its training arm known as the Egyptian Banking Institute (EBI) which was established by Law 88/2003:

> The banking institute shall be established and be affiliated to the central bank … the banking institute shall be concerned with the development of skills in the fields of banking, financial and monetary aspects, and combating of money laundering, for staff of the central bank, banks and other parties … with the aim of keeping abreast of world developments and firmly establishing sound professional rules. (Law 88, 2003, Article 45: 21)

Since the late 2000s the EBI has taken the initiative to increase corporate governance awareness in the EBS by organising seminars. However, more recently this role has witnessed a major development through the creation of a corporate governance unit. The unit was created in 2011 concurrently with issuing the corporate governance code of the CBE in the same year. According to the EBI (2015):

> In light of the current changes in the global and regional markets and increasing the importance of sound Corporate Governance practices, the Central Bank of Egypt has launched the Corporate Governance regulation on the 23rd of August 2011 requiring banks to comply with its provisions. Therefore, the Egyptian Banking Institute has established a Corporate Governance Unit dedicated to raise the awareness on Corporate Governance principles, systems and applications and to assist the organizations to implement sound Corporate Governance practices.

Of course, this marks a tangible development towards creation of the corporate governance culture and reflects a real interest from the CBE and its training arm to promote this concept. This unit aims to achieve a number of goals, namely 'to raise awareness on Corporate Governance and its related topics; to support the business community to apply/enhance good governance practices through providing high quality of services; to enhance the cooperation between the EBI and the regional and international organizations working in the field of Corporate Governance' (EBI 2015).

Auditing firms also exert pressure on the banking sector in relation to their corporate governance practices, though only to the limit stipulated by law and regulation and as enforced by the CBE. Here it should be noted that auditing firms' pressure is derived from the authority of the regulator (CBE), since the banking law has determined the role of the external auditing firm as follows:

> Bank accounts shall be audited by two auditors … each bank shall determine the procedures to be applied for facing irregular finance and credit facilities. The management of each bank shall comply with these standards & implement these procedures. The auditors shall also verify the compliance of the bank management with these standards (ibid., p. 11).
>
> The two auditors shall prepare their report on auditing the banks financial statements, the extent of adequacy of internal control … any regulatory or supervisory standards that the Board of directors of the central bank requires the auditors to verify bank's compliance with. (ibid., pp. 37–38)

As such the auditor exerts a pressure on banks to comply with banking regulations, including corporate governance related, as they are required to verify a bank's compliance with applicable laws and regulations. In case of non-compliance the two auditors are responsible for communicating the case to the CBE and the bank's general assembly. This can possibly lead to penalising the bank by the CBE. However, it is worthwhile mentioning that cases of non-compliance might be a grey area, especially with the more principles-based approach followed by the CBE in relation to corporate governance as will be discussed in the next section of the chapter.

Finally, international organisations exert pressures on the EBS regarding its corporate governance practices. International organisations exert a normative pressure[1] by establishing standards that constitute good corporate governance. In fact, international organisations play a role in stimulating compliance with international standards of corporate governance. On the one hand, requiring the compliance with these standards as a condition for donation encourages banks that seek the international organisation's funds to show compliance with these standards. On the other hand, international organisations establish corporate governance standards that over time become the norm of the international banking community. In fact, following the global crisis (2007) the emphasis on corporate governance reform was an unprecedented detrimental effect of 'failures and weaknesses in corporate governance arrangements' (Kirkpatrick 2009, p. 1). Thus, enormous efforts were made by international organisations such as the Basel Committee on Banking Supervision (BCBS) and the Organisation for Economic Co-operation and Development (OECD) as well as the European Union to reform further corporate governance in banking sectors (Dermine 2013). This has created ongoing pressure from such organisations on the EBS to continue reforming its corporate governance and create a corporate governance culture, as became an obvious necessity for any sound banking sector.

---

[1] Here normative pressures refer to the pressure created on banks as a result of corporate governance standards established by international organisations. These standards create an institutional pressure based on a binding expectation that banks should comply with these corporate governance standards to be perceived as appropriate within the international banking domain (Scott 2001). Also, international organisations normally use these standards as a benchmark for a well-governed banking organisation. More precisely, international organisations would use these standards when making donations to well-governed banks.

Pressure by Governmental Entities

Governmental entities are another source of pressure on the EBS in relation to corporate governance. In fact, the Ministry of Investment started corporate governance reform in Egypt by asking the World Bank to assess it in Egypt (ROSC 2001, 2004). Upon the recommendations of these assessments, the Ministry of Investment undertook serious steps to improve corporate governance in Egypt. For instance it established the EIOD with the responsibility to 'spread awareness, knowledge and best practices of corporate governance in Egypt' (EIOD 2009, online). The EIOD has made a genuine contribution towards reforming corporate governance in Egypt by issuing codes in 2005 and 2011. These codes assigned the responsibility of corporate governance promotion to banks.

In conclusion, banks are all affected by the above mentioned pressures; and they do respond to them. These responses are basically related to being perceived as legitimate by the CBE and shareholders. However, given its coercive power, the CBE seems to have the most significant pressure on the banking sector towards adoption of particular corporate governance arrangements. The pressures of international organisations impact on the banking sector indirectly through the CBE. Organisations such as the World Bank and the Basel Committee identify corporate governance of banks as a measure of soundness and appropriateness. Moreover, they can directly impact on banks by requiring good corporate governance as a prerequisite for donation. However, the former case occurs over time and is likely to bring about more change because they induce the CBE to change the regulatory framework in accordance with international standards. As such, one could conclude that, although international organisations exert pressure on the banking sector, its impact can only be felt over time. This can be noticed over the last decade, with the CBE issuing the first bank corporate governance regulation (code) in 2011 as a response to these pressures. The EBI should play a role in the promotion of corporate governance through its professional training services; however, this role, although started humbly in the late 2000s, has seen a major development in what it can offer, clearly signified by the creation of a specialised corporate governance unit as mentioned above.

The Protection of Interests

Interest refers to the ''material right, benefit, asset, or share possessed by fiduciary or by others with whom he/she is legally or closely associated (family members, business partners, employers, benefactor, client, or the like)' (Luebke 1987, p. 69, cited in Martin and Gabard 2001, p. 315). As such, it refers here to the stakeholders' interests that are central to the corporate governance of banks. Stakeholders of a bank can include many parties, such as shareholders, depositors, regulator, employees and society. However, the study revealed a consensus that corporate governance mechanisms have to protect shareholders because they are the owners of the bank. However, this does not mean that shareholders are actively seeking corporate governance improvement in all cases, as some shareholders are not really aware of the corporate governance concepts, while others can be free riders. Although, shareholders would be given primary, the special nature of the banking industry, mandates serving other stakeholders, namely the regulator (CBE) and depositors. Clearly, the CBE plays a pivotal role in putting in place the corporate governance arrangements to maintain the protection of depositors' funds. Here, the depositors' interests became an overriding objective of the CBE and consequently a fundamental reason for improving corporate governance in banks.[2] The study revealed that other stakeholders, such as employees, local communities, the environment and borrowers, would have lower salience. Notably, it was revealed that they do not have enough power nor can they threaten the legitimacy of banks in order to have the same salience as depositors or the regulator. In conclusion, this clarifies that corporate governance is primarily driven by the power of the CBE and shareholders. Depositors themselves are not powerful in relation to inducing corporate governance change because in most of the cases they are unaware of it. But the CBE considers that

[2] Protecting depositors' funds has become a priority for the CBE, especially after corporate-governance-related bank failures occurred during late 1990s, leading to a huge NPL problem. So here protecting depositors is a priority for improving bank corporate governance in the EBS, though not because the depositors themselves are aware of what good corporate governance can offer them. These failures have cost the CBE high bail-out costs to compensate depositors for their lost funds.

their protection is an overriding objective. In fact, this can clarify how corporate governance can be defined within the context of the EBS, as the debate is always whether corporate governance arrangements should serve shareholders solely or serve a wide range of stakeholders (Solomon 2014). This category has identified whose interests corporate governance should serve, based on the power they have. In fact, this agrees with the scope of corporate governance identified by the EBI (2006) in confromance with BCBS (2005, p. 4) definition of corporate governance as "the manner in which…banks…meet the obligation of accountability to their shareholders and take into account the interests of other recognize stakeholders (supervisors, governments and depositors)". Indeed, this reflects the fact that the prevailing corporate governance model in the EBS is likely to be a pluralistic model that serves recognised stakeholders, namely shareholders, regulator and depositors.

Banking Laws and Regulations

No doubt, laws and regulations play an inevitable role in shaping corporate governance practices within any sector of the economy. Here, we pay particular attention to laws and regulations issued by the CBE as the sole regulating authority of the banking industry in Egypt. According to the Basel Committee (BCBS 2005, 2010) governments can play a vital role in promoting good corporate governance in banks, specifically through 'laws, regulations, enforcement' (BCBS 2005, p. 19). According to Sorour (2011) the dimension of the laws and regulations of the substantive theory (ST) can be explored in terms of two properties: corporate governance content and enforcement.

Corporate Governance Content

An effective legal and regulatory framework is essential to promote good corporate governance practices within any banking sector (BCBS 2005). Here, the ST evaluated the current legal and regulatory framework on the basis of its corporate governance content, with the main reference made to the law of Central Bank, The Banking Sector and Money number 88/2003, as the principal legal document governing the banking sector. As such, if a legal framework is to promote corporate governance of the banking sector, it should explicitly be issued by the Central Bank. Although the Egyptian Codes of Corporate Governance (2005) is applicable to banking organisations, as stated in the code's scope of application, 'it is also applicable to ... banks, insurance companies, and real-estate financing companies' (ECOCG 2005, p. 5), the study did not document any reference to the code by the participants. This indicates that corporate governance regulations that address the banking sector amongst a number of organizations do not have a strong impact, especially if they are voluntary and not endorsed by the CBE, whereas those endorsed or enforced by the CBE are more effective in bringing change.

Reviewing Law 88/2003 and its executive regulation indicates the absence of the term 'corporate governance' from both documents, with few aspects that can be considered corporate governance related, such as ownership rules, audit committee formation and the role of auditors in reviewing the internal controls of banks. Meanwhile, some other corporate governance related regulations were enacted by the CBE, such as the guidelines for the evaluation of creditworthiness of customers and the control and supervision guidelines. However, none of these regulations deal with corporate governance in a comprehensive manner. This demonstrates the limited corporate governance scope within the banking laws and regulations cited above. On the other hand, the study reveals that the role of the regulator is to set the rules that can be applied equally to all banks and allow for differences between banking organisations in terms of size and abilities. That said, the need for a corporate governance code to fill the gap in the applicable regulations was evident.

As such, and showing the validity of the above contentions, the CBE board of directors issued a corporate governance directive in 2011 (referred to as the corporate governance code hereafter in the chapter). The CBE indicated that the code is applicable to all registered banks, which had to comply with the code provisions before 1 March 2012 (CBE 2011).

Enforcement of Corporate Governance

According to the Electronic Longman Dictionary 'enforcement' refers to the ability to achieve obedience to a rule or a law. Enforcement requires having coercive power that refers to the ability to force someone to comply with an order (law) through the threat of punishment (French and Raven 2001). Indeed, enforcement is an essential property of laws and regulations. Here, enforcement refers to the ability of the CBE to force banks to comply with relevant corporate governance laws and regulations to promote good corporate governance practices and help create a corporate governance culture. The study stressed the need for effective enforcement mechanisms that can bring about real change in corporate governance practices. However, one interesting point highlighted was the CBE approach to bring about compliance. Effectively, the study revealed that the general approach to enforcement was to issue rules but follow a flexible approach in implementation (similar to a principles-based approach of corporate governance). Here, this approach is one that does not discriminate between banks, but would allow them to adopt rules in accordance to their size and capabilities. Notably, the study documented also an opposite view that favours a stringent application of corporate governance rules (more of a rule based view of corporate governance). Here, the CBE faces the challenges of achieving competing objectives, on one hand sustaining the stability of the banking sector and on the other creating a corporate governance culture. From a CBE point of view, both would be difficult to achieve, if too tight corporate governance measures were enforced. So, the CBE tries to achieve balance between banking sector safety and stability. The CBE approach is to modernise the banking sector and endorse good practice guidelines, yet to do this gradually after ensuring that the CBE itself has the capabilities to support the new concepts. This is essential to avoid shocks or technical problems. This approach was followed by the CBE when they issued the corporate governance code (2011). Although the code states that all banks registered with the CBE have to put in place or develop their corporate governance systems in accordance to the code provisions, banks have to comply with the code to the extent that it is relevant to their volume of business and the complexity of their business models, internal policies and risk for appetite. The code also states that, in cases where it has became impossible to comply with the code provisions, the bank has to report this to the CBE, explaining the compelling reasons for such instances.

Supervision of Banks

This category indicates the processes or mechanisms undertaken by the CBE to enhance corporate governance practices within the EBS. In an organisational context, supervision indicates the act of 'oversight that is necessary … to prevent wrong doing that may go unnoticed' (*Encyclopaedia of Management* 2009, p. 20). This category has emerged to demonstrate supervision as the principal mechanism utilised by the CBE to make sure that banks comply with corporate governance regulations. It is a measure of safety and soundness in banks. Moreover, this function is being upgraded by the CBE to bring about more compliance with corporate governance laws and regulations. According to Sorour (2011) upgrading supervision can be discussed through two properties: *supervision processes* and *efficiency and effectiveness of supervision.*

Supervision Processes

'The CBE is an autonomous public legal entity which regulates monetary, credit and banking policy, and supervises its implementation in accordance with the banks and credit law, the law of the central bank and banking system, and the regulations of the Board of the CBE promulgated under these laws' (CBE 2010, online). Therefore, one of the CBE's main functions is to supervise the implementation of laws and regulations. The focus here is corporate governance practices and what supervision has to do with it. According to BCBS (2010), the role of enhancement of bank corporate governance practices is related to the supervisory role of the regulator:

> Supervisors should provide guidance to banks on expectations for sound corporate governance … [through establishing] guidance or rules … espe-

> cially … where national laws, regulations, codes, or listing requirements regarding corporate governance are not sufficiently robust to address the unique corporate governance needs of banks … [Meanwhile] supervisors should regularly perform a comprehensive evaluation of a bank's overall corporate governance policies and practices and evaluate the bank's implementation of the principles. (BCBS 2010, p. 29)

As such, the CBE issued a corporate governance regulation (code), as previously mentioned, to avoid corporate governance related troubles as well as meeting the expectations of the international banking community. However, issuing a corporate governance code does not automatically guarantee banks' compliance with such regulations. Hence, the supervision function plays a crucial role in this context. It should include regular and comprehensive evaluation of banks' overall corporate governance policies and practices (BCBS 2010). Additionally, regulators should 'supplement their regular evaluation … By monitoring a combination of internal reports and prudential reports … require effective and timely remedial action by a bank to address material deficiencies in its corporate governance' (BCBS 2010). Here, there are many supervision mechanisms utilised, such as on-site supervision, off-site analysis and prudential surveillance (see more details in CBE 2010). Moreover, the CBE has a range of corrective measures when banks violate laws and regulations, ranging from reduction or suspension of credit facilities to dissolving the board of directors and appointing a commissioner (CBE 2010, online). Note that the approach of supervising corporate governance regulations seems to be more inclined to the comply or explain approach, as indicated in the corporate governance code (2011), where banks have to explain to the CBE why they did not comply with a particular code provision. That said, there is no information available about what happens in cases of non-compliance.

Efficiency and Effectiveness of Supervision

Efficiency and effectiveness of supervision complement the previous subcategory of supervision processes and aim to show how the supervision function has been subject to upgrading and how this will affect corporate governance of the EBS.

'Efficiency is doing things right and effectiveness is doing the right things' (*Encyclopaedia of Management* 2009, p. 217). In the context of the efficiency of supervision operations, participants have questioned the competence of the CBE examiners, especially in relation to corporate governance, given its recency. This would certainly affect the efficiency of supervision, as less competent examiners would not be able to do 'things right'. Thus, the CBE decided to upgrade the supervision function as part of the overall banking sector reform. During the first stage of reform the objective was 'upgrading of the supervision sector of the CBE' (CBE 2009, p. 17), while during the second stage[3] of reform the CBE has been more specific in addressing the crucial issues of effective and efficient supervision. Then, the CBE added qualitative standards that ensure the safety of depositors' funds rather than depending on quantitative measures only. For the first time 'good governance rules, information system efficiency and the appropriate competency standards for officials and managers of banks' key sectors' (CBE 2009, p. 13) will be areas to be assessed within the supervisory framework. This will directly affect effectiveness and efficiency of supervision in relation to corporate governance by, firstly, including corporate governance explicitly in the scope of supervision, which will enhance effectiveness; and secondly, addressing the competency of both officials (CBE examiners) and bank management teams, which will affect efficiency. That said, the new corporate governance code (2011) and its disclosure requirements will also contribute to the effectiveness of supervision as banks are now expected to be transparent regarding their corporate governance practices as will be investigated later in the chapter.

Hawkamat Al-Sharikat Culture

Hawkamat Al-Sharikat is the Arabic translation of corporate governance (World Bank 2015, online) which came into existence during the early

[3] Covers the period of 2009–2011.

2000s, showing the relative recency of the concept. Culture refers to 'a pattern of shared basic assumptions that was learned by a group as it solved its problems of external adaptation and internal integration, that has worked well enough to be considered valid and, therefore, to be taught to new members as the correct way to perceive, think, and feel in relation to those problems' (Schein 2004, p. 17). Culture includes some essential elements, such as history sharing, structural stability, depth, breadth and patterning or integration (Schein 2004, p. 17). Having said that, corporate governance culture refers to a mode of behaviour of the principal players in governance systems (i.e. stakeholders) that must reflect a deep and abiding commitment to governance—a commitment which comes naturally' (Dey 2001, p. 4). As such, one could argue that corporate governance culture in the EBS would truly exist if and only if banks and their stakeholders, such as customers, regulator, suppliers and the wider community, are naturally committed to good corporate governance practices. A closely related concept to culture is leadership, for some authors such as Schein (2004, p. 17), the two concepts "are two sides of the same coin; neither can really be understood by itself. The reason being that culture defines who will be accepted as a leader and as such can attract followers' attention (Schein, 2004). On the other hand, leaders can create, manage or destroy culture if considered dysfunctional. Therefore, Sorour (2011) has observed the category of corporate governance culture (or *Hawkamat El-Sharikat* culture) in the light of the following properties: the role of reformers and the role of public governance.

Role of Reformers

As leadership is crucial to culture formation, one can argue that if *Hawkamat El-Sharikat* culture exists, leaders of the EBS would have had a role in building this culture. Moreover, if this culture exists this would imply the natural and deep commitment to governance as indicated above. Sorour (2011) indicated that this culture is still at the early stages of formation and is a long term objective that requires true and serious work by the EBS reformers, especially the CBE. In fact, cultural formation is very much related to leadership action. Here the CBE plays the role of the leader, and not only as the regulator, by starting reforms that would eventually lead to a corporate governance culture. In essence, this implies that dysfunctional cultures change, such as through the rejection of a corporate governance culture and/or a board of directors' resistance to change or a resistance to learn new concepts.

The cultural aspect of reform can be observed in the restructuring of state-owned banks for instance. Here, restructuring started by replacing top management at these banks with more competent figures, who are able to lead culture change in their banking organizations, including creating a corporate governance culture. As such new management of state-owned banks has started this culture change, with enhanced internal control systems including risk management, internal audit and compliance functions. In essence this not only requires the change of the systems, but also the change of the culture where these new systems are operating. The relatively low corporate governance quality in state banks is partially blamed on the cultural aspect, as this quality is still prevailing, even though systems have changed.

Two important developments took place in the EBS since Sorour's (2011) study: issuing the bank governance code (2011) by the CBE and establishing a new corporate governance unit by the EBI. This code followed a 'comply-or-explain' approach, mandating that banks comply with the code provisions or explain to the CBE the reasons for non-compliance. Although the code prescribed the requirements of good bank governance, the code was quite flexible in permitting every bank to choose the most effective approach to adopt the code principles, taking into consideration its size and level of operational complexity (CBE 2011). The code states that every bank should first build a corporate governance culture through developing an internal code of conduct to direct the bank on how it discharges its responsibilities towards shareholders and depositors. Unsurprisingly, the code has been influenced by both the OECD principles of corporate governance (2004) and the Basel Committee's principles for enhancing corporate governance in banking organisations (BCBS 2006, 2010). We noticed a significant influence in relation to the definition of corporate governance, as well as provisions related to the following areas: the board of directors, effective utilisation of the work conducted by the internal auditors/external auditors/internal control functions, disclosure and transparency, and oversight on complex structures/processes through the implementation of a corporate governance framework (CBE 2011). While this is considered an important step towards creating a corporate governance culture, no previous studies assessed the level of banks' compliance with the code provisions, a gap in the literature that this chapter will address in the following section.

Role of Public Governance

Public governance is the concept related to 'the process by which a society organizes its affairs and manages itself' (Manning and Kraan 2006, cited in UN 2007, p. 2). It implies that the supply of public goods occur in agreement with democracy, transparency and accountability principles (UN 2007). According to Euromoney (2006) poor public governance can have a quite negative impact on corporate governance, simply because it would be very difficult to ask people and organisations to be committed to good corporate governance practices while the wider environment is corrupt. It must be mentioned here that the political arena in Egypt has witnessed fundamental changes during the last four years, with upheavals taking place in 2011 and 2013. Unprecedented changes took place since President Mubarak surrendered power in February 2011 (*The Guardian* 2011, online) up until the final presidential elections won by President Al Sisi in 2013. It is fair to say that efforts to fight corruption in Egypt is easier said than done; for instance in 2011 Egypt was ranked 112th in the Transparency Corruption Index (CPI) which indicates that 'access to information, bribery of public officials, kickbacks in public procurement, and the enforcement of anti-corruption laws' (Transparency-International 2011) still requires enormous work. On a positive note there has been considerable improvement in public governance, as Egypt ranked 94th on the CPI; however, there is still one caveat in the CPI, that it is based on experts' perceptions rather than factual data which for obvious reasons could be unrealisable.

Evaluation of Banks Compliance with the CBE Disclosure Requirement

In the previous sections the chapter has shown that although bank governance is a relatively new phenomenon in the EBS, there are many drivers and developments that have successfully led to progress in bank governance reform. So far, we have shown that over the last five years these developments have pushed the evolution of bank governance forward towards the creation of a corporate governance culture helped by the reform process. This section of the chapter aims to assess how far this culture has been created. Based on Dey's (2001) definition of corporate governance culture, we assumed that such a culture would exist if good corporate governance practices became a naturally occurring practice, i.e. when non-complying banks are noticed to be illegitimate. Towards this objective this section investigates the level of compliance of banks with the bank governance code (2011) provisions in relation to compulsory disclosures. Under the title of 'disclosure and transparency' the bank governance code mandates that banks disclose the following information:

1. The composition and structure of the bank's board of directors;
2. The board members' expertise and qualifications;
3. Responsibilities of the board of directors;
4. The bank's ownership structure;
5. The organisational structure of the bank; for example, the overall structure of jobs, business sectors, subsidiaries and especially board committees;
6. The bank's code of conduct;
7. The bank's policies with respect to conflict of interest and internal transactions and transactions with related parties;
8. The bank's policy for corporate governance and its practices;
9. The bank policies related to salaries and bonuses, including the disclosure of the total amount of remenuration received by the largest 20 employees of the bank (includes salaries, allowances and benefits in kind and shares and any other benefits of a financial nature);
10. The bank's social responsibility policies and its practices.

Following the Basel Committee guidance on enhancing corporate governance for banking organisations (BCBS 2006, 2010) the code mentioned that disclosures can be made, for example through banks' annual reports and websites, and also through reports to the regulatory authorities. Here, the main purpose of transparency is to enhance the ability of various stakeholders to monitor effectively the soundness of banking organisations (BCBS 2006). Websites and annual reports became the main channels for communication with the wider stakeholder's community (Barakat and Hussainey 2013). It is worth mentioning that the code equating annual reports and websites with reports to regulatory authorities undermines the concept of disclosure and transparency as these reports would not be really accessible by wider stakeholders. As such, we assume that it is a matter of custom and practice that companies report their corporate governance compliance through their websites and annual reports. That said, this might be a limitation that we should acknowledge as well.

Our study has investigated corporate governance disclosures of 38 banks which represents the whole population of banks registered with the CBE as of September 2015 (CBE, 2015), except two banks that have stopped operations in Egypt. Our methodology was based on analysing the content of the official websites of the 38 banks in relation to the disclosure and transparency aspects required by the bank governance code and as listed in Table 4.1. We have followed a simple methodology which is common in corporate governance studies, by assigning a value of 1 in the case where the bank discloses the item required, and 0 if the item is not disclosed.

Findings

Analysis of the annual reports and websites of the 38 banks have revealed that there is a relatively weak overall level of disclosure as only 55 % of banks have disclosed four items or more of the ten items required by the bank governance code. Moreover, the analysis shows that only 3 % of banks (one bank) have disclosed the nine items. Of note, only 3 % of banks have not disclosed any item. See Table 4.1.

It seems that the most popular disclosure is related to the structure and composition of the board of directors, as 92 % of banks have dis-

Table 4.1 Corporate governance disclosures made by banks in Egypt

No. of items disclosed	No. of banks disclosing the item	%
0	1	2.6
1	6	15.8
2	2	5.3
3	8	21
4	5	13.2
5	4	10.5
6	4	10.5
7	4	10.5
8	3	8
9	1	2.6

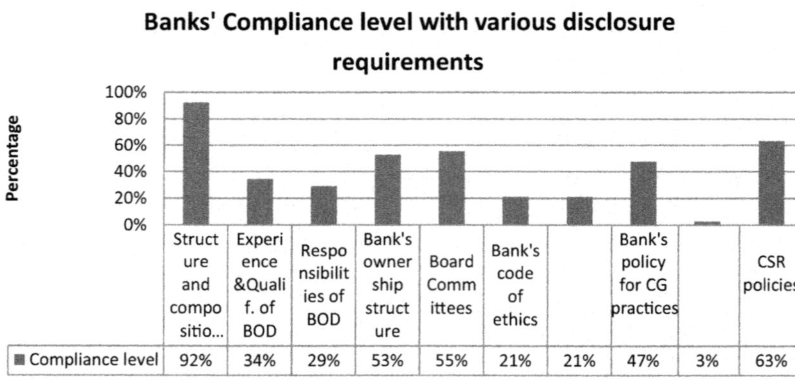

Fig. 4.1 Bank compliance level for various disclosure requirements. *Source*: Authors (2015)

closed this item, as shown in Fig. 4.1. CSR policies were the second most disclosed item, followed by board of directors' committees and the ownership structures of banks. That said, 34 % of banks disclosed the experience and qualifications of the board of directors and 55 % disclosed their organisational structure including board committees. In contrast, only one bank (3 %) disclosed its compensation policy and the figures of the highest paid officials. Finally, 47 % of banks disclosed their policy on corporate governance practices and 21 % disclosed their policy in relation to conflict of interests and the transactions of related parties.

The above analysis shows that the overall level of compliance is not as it would be expected with a code of corporate governance. The results do suggest that more stringent enforcement and supervision would be necessary to bring about greater compliance. Still, one has to acknowledge that with 50 % of banks disclosing five items one can argue that there is a very slow progression towards the formation of a corporate governance culture within the EBS. One reason for these results would be the special political and economic circumstances that Egypt witnessed over the last few years and since the issuance of the code.

In fact, the CBE role has seen many challenges since the 2011 upheavals in the light of withdrawal of more than USD21 billion from the country's foreign currency reserves. This has created 'a series of financial, economic and social challenges ... which the central bank is expected to help address, particularly since the goals set by central banks after the world financial crisis of 2008 are no longer confined to guaranteeing monetary stability, protecting the national currency from inflation and safeguarding the banking sector. These goals have instead evolved to exploit fiscal policies for the benefit of revitalizing the economy, promoting growth and working toward securing economic and social stability' (Almonitor 2015).[4] This has put enormous pressure on the CBE to rearrange the priorities of the reform process initiated in 2004 (Nasr 2012). That said, acknowledging these challenges is not a synonym for forgoing the need to continue 'strengthening the regulatory and supervisory framework, institutional structure, and the legal and institutional environment through governance and transparency' (Nasr 2012, p. 26).

On the other hand, positive developments have taken place in relation to capacity building and corporate governance awareness raising as demonstrated by establishing a corporate governance unit in the EBI. This unit has nine corporate governance courses on offer in addition to a certificate for 'the effective board member' (EBI 2015). Still the effect of this important development is not reflected in the above results. Essentially, this goes against the undisputed importance of corporate governance fol-

[4] http://www.al-monitor.com/pulse/business/2015/05/egypt-central-bank-role-social-economic-development.html#ixzz3oMmpTSMC.

lowing the global financial crisis (see Kirkpatrick 2009; Aebia et al. 2012; Dermine 2013; Grove et al. 2011). It is worth mentioning that both systematic failures in corporate governance systems as well as insufficient implementation of corporate governance were amongst the reasons that led to the global financial crisis (Sun et al. 2012). This systematic failure can include issues in the various realms of corporate governance that according to Blair (1995) can include 'legal, cultural and institutional arrangements' (Sun et al. 2012, p. 8). In conclusion, in the Egyptian case, one can argue that these three aspects might pose significant challenges to the creation of a corporate governance culture where compliance becomes the norm.

Conclusion

Corporate governance reform and culture creation within the EBS has witnessed serious efforts in the last decade. This has been due to pressures from the CBE, international organisations such as the World Bank and the Basel committee and the Egyptian government. The bank governance reform process was seen as imperative to ensuring a safe and healthy banking system and to provide reasonable assurance that the 1990s banking scandals would not recur. Although many developments can be seen as the building blocks of corporate governance culture, two of these have marked a significant leap towards this end: issuing the corporate governance code and the creation of a corporate governance unit at the EBI. However, our results have shown that current compliance levels with the required disclosures is relatively low, suggesting that awareness problems along with lax enforcement are challenges that need to be addressed. It must be noted that recent political and economic turbulence has interrupted the reform efforts and seem to have forced the CBE to reassess priorities. Here, the CBE leadership should ensure stronger enforcement of the corporate governance code and at the same time encourage bank leaders to further engage in the corporate governance agenda as well as cascade the message throughout their respective organisations.

References

Aebia, V., Sabato, G., & Schmid, M. (2012). Risk management, corporate governance, and bank performance in the financial crisis. *Journal of Banking & Finance, 36*(12), 3213–3226.

Almonitor. (2015). *The role of Egypt's central bank*. http://www.al-monitor.com/pulse/business/2015/05/egypt-central-bank-role-social-economic-development.html#

Ardalan, K. (2007). Corporate governance: A paradigmatic look. *International Journal of Social Economics, 34*(8), 506–524.

Barakat, A., & Hussainey, K. (2013). Bank governance, regulation, supervision, and risk reporting: Evidence from operational risk disclosures in European banks. *International Review of Financial Analysis, 30*, 254–273.

BCBS. (2005). *Enhancing corporate governance for banking organisations*. http://www.bis.org/publ/bcbs117.pdf

BCBS. (2006). *Enhancing corporate governance for banking organisations*. http://www.bis.org/publ/bcbs122.pdf

BCBS. (2010). *Enhancing corporate governance for banking organisations*. http://www.bis.org/publ/bcbs117.pdf

Blair, M. M. (1995). *Rethinking Assumptions Behind Corporate Governance*. http://www.jstor.org/stable/40721647

Buchs, T. D. (2009). *New Corporate Governance in the Post-Crisis World*. Washington, DC: http://www.ifc.org/wps/wcm/connect/f171e80048a7e726aa47ef6060ad5911/GCGF%2BPSO%2Bissue%2B16%2B1-7-10screen_FINAL.pdf?MOD=AJPERES

CBE. (2015). *List of registered banks*. http://www.cbe.org.eg/English/Banking+Supervision/Licensing+Lists/

CBE. (2009). *Annual report*. http://www.cbe.org.eg/nr/rdonlyres/eb4d01a8-e30b-4458-bed7-d97e43d882c5/1215/annualreport2009_2010e.pdf

CBE. (2010). http://www.cbe.org.eg/English/

CBE. (2011). *Instructions on banks governance*. http://www.cbe.org.eg/English/Banking+Supervision/Prudential+Regulations/

CIA. (2015). *The world factbook Egypt*. https://www.cia.gov/library/publications/the-world-factbook/geos/eg.html

Dermine, J. (2013). Bank corporate governance, beyond the global banking crisis. *Financial Markets, Institutions & Instruments, 22*(5), 259–281.

Dey, P. (2001). *What qualities should directors possess, and how do companies find competent directors?* Paper presented at The Objective: A Culture of Corporate Governance, Outline of Comments to Be Made to the Third Asian Roundtable on Corporate Governance the Role of Boards and Stakeholders in Corporate Governance. http://www.oecd.org/corporate/ca/corporategovernanceprinciples/1872786.pdf

EBI. (2006). http://ebi.gov.eg/

EBI. (2015). http://ebi.gov.eg/

ECOCG (Egyptian Code of Corporate Governance), (2005). *Egypt Code of Corporate Governance: Guidelines and Standards*. Egyptian Institute of Directors.

EIOD. (2009). http://www.eiod.org/default.aspx

El-Said, H. (2009). *Overview of corporate governance in the Egyptian banking sector*. Paper presented at the Corporate Governance in Banking Sector, the Safe Guard, Marriott Hotel Cairo.

El-Shazly, A. (2001). Incentive-based regulations and bank restructuring. In *Egypt: Topics in Middle Eastern and North African Economies* (p. 3). http://ecommons.luc.edu/cgi/viewcontent.cgi?article=1028&context=meea

Euromoney (2006). *Corporate governance 2006: Caveat creditor*.

French, J., & Raven, B. (2001). The bases of social power. In I. Asherman & S. Asherman (Eds.), *Negotiation source book*. Amherst: HRD Press.

Grove, H., Patelli, L., Victoravich, L. M., & Xu, P. T. (2011). Corporate governance and performance in the wake of the financial crisis: Evidence from US commercial banks. *Corporate Governance: An International Review, 19*(5), 418–436.

Guba, E., & Lincoln, Y. (1989). *Fourth generation evaluation*. Thousand Oaks, CA: Sage.

Howell, K. E. (2000). *Discovering the limits of European integration: Applying grounded theory*. New York: Nova Science.

Huang, R. (2006). *Bank disclosure index: Global assessment of bank disclosure practices*. World Bank. http://papers.ssrn.com/sol3/papers.cfm?abstract_id=1425915

Kalhoefer, C., & Salem, R. (2008). *Profitability analysis in the Egyptian banking sector*. Cairo: German University in Cairo. http://mgt.guc.edu.eg/wpapers/007kalhoefer_salem2008.pdf

Kirkpatrick, G. (2009). The corporate governance lessons from the financial crisis. *OECD Journal: Financial Market Trends, 2009*(1), 61–87.

Luebke, N. R. (1987). Conflict Of Interest as a Moral Category. *Business And Professional Ethics Journal 6*, 66–81.

Martin, M. W., & Gabard, D. L. (2001). Conflict of interest and physical therapy. In M. Davis & A. Stark (Eds.), *Conflict of interest in the professions* (pp. 314–332). New York: Oxford University Press.

Mohieldin, M., & Nasr, S. (2007). On bank privatization: The case of Egypt. *Quarterly Review of Economics and Finance, 46*(5), 707–725.

Nasr, S. (2012). The Egyptian Banking System Post January 25th Revolution. Paper presented at the Cambridge Business & Economics Conference (CBEC).

Oldham, M., & Benaddi, O. (2005). *The Egyptian banking sector: The long road to reform*. Fitch Ratings Special Report, New York.

ROSC. (2001). *Report on Observance of Codes and Standards (ROSC) corporate governance country assessment, Egypt*. http://www.worldbank.org/ifa/Egyptrosc.pdf

ROSC. (2004). *Report on Observance of Codes and Standards (ROSC) corporate governance country assessment, Egypt*. http://www.worldbank.org/ifa/rosc_cg_egyp2.pdf

Rwegasira, K. (2000). Corporate governance in emerging capital markets: Whither Africa? *Corporate Governance: An International Review, 8*(3), 258–267.

Schein, E. H. (2004). *Organizational culture and leadership*. San Francisco, CA: John Willey.

Schwandt, T. (1998). Constructivist, interpretivist approaches to human inquiry. In N. K. Denzin & Y. S. Lincoln (Eds.), *Landscape of qualitative research theories and issues*. Thousand Oaks, CA: Sage Publications.

Scott, W. R. (2001). *Institutions and organizations ideas, interests, and identities*. Stanford University, USA.

Solomon, J. (2014). *Corporate Governance and Accountability*, John Wiley & Sons, Ltd.

Sorour, M. K. (2011). *An exploration and analysis of the evolving bank corporate governance practices in Egypt: A grounded theory approach*. PhD thesis, University of Plymouth Business School.

Sorour, K. (2014). Corporate Governance Reform in Egypt: Achievements and Challenges Ahead. In S. O. Idowu & K. T. Çaliyurt (Eds.), Corporate Governance (pp. 143–155): Springer Berlin Heidelberg.

Sorour, M. K., & Dey, B. L. (2014). Energizing the political movements in developing countries: On the role of social media. *Capital & Class, 38*(3), 508–515.

Strauss, A. L., & Corbin, J. M. (1990). *Basics of qualitative research: Grounded theory procedures and techniques*. Thousand Oaks, CA: Sage.

Strauss, A. L., & Corbin, J. M. (1998). *Basics of qualitative research: Groimded theory procedures and techniques* (2nd ed.). Thousand Oaks, CA: Sage.

Sun, W., Stewart, J., & Pollard, D. (Eds.). (2012). *Corporate governance and the global financial crisis: International perspectives*. Cambridge University Press.

Theguardian. (2011). *Hosni Mubarak resigns—and Egypt celebrates a new dawn*. http://www.theguardian.com/world/2011/feb/11/hosni-mubarak-resigns-egypt-cairo

Transparency-International. (2011). *Corruption perceptions index*. http://www.transparency.org/cpi2011/results

UK Government. (2015). *2010 to 2015 government policy: Bank regulation*. https://www.gov.uk/government/publications/2010-to-2015-government-policy-bank-regulation/2010-to-2015-government-policy-bank-regulation

UN. (2007). *Public Governance Indicators: A Literature Review*. New York: https://publicadministration.un.org/publications/content/PDFs/E-Library%20Archives/2007%20Public%20Governance%20Indicators_a%20Literature%20Review.pdf

World Bank. (2015). *Translating 'governance' into Arabic*. http://web.worldbank.org/archive/website01020/WEB/0__CON-6.HTM

5

Ethical Dimensions of Corporate Governance Practice in Ghana: Developing a Theoretical Perspective

Mark Boadu

Introduction

During the last three decades, corporate governance has received growing attention at both the national and international levels. This is mainly due to the increasing corporate financial scandals and the growing acknowledgement that improved corporate governance was crucial for economic growth and development. In Ghana, the enactment of the corporate governance code (2002) by the Securities and Exchange Commission (SEC) resulted in numerous interpretations regarding codes of best practices. However, due to unethical governance activities and decisions, compliance with the codes and enforcement by the SEC and other regulators has become an issue of growing concern. This chapter presents the ethical dimensions of corporate governance practice in Ghana. Using a construc-

M. Boadu (✉)
Plymouth University, Plymouth, UK

College of Technology Education, Kumasi,
University of Education, Winneba, Ghana

K.E. Howell, M.K. Sorour (eds.), *Corporate Governance in Africa*,
DOI 10.1057/978-1-137-56700-0_5

tivist grounded theory methodology the study develops a substantive theory of corporate governance which identifies the dominant influence of national culture on corporate governance practices. In the context of Ghana, corporate governance is socially constructed, thus understanding the behaviour of the board of directors is vital for comprehending how corporate governance is practised and serves as a useful guide to investors and corporations both locally and internationally.

In Ghana, corporate governance issues have mainly focused on listed and large companies (Abor and Adjasi 2007; Kyereboah-Coleman and Biekpe 2005; Tsamenyi et al. 2007) while little or no attention has been paid to the public sector (state owned enterprises and state institutions). However, corporate governance is equally important in public sector organisations as well as in public limited companies (Boadu and Sorour 2015). This is because the Ghanaian public sector organisations contribute over 70 % of the labour force (Baah 2007; Ofori 2009). Additionally, shareholder accountability and minority shareholder-protection systems in most public sector and unincorporated businesses appear to exist on paper, leaving room for much insider-dealing by corporate management (Prempeh 2002a). Although there have been reforms over the years, these have not precipitated major changes to the operations of state-owned enterprises. The Report on the Observance of Standards and Codes (ROSC 2005) maintained that business practices in Ghana still fell short of promoting an ethical, responsible and transparent corporate governance environment. Given these findings, this chapter examines the ethical dimensions of corporate governance practice in the Ghanaian public sector and unincorporated businesses.

This study is important for Ghana because issues of corruption and mismanagement of the public sector financial systems remain a major concern. Issues of corruption and mismanagement can be viewed through cultural and ethical perspectives and practices. Indeed, it is interesting to note that the nature of the Ghanaian business environment allows traditional cultural values to permeate governance practices (Odotei and Aweodoba 2006; Okike 2007). This has implications for compliance, enforcement and ethical concerns for existing and developing corporate governance systems (Giurca 2008; Prempeh 2002b).

Using grounded theory methodology, data was collected through 28 semi-structured interviews with board directors and senior officials, and group discussions with nine participants (mainly directors and officials involved with the Ghanaian corporate governance system). Through a constant comparative method of open coding of interviews, categories emerged which were subsumed into main categories. This formed the basis for the selective coding, which identified the core category and its relationships with the sub-categories and developed a substantive theory of corporate governance practice.

Overview of Corporate Governance in Ghana

The origin of the Ghanaian corporate governance system can be traced to colonial variables as following independence Ghana inherited numerous existing rules and regulations (Adegbite 2012). Thus, the Ghanaian Companies Code (1963, Act 179) is based largely on the British Companies Act of 1948 (Adda and Hinson 2006) and the corporate governance system follows the 'Anglo-Saxon' model reflected by a path-dependent colonial past (Okike 2007). Despite the fact that the Code has undergone transformations since it was first enacted, these changes have been mostly superficial or cosmetic (Adegbite 2012). Essentially, the legal and regulatory frameworks of the Ghanaian corporate governance system include:

1. The Company's Code established in 1963 (Act 179) to regulate all companies incorporated in Ghana. The Code anticipated and provided adequately for the central issues of corporate governance in the Ghanaian private sector.
2. The Securities Industry Law (1993, 333) and the Securities Industry (Amendment) Act, 2000 (Act 590) created the Securities and Exchange Commission, Ghana. The two laws, as well as the Ghana Stock Exchange (GSE), regulate stock exchanges, investment advisors, securities dealers and collective investment schemes, licensed under the SEC.

The Companies Code (1963, Act 179) outlined certain provisions relating to the composition of the Board of Directors discussed under membership, independence and the expertise of directors. Every public limited company, and every private company that is a subsidiary of a public limited company, must have at least two directors with the maximum to be fixed by each company representing the shareholders. Directors have fiduciary roles and the code provides sanctions in the event of breaches. In appointing boards of directors, the code has no requirement to appoint independent directors elected by the shareholders at the annual general meeting (Companies Code 1963, Act 179).

Similarly, the Securities Industry Law (1993, 333) gives the SEC regulatory authority over institutions and persons operating in the industry, for example stock exchanges, investment advisers and securities dealers. The primary goal of the SEC is to protect investors and maintain the integrity of the securities market. The SEC is an active and effective regulator that has suspended market participants that break the rules. Additionally, the GSE regulates listed entities under the Stock Exchange Act (1971) and the Listing Regulations (1990). Listed companies are required to comply with corporate governance guidelines by the SEC, Ghana and the Listing Regulations. The GSE has only 35 listed companies who are predominantly foreign and multinationals and operate under mandatory regulations. As a result, most companies tend to be compliant with the requirements and the international corporate governance principles of best practices (ROSC 2005). Furthermore, the Bank of Ghana (BoG) regulates financial reporting by banks and non-bank financial services under the accounting and auditing requirements set by the Banking Law (1989). The BoG is the overall supervisory and regulatory authority in all matters relating to banking and non-banking financial services in Ghana. The BoG strongly enforces relevant regulatory provisions which have extensive sanctions available to impose on banks fines, revocation of licence (in extreme cases), variations in the terms and conditions of licensing, as well as civil and criminal penalties for non-compliance.

In addition, the State Enterprises Commission (SEC) is the overall supervisory authority in all matters relating to public sector organisations (state owned enterprises and state institutions). The public sector is not governed by the Companies Code (1963, Act 179), but the Securities and Exchanges Commission guidelines on corporate governance.

Prempeh (2002b) argued that the commission is impotent when it comes to enforcement and ensuring compliance with the guidelines. The weak enforcement environment has been blamed on the lack of a strong corporate culture and the non-mandatory nature of the SEC guidelines on corporate governance for public sector organisations. It has been argued that the nature of the governance regulations, being non-mandatory, tends to encourage non-compliance. Thus, public sector boards of directors tend to bear no responsibility for non-performance.

Research Methodology

As stated by Collis and Hussey (2003), our personal research paradigm helps us to determine which methodology to adopt and, in turn, determine methods of collecting data. Paradigms have implications for the methodology chosen and the outcome or results of the research. I adopted a combination of phenomenological and constructivism paradigms of inquiry. Phenomenological paradigm is a qualitative research approach employing an inductive process concerned with understanding human behaviour from the participant's own frame of reference. Constructivists argue that people construct knowledge by developing concepts, models and schemes of the world. Hence, the study adopted a combination of phenomenology and constructivism to identify behaviour/actions, attitudes or knowledge of boards of directors, primarily in Ghanaian public sector organisation settings in relation to corporate governance practice. The grounded theory methodology was used for this study because it offers a comprehensive and systematic framework for inductive theory building. The constructivist approach to grounded theory facilitates the continuous interplay between the researcher and the participant and the incorporation of multiple perspectives in writing the emerging theory (Corbin and Strauss 2008; Graham and Thomas 2008; Strauss and Corbin 1994). The researcher and researched interact 'so that the "findings" are literally created as the investigation proceeds' (Graham and Thomas 2008, p. 111). The nature of grounded theory is such that the theory to emerge 'will be abstract enough and include sufficient variation to make it applicable to a variety of contexts related to the phenomenon'

(Strauss and Corbin 1990, p. 23). The researcher used grounded theory methodology to investigate empirically the corporate governance practice of boards of directors and senior officers of public sector organisations and develop a substantive theory of corporate governance.

Using the three phase grounded theory method of open, axial and selective coding, data from the semi-structured interviews and group discussion were analysed along with the written notes. During open coding, 'data are broken down into discrete parts, closely examined, and compared for similarities and differences' (Strauss and Corbin 1998, p. 102). This process uncovers the thoughts, ideas and meanings attached to concepts. Interview transcripts were coded sentence-by-sentence to allow concepts to emerge. A number of concepts emerged as the interview process progressed. Open coding analysis was also applied to the group discussion to identify emergent concepts here. Through the process of simultaneously comparing concepts to identify similarities and differences, eight open categories emerged in terms of its properties and dimensions based on the interview questions. These included: board effectiveness, cultural influence, ethical concerns, board accountability, government interference, regulations, training and education, and weak institutions and poor leadership.

Board Effectiveness

Ghana's corporate governance guidelines on best practices state that boards of directors are charged with the responsibility of ensuring effective corporate governance practices (SEC 2009). An effective board is expected to ''develop and promote the collective vision of a company's purpose, its culture, its values and the behaviours it wishes to promote in conducting its business' (Financial Reporting Council 2011, p. 2). In order to improve the overall effectiveness of the board, its committees and individual members, companies' boards of directors are required to undertake training and voluntary self-evaluation (SEC 2009). The Ghana Institute of Directors (GIoD 2010) states that organisations should consider periodic and rigorous board evaluation processes as best practice. This is achieved by using the dynamics of board behaviour regarding strategic decision-making which comprises the oversight of strategy formulation and execution, the teamwork of board members and their interaction with management (Huse 2005).

Board Evaluation

Board Evaluation is defined as improving effectiveness through assessing the strengths and weaknesses of programmes, policies, personnel, products and organisations (American Evaluation Association 2004). This refers to the systematic collection and analysis of data needed to make decisions. The purpose of board evaluation is to penetrate the inner workings of the boardroom in order to assess the extent to which the board is capable of delivering good governance while providing appropriate direction to the enterprise, in both the short and long-term contexts.

The majority of the directors interviewed identified the following areas where board evaluation is required: roles and responsibilities, structures and procedures, strategy setting, risk management and appropriate board behaviours. In order to appraise these processes, the board and its committees analyse the extent to which they are successful in fulfilling their key roles and responsibilities together with the individual director's contribution to the achievement of the organisation's objectives. They also intimated that the board and its committees consider the extent to which they adhere to best practice in their structure and procedures, culture and behaviour patterns that support the effective functioning of the board. It was revealed that board evaluations are mainly conducted in-house and at three levels, namely: board level, board committee level and individual director. In most of the private companies where self-assessments are institutionalised, board members usually meet on an annual basis to question their own performance and identify potential improvement regarding issues such as quality of discussions at board meetings, support provided to the executive management, effective financial reporting, interaction within the board and with the management, appropriate board behaviours, reviewing the company's short-term and long-term goals, maximising return on shareholders investments and increasing shareholders' wealth. However, in public sector organisations the situation is different and board evaluation is rarely conducted, even though directors are aware of the importance of evaluation in ensuring board effectiveness. The few state-owned enterprises that conducted board evaluation focus on committee reports to the board upon committee meetings.

Shareholders expect that boards of directors scrutinise their own performance in carrying out their corporate governance responsibilities on a regular basis. This enables boards to monitor effectively managements' operations and ensure accountability to shareholders through 'interactions with institutional investors, financial markets, government departments, trade unions, and other stakeholders, and reporting on corporate social responsibility to their stakeholders groups' (Nwanji 2006, p. 267). In general, boards of state-owned enterprises barely perform self-evaluation to identify potential weaknesses and provide appropriate measures to improve the effectiveness of their boards. However, it was revealed that some public companies perform board evaluation at the board level.

It is recommended that effective board evaluation should be both internally and externally facilitated (Schmidt and Brauer 2006) since over reliance on internal assessment could lead to deterioration rather than an improvement of board effectiveness. Boards of directors tend to be 'more lenient, less variable, more biased, and show less agreement with the judgement of others' (Carcio 2004, p. 100) during internal assessment. It could be argued that such an evaluation runs the risk of being politically shaped and based on board members' hesitation to challenge each other's performance in peer evaluations (Schmidt and Brauer 2006). In addition, the involvement of external consultants to facilitate the self-assessment might ensure objective professionalism in the evaluation process.

Board Issues

Concepts that are explored under board issues include: politicisation of appointments onto boards, levels of professionalism, roles and duties, and board and management relationships.

The politicisation of boards refers to manipulation for political ends. The key to good governance of any modern corporation is an informed and well-functioning board of directors (Prempeh 2002a). In assessing the eligibility for membership of boards, Prempeh (2002a, p. 5) recommended that 'appointing authorities should regard a prospective nominee's political credentials as a "plus factor" at best, not as an outcome-determinative qualification'. Also, in order for boards to fulfil effectively their responsibilities, they must have some degree of independence from shareholders (SEC 2009, p. 7). Ensuring board independence empowers board members to contribute significantly to the decision-making processes. While rules on appointment and termination of board members are not strictly related to board member's independence, they are a quintessential aspect of their true independence of judgement (Prempeh 2002b). If independent board members can be appointed directly by those from whom they are supposed to be independent, the due process to ensure independence is severely put at risk.

The majority of directors in Ghana are of the view that appointments onto public sector organisation's boards are not meritocratic and extensively based on opportunities to allocate patronage to party loyalists and political cronies. Such situations may undermine the independence of the board. Indeed, board members' ability to challenge or question the authority of the CEO or the managing director can be compromised especially if they are looking for another term of office. It is believed that appointments onto boards are politicised in both private and public institutions, but the situation is more pronounced in the latter.

Furthermore, in the Ghanaian context, board members cannot often openly challenge the questionable actions of CEOs or other board members without fear of retribution. They often want to ensure they keep their positions in the coming years irrespective of the government in place. This is especially true of directors of public institutions since they also derive their authority from the same source as the members of the board. Members of parliament or ministers of state appointed to boards of state-owned enterprises complicate board accountability and appropriate the chain of command. These high ranking politicians on boards with a CEO appointee make it difficult for the board to isolate or apportion responsibility when there are problems because they often make other members of the board feel intimated and make it difficult for the CEO to be free to implement policies that would be in the best interest of the organisation. This practice impinges on the competence, professionalism and quality of contributions by members. In addition, parliamentarians' overseeing responsibilities extend to public institutions and state-owned enterprises. This may create serious conflicts of interest and affect good corporate governance practices. In some cases, individual board member's ability to challenge and question issues during board meetings are greatly impaired. This undermines the primary role of boards to provide direction and establish the frameworks for aspirations, goals, values and policies. This makes it difficult for board members to provide management with professional expertise and leadership.

Cultural Influence

Culture describes the environment in which people live and is composed of their learned and shared behaviour patterns, values, norms and material objects. Takatera and Yamamoto (1987) defined culture as an expression of norms, values and customs which reflect typical behavioural characteristics. Indeed, most of the traditional definitions of culture revolve around values, rituals, symbols, beliefs and expectations which are developed over time and passed down through previous generations (Hofstede 2001; De Wit and Meyer 1998). Culture is a dynamic phenomenon that surrounds us at all times, being constantly enacted and created by our interactions with others and shaped by leadership behaviour, and a set of structures, routines, rules and norms that guides and constrains behaviour. That is, a group is said to have a culture when it has enough shared history to have formed a set of basic assumptions, which serve as a psychological mechanism that keeps the group functioning. Thus, 'the society that people grow up in shapes their basic beliefs, values, and norms' (Kotler 1991). Cultural values shape an individual's actions, behaviour and judgements of what is right or wrong, and the selection of the social goals or ends that are desirable (Muenjohn and Armstrong 2008; Yücel et al. 2009).

A society's shared learned behaviour is transmitted over time from one group or generation to another through social interaction and can be interpreted as a set of standards for behaviour considered authoritative within a society. From this perspective, national level cultural values are said to have a substantial influence on the behavioural responses of individuals. This may influence a wide range of behaviours and actions of individuals within a given cultural environment. Thus, differences in corporate governance practices can be explained by differences between national cultures (Li and Harrison 2008; Licht et al. 2005; Oghojafor et al. 2012).

Gift Giving/Receiving

Gift giving is viewed as a central part of human behaviour and culture (Mysterud et al. 2006) and continues to play an important role in today's society. According to Mauss (1954), exchange takes place between two groups and not individuals and includes goods and wealth, real estate and personal property and other things of economic value. In an attempt to distinguish between the two types of exchange relations, Gregory (1982) maintained that exchanges of gifts creates 'personal relations between people, while commodity exchange creates objective relations between things' (p. 8).

According to Mauss (2002) gift giving generates an obligation to reciprocate through the 'norm of reciprocity'. During the process of gift giving, individuals contribute to the general welfare of recipients. The assumption is that the receiver or the giver hopes to repay something based on past generosity or expected future generosity. Further, Basu (2001) argued that this social norm may produce gift anxiety which needs to be followed; indeed, if violated it may result in individuals being directly punished by others and made to feel guilt, shame, embarrassment and anxiety.

The act of gift giving and gift receiving is a common practice in every sector of the Ghanaian economy. Gift giving and receiving assist in establishing or enhancing all types of relationships. These include demonstrating gratitude towards stakeholders for good work, recognising talents and achievements, and establishing stronger ties with stakeholders. Indeed, gift giving has a great impact in maintaining social ties and serves as a means of symbolic communication in social relationships (Ruth et al. 1999).

Examining the influence of Ghanaian culture on corporate governance regulations in the country reveals that such regulations do not fully reflect the culture. This is because the regulations are often imported from the developed world, including colonial influences, through which the concept of corporate governance was initially introduced. After examination, we can reveal that Ghanaian cultural values and norms influence corporate governance practices. For example, Ghanaian society is a gift-giving society and so giving and receiving gifts is culturally accepted. This has implications for effective corporate governance practice. Even though participants argued that gift giving demonstrates gratitude and reward for good work done, the practice leads to ''politicking' and consequently unethical practices in corporate governance.

However, most of the Ghanaian directors interviewed argued that the act of gift giving does not necessarily create a compulsion to either return or violate another person's right to refuse to reciprocate. For example, during festive occasions——Christmas, Easter and other corporate celebrations——most organisations in Ghana offer gifts to stakeholders to demonstrate appreciation of their contribution to the growth and development of their organisations. Indeed, the act of gift giving has unofficially become part of business practice and has influence on corporate governance practices. This notwithstanding, we do acknowledge that gift giving as a practice in the corporate world is not an unethical practice in itself, but needs to be managed to minimise the abuse of it; in some contexts it has potential to encourage corruption and bribery.

To determine the extent to which gift giving or receiving could be ethical or unethical, participants identified four factors. These include the intent behind the act, the amount involved, the context, and the timing of the gift. For example, if the gift is intended to influence a decision or to receive a favour in return, or the amount involved in the act is above a defined minimum, or it was given in secrecy, or the gift was given or received before a contract, then the act can be said to be unethical. However, if the reverse is the case, the gift giving or receiving cannot be said to be unethical. Thus, the act of gift giving and gift receiving is not unethical governance practice in itself.

In the Ghanaian context, it is interesting to note that rejecting a gift is considered an insult or a rejection of the giver of the gift and this has implications for establishing relationships and social acceptance. It is worth noting that some leaders in government and corporations in the country have made several attempts to curtail the act of giving or receiving gifts in the corporate context but to no avail. This is not surprising because, as has been asserted by Gibson and Barsade (2003), culture is indeed difficult to change. For instance, ex-President of the Republic of Ghana, John Evans Atta Mills, in 2010 prohibited gift giving and receiving within the public sector, but which was ultimately unsuccessful.

Some of the directors interviewed believed that the act of giving and receiving gifts is cultural and should not be equated to bribery. However, many of the participants argued that if encouraged the act of gift giving and receiving has the potential of becoming a dangerous practice. However, the Internal Revenue Service Act (Act 592:143) states the accepted limit for a gift in public sector organisations, and any gift valued above that amount is subject to tax. Unfortunately, this section of the Act is difficult to enforce. In an attempt to manage the practice of gift giving and receiving, the highly regulated companies (banks and non-bank financial institutions, pharmaceutical and manufacturing companies) introduced the gift registry. Participants indicated that this register is hardly used to record any gift. It is important to note that the new Income Tax Act, 2015 (Act 896) does not capture gift tax.

The Internal Revenue Service Act (2006, Act 592) defines the maximum value of a gift (less than or equal to GH¢50.00) for acceptance beyond which the recipient pays tax of 10 % when declared, though this regulation is rarely enforced. Some people receive gifts of over GH¢50.00 but never declare it due to fear of reprisal. This means that organisations with a corporate gift register 'rarely' capture any at all. Gifts received were not disclosed in the gift registry and approval for such gifts had not been obtained. The act of gift giving and gift receiving could have both positive and negative influences on corporate governance practice. In relation to the positive effect, organisations give and receive gifts due to the great impact it has in maintaining social ties and serving as a means of symbolic communication in social relationships. On the other hand, there may also be a negative effect in relation to the tendency to promote unethical business practices such as bribery and corruption and the issue of ''gift anxiety' (*norm of reciprocity*).

Moreover, the act of gift giving and gift receiving as a social norm does influence governance practices in terms of the actions and behaviours of boards of directors. This influence of gift giving and receiving on governance practice could be positive (ethical) and negative (unethical). Thus the practice of gift giving and receiving could be measured along positive and negative effects. In general, it was concluded from the survey that the Ghanaian culture of gift giving and receiving influences corporate governance practices within the country, but the extent of the influence could not be determined from the survey conducted. The aspect of this finding is in agreement with existing literature which identify national level cultural norms and values of gift giving as a factor that strongly influences corporate governance practices (Djankov et al. 2008; Dyck and Zingales 2004).

The majority of the directors interviewed agreed to give gifts to stakeholders as well as receiving. Few of the participants interviewed claimed that their organisations do not support gift receiving but do give gifts to stakeholders during festive occasions. They believe that receiving gifts has the potential to influence decisions which could be unethical. Governing boards support gift giving because it is used to demonstrate gratitude and motivation to stakeholders and also establish interpersonal relationships. Indeed, giving and receiving of gifts, particularly during festive occasions, as already stated, has become part of accepted business practices in Ghana.

It was revealed that the level of regulation of corporations affects the extent of the influence of cultural norms and values on their corporate governance practices. The highly regulated companies tend to minimise the influence of culture on their governance practices. Nonetheless, the governance practices of less-regulated companies are greatly influenced by culture. Participants concluded that corporate governance practices in Ghana are greatly influenced by cultural norms.

Family Systems

A family refers to a group of people bound together by blood ties or through adoption in which the older people take care of the younger ones (Ardayfio-Schandorf 1994, p. 5). Hendricks (2000, p. 5) refers to a family as 'an intimate room where the core values, culture as well as ethical climate of the family as well as of the broader environment is shaped, and where the first social relationships are formed, which differ from relationships with people outside the family circle'. Thus, family systems provide a set of social arrangements and interrelationships that allow people to live cooperatively and in harmony, and to pursue orderly social life (Klomegah 1997, p. 76). A family system establishes a strong bond among members and is the primary source of identity, loyalty and responsibility of individual members. Indeed, individual members achieve recognition and social standing through their extended family. Consequently, the family system forms fundamental principles, core values, which can be seen as the guidelines in setting the vision, mission and goals of a family enterprise.

The extended family system tends to place much responsibility and pressure on governing boards in terms of social demands and support. Family ties, relationships and cronies influence governing action or behaviour to some extent, in terms of employment. These pressures act as a negative influence on corporate governance practices. These pressures are perceived to be prevalent in most state-owned enterprises and private sector organisations. The strong cohesion of family systems was also identified as being the motivation (financial and emotional) for the success of family businesses.

A family business can generally be described as a business which is controlled by one or more members of one or more families. The family (through its core values) influences the business system and ethical behaviour of its enterprise (Hendricks 2000; Klein et al. 2005). Participants believed that family businesses tend to be one area where a large number of firms operate but are not adequately regulated. It was discovered that most Ghanaian family businesses do not operate under the corporate governance regulations of the country. Considering the number of family businesses operating in Ghana, it is important to have them properly regulated. The proper regulation of family businesses would have a positive influence on their corporate governance practices. The existing Companies' Code (1963, Act 179) does not fully address the peculiar corporate governance situation of family owned enterprises. However, it is argued that the ownership structure of a family business is considered an internal control mechanism that can help to monitor the behaviour of managers and, likewise, to avoid the inefficient use of resources (Stiglitz 1985). The property of a close family system is expressed in terms of its dimensions as positive and negative influences.

Family businesses tend to receive much support and influences from the extended family system. The corporate governance practice in most family businesses and private companies is influenced by cultural values and norms. This influence could be positive in terms of providing financial, moral and professional support and encouragement to the board of directors. This has served as motivation for the boards of most private and family businesses to succeed. A participant interviewed agreed that sometimes there is interference from family members on governing action or decisions, which has the potential to be unethical.

Respect for Authority

Ghanaian society is hierarchical with unequal relationships between people. People are granted respect because of their age, experience, wealth and/or position. This reflects the views of directors and senior managers in relation to respect for traditions. Tradition can be conceptualised as a number of interrelated ideas such as beliefs, objects or customs that are performed or were believed in the past, or originate in the past, and are transmitted through time by being taught by one generation to the next, and are now performed or believed in the present (Green 1997; Shils 1971). Chiefs, by the nature of their position, power and influence in society, are granted respect and recognition in their communities. Organisations honour the custodians of the traditions through contributions (monetary and non-monetary) especially during festive occasions. This is done during ceremonies and other festive occasions.

Honouring traditional leaders involves paying homage during festive seasons and national occasions. This is provided through gift giving and social responsibility in cash or kind. As custodians of culture and tradition, leaders play significant roles in influencing members of society. Honouring traditional leaders as a cultural practice creates positive social relationships between organisations and their larger stakeholders. Directors interviewed indicated that these practices are more pronounced in industries where they are less regulated, such as mining and construction companies. Directors pay homage to traditional leaders to ensure that stable and trusted relationship exist between the community and the organisation.

Most shareholders are not culturally encouraged to question the decisions of the board of directors. Shareholders regard their board of directors as superiors and grant them unquestioned respect. However, this practice does not promote board accountability and tends to make directors less accountable. This has implications for good corporate governance practice. The situation tends to be more pronounced in private sector organisations where shareholders find it culturally challenging to question the decisions of the Chief Executive Officer (CEO). This is in agreement with existing literature that shareholders are not culturally empowered to serve as a check on the board of directors (Amao and Amaeshi 2007; Bruner 2011).

Ethical Concerns

Ethics defines the rules and practices underpinning responsible conduct between individuals and groups by making systematic sense of individual and social moral experience (De George 2000). Ethical values such as trust, honesty, truthfulness, fairness and/or kindness are usually used in making ethical judgements of rightness and wrongness in human behaviour which underlies business ethics. Unethical behaviour involves the opposite: 'distrust', 'deception', 'dishonesty', 'lying', 'greed', and so on. Knowledge of individual values provides 'general expectation of their behaviour' (Jackson and Thomas 2005, p. 3). Schein (2004) argues that our values influence what we will determine as ethical. Behaving ethically depends on the ability to recognise that ethical issues exist.

Board Responsiveness to Stakeholders

Responsiveness occurs when institutions and processes try to serve all stakeholders using a proactive manner regarding complaints and public criticism (Graham et al. 2003). This is done through the level of perceived responsiveness of companies to stakeholder complaints. A stakeholder refers to 'any identifiable group or individual who can affect the achievement of an organisation's objectives or who is affected by the achievement of an organisation's objectives' (De Wit and Meyer 2004, p. 832).

Boards of directors of state-owned enterprises are less responsive to stakeholder complaints. Goods and services are either provided late or not provided at all. They believe boards of directors are just less concerned or do nothing at all to make the system work. The 'free rider' role of board of directors in organisations, particularly state-owned enterprises, will continue until somebody is held accountable for work not done. Generally, directors within the Ghanaian context have demonstrated less commitment and responsiveness to ensuring efficient service delivery.

Code of Ethics

A code of ethics can be defined as 'a written set of guidelines issued by an organisation to its workers and management to help them conduct their actions in accordance with its primary values and ethical standards' (*Business Dictionary* 2011). This suggests that a code of ethics is considered the manifestation of a company's morality, or at minimum a company's intentions or commitment to act ethically. Codes of ethics are used to establish a baseline for action within the corporation. This provides a platform to demonstrate social responsibility, a corporate culture that promotes anti-criminal behaviour patterns, and the possibility of self-regulation which establishes a relationship with behaviour (Carasco and Singh 2003). ROSC (2005) maintains that business practices in Ghana still fall short of promoting ethical, responsible and transparent corporate governance practices.

What constitutes an ethical or unethical governance action or practice is an on-going debate. Boards that are ethical give a reflection of good leadership and create a good corporate culture to motivate management and other workers to meet the needs of all stakeholders. On the other hand, unethical boards promote unethical practices and actions which give a negative public image to the organisation if not a complete collapse. They deemed most public sector organisations' boards of directors to be unethical but the extent of this was not established. Most of the state-owned enterprises either had no written code of ethics for their boards or the boards were unaware of such official documents; instead unwritten grand rules are used to guide behaviour, particularly in state-owned enterprises and private sector organisations.

These rules largely depend on the integrity of board members. Although there were no codes of ethics, directors used the rules to avoid conflict of interest. However, some directors acknowledged the significance of a code of ethics in ensuring ethical governance practices, though commitment to their establishment was surprisingly low. Directors in Ghana admit that even though codes of ethics define acceptable standards, little importance is attached to their existence and applicability. Some organisations have written a code of ethics for both management and directors and encouraged them to comply at all times. That said, the level of commitment to the code in terms of their establishment and compliance is better developed in public companies than it is in private sector organisations.

Participants contended that the lack of regard for codes of ethics by boards makes it difficult to address issues of business ethics. Even though a majority of participants argued that having a code of ethics is just a means to an end, but not the end in itself, they admitted the necessity for organisations to have a code and compliance with the code. It was observed that a strong corporate culture promotes the provision of a code of ethics and its subsequent compliance. Participants claimed that some organisations, particularly the publicly traded companies, have codes that define their ethical business practices.

Corporate Social Responsibility

Corporate social responsibility refers to 'a commitment to improve community well-being through discretionary business practices and contributions of corporate resources' (Kotler and Lee 2005, p. 3). Additionally, participants were of the view that the private sector has performed considerably well in relation to the provision of corporate social responsibility given the lack of national policy guidelines. Indeed, corporate social responsibility is characterised as:

> the continuing commitment by business to behave ethically and contribute to economic development while improving the quality of the workforce and their families as well as of the local community and society at large. (Holme and Watts 2000, p. 3)

Most public institutions, particularly state-owned enterprises, provide less corporate social responsibility. Corporate social responsibility of state-owned enterprises is factored into government overall policy However, public companies provide corporate social responsibility despite the lack of national policy guidelines. For some organisations, their commitment is motivated by the benefits they get through tax exemption and societal recognition.

Despite the lack of national policy guidelines, organisations have adopted different models to ensure effective provision of social responsibility to their stakeholders. However, challenges encountered include a lack of coordination, monitoring and supervision, and inadequate community or stakeholder involvement. That said, organisations undertake what they consider to be socially responsible and relevant to the community. There are high levels of tokenism and self-interest in the provision of social responsibility. Organisations use the provision of corporate social responsibility for profit maximisation and tax exemptions. The absence of national policy guidelines is a critical factor in developing meaningful corporate social responsibility in Ghana and ethical business practices. Its provision is perceived to be high in private sector organisations and low in public sector organisations. However, it was noted that the provision could be linked to the Ghanaian culture of gift giving, regardless of the lack of national policy guidelines.

Board Accountability

Accountability is generally defined as an:

> obligation of an individual, firm, or institution to account for its activities, accept responsibility for them, and to disclose the results in a transparent manner, including the responsibility for money or other entrusted property. (Business Dictionary 2011)

Accountability requires that officials answer to stakeholders on the disposal of their powers and duties and accept responsibility for failure, incompetence or deceit. Transparency involves sharing information and acting in an open manner (Graham et al. 2003). The two concepts of accountability and transparency are two sides of the same coin. The public sector is generally characterised by low levels of transparency and accountability (Bovens 2007). However, the principles of fairness, transparency and accountability, and responsibility have been recognised in all corporate governance principles as tenets of a good corporate governance system. The Organisation for Economic Co-operation and Development (OECD 2004) principles of corporate governance strongly maintain that member countries adhere to these key principles in their regulations to ensure good practices. Good corporate governance rules and practices govern the relationship between the managers and shareholders of corporations on the one hand, and the larger stakeholder groups on the other hand in contributing to economic growth, market confidence, and financial and market integrity. If government wants state-owned enterprises to be effective and accountable, then it should consider reviewing the appointment process of boards; perhaps an independent committee would encourage organisations to be competitive by defining and enforcing sanctions for the non-performance of boards.

Minority Shareholder Education

Stock market rules clearly specify the protection of the rights of minority shareholders. However, its awareness and enforcement has not received much attention. Minority shareholder rights are crucial for the protection of investors against poor management practices. Unfortunately, these laws are not strictly enforced and often disregarded because shareholders are generally unaware of their rights. The concern is that the lack of awareness and low level of financial literacy render minority shareholders unable to effectively hold directors accountable. This brings to the fore the issue of minority shareholder education and awareness.

Government Influence

Government signifies the formal institutions of the state and their monopoly of legitimate coercive power. That is, the concept is understood to mean the formal and institutional processes which operate at the level of the nation or state to maintain public order and facilitate collective action; while governance is concerned with creating the conditions for ordered rule and collective action (Stoker 1998, p. 19). Government can be described as the act or process of governing. Government interference refers to an act or instance whereby government hinders, obstructs or impedes an organisation's governance action or behaviour (*Business Dictionary* 2011).

Government Influence

Government intervention is a regulatory action taken to affect decisions made by individuals, groups or organisations regarding social and economic matters. Government intervention is viewed, within the context of a free market economy, as the deliberate action taken to influence the economy by means of 'legislation, fiscal and monetary policy as well as direct government participation' in the productive sectors of the economy (Prempeh 2002a, b, p. 8). Government interventions such as statutory monopoly, budget support and government guaranteed loans and bailouts have kept alive many uncompetitive and badly managed state-owned enterprises in Ghana. Indeed, it may be argued that these continuous interventions by government weaken the institutional capacity for state-owned enterprises to be competitive and productive consistently.

Exposing public institutions to the dynamics of the market stimulates good corporate governance in the public sector. Although the interventions may not directly lead to interference, it has the potential to promote it. As institutions go to the government for financial support, governing boards become vulnerable to government interference, with regard to governance decisions. There has been an improvement in permitting private competition in a market previously protected for state-owned enterprises by government. State-owned enterprises charge commercial rates for their services, despite the government's interference in their pricing. So, there is no rational justification for government to continue to provide those financial supports. State-owned enterprises should be and in certain contexts are encouraged to be self-supporting, productive and responsible.

Government Interference

There is a high degree of government interference regarding the behaviour of state-owned enterprises. Selection and appointments of public boards are not meritocratic but are extensively based on patronage to party loyalists and political cronies. Participants believe that appointments to boards are politicised in both private and public institutions within the Ghanaian context, but the situation is pronounced in the latter. Thus generally, independence of boards in the country is undermined due to their politicisation. Board members' ability to challenge or criticise the authority of the CEO or the managing director is endangered if individual board members want to protect their position.

Undeniably, government interference in the governance of state-owned enterprises makes them vulnerable, uncompetitive, less effective and often unaccountable. In addition, weak governance and lack of moral commitment to be responsive to stakeholders are also contributing factors to poor corporate compliance with governance regulations. Consequently, some of the major problems in public sector corporate governance practices in the Ghanaian context are interference by government, a cultural milieu that impedes effective corporate governance practices, and poor leadership and management of public sector organisations coupled with weak regulatory institutions.

Regulations

In order to ensure good corporate governance practices, it is fundamental that an appropriate and efficient legal, regulatory and institutional framework be established upon which all market participants can rely and establish their contractual relations (OECD 2004). The OECD principles of corporate governance clearly specify legislation, regulation, voluntary commitments and business practices that underlie a country's specific circumstances such as history and tradition.

Content

The intent of the code is clear enough and the content is adequate to facilitate a good governance framework. Compliance to the code is mandatory for all public companies and some state-owned enterprises that have become limited companies. The intent of the code is to meet current challenges. Participants in the survey believe that the legal and regulatory framework of corporate governance within the country is compliant with international regulations. One participant stated that:

> Our laws are fairly in consonance with the best practices in the world to the extent that we are now a signatory B to the IOSCO MOU. After the draft bill has been passed into law we will be able to attain the signatory 'A' status of the MOU which will mean that our laws are fully now compliant with international standards.

Therefore, if the legal and regulatory framework seems ineffective, it is due to weak monitoring and enforcement mechanisms and poor compliance to the code.

Compliance and Enforcement

According to the World Bank's (2004) report on corporate governance, most developing and transition economies have failed to enforce laws, rules and regulations regarding corporate governance consistently and evenly. Not surprisingly therefore, a poor compliance and weak enforcement environment have characterised Ghanaian corporate governance practices. The Companies Code (1963, Act 179) provides the basic requirements regarding preparation and publication of financial statements, disclosures and auditing, among other provisions for good corporate governance practice of public companies within the country. The Registrar-General is responsible for the enforcement of the Companies Code, and can impose penalties on defaulting persons; however, it hardly implements these enforcement requirements.

Enforcement of governance regulations by boards tend to be effective in industries or sectors that are highly regulated. For instance, the Bank of Ghana and the Ghana Stock Exchange were thought to be able to enforce effectively their regulations due to the fact that these regulatory institutions are independent and tend to have the necessary enforcement powers. Participants believe these institutions have the required resources to enforce the regulations and metre out appropriate penalties to offending corporations. Some directors from public institutions and state-owned enterprises indicated that in an attempt to ensure that regulatory agencies are more efficient, government employs a legislative overhaul or decree to establish new regulatory agencies. However, it takes more than legislative overhaul or decrees to make regulatory agencies more efficient. There is the need to empower institutions and indicate their functions to include their enforcement powers. There is the need to strengthen institutions and make them more effective in satisfying their stakeholders. Further, some of the factors that could be used to make the regulatory institutions stronger are financial independence, minimising governmental interference, a strong organisational culture and an ethical leadership.

As has been established, compliance with governance regulations within the Ghanaian context is at best non-existent even though the contents of the regulations are adequate and clear. This weak enforcement has been due to the lack of a strong corporate culture, the non-mandatory nature of the corporate governance guidelines for public sector organisations and the private sector. It was argued that the nature of the governance regulations, being non-mandatory, tends to encourage non-compliance. Thus, public sector boards of directors tend to have no responsibility for non-performance.

The World Bank corporate governance country assessment of Ghana states that 'awareness of corporate governance is in its incipient stages and compliance with corporate governance practices are slightly low with little enforcement' (ROSC 2005, p. 3). It is not surprising therefore that the World Bank (2005) has pointed out that developing and transition economies have failed to enforce laws, rules and regulations regarding corporate governance consistently and evenly.

Boards of directors can only be encouraged to be compliant with the guidelines and the principles they are equipped with during the training programmes organised for them. They should be encouraged to educate and create ethical and legal awareness on corporate governance practices of the corporations they are given oversight responsibilities over. To guide corporate governance in Ghana, there are a number of laws that can aid in this direction, including the Companies Code of Ghana (1963), which is based on the UK model, and the Securities Industry Law (1993), which created the Securities and Exchange Commission (SEC), Ghana. The two laws, as well as the GSE rules, are mandatory governance regulations for the country. In addition, there are corporate governance guidelines on best practices for corporations in Ghana, which are voluntary. These mandatory and voluntary regulations and guidelines could aid greatly in improving corporate governance within the country. Indeed, the legal and regulatory framework of corporate governance is adequate and far from needing reform (ROSC 2005).

Board Training and Minority Shareholder Awareness

The corporate governance guidelines on best practices recommends director training for all organisations (SEC 2009). The Ghana Institute of Directors (IoD) has published a code of ethics for all directors and provided certified training programmes, but there was no formal recognition by the Securities and Exchanges Commission of such certification programmes. The OECD (2004) principles recommend that, in order to improve board practices and the performance of board members, countries should increasingly encourage companies to engage in board training and voluntary self-evaluation that meet the needs of individual companies. Indeed, board training plays a critical role in ensuring effective corporate governance practices. In Ghana, training and orientation programmes are organised for boards of directors before they take office. This is because adequate knowledge of board appointees, CEOs and managing directors on critical corporate governance matters is critical for good public sector governance practice. Some of these matters concern the role of the board vis-à-vis the managing directors, the fiduciary duties of directors, the legal liability associated with a breach of such duties, and the financial audit and reporting obligations of boards.

The State Enterprises Commission and GIoD are some of the bodies that have been organising series of training programmes to equip especially board directors of public institutions before they take office or even while in office. Such training programmes are increasingly receiving recognition and increased attendance, particularly in public institutions including state-owned enterprises. In order to make the programmes effective, organisers conduct follow-up programmes based on the feedback received and monitor the progress of the programme.

It is important that the right calibre of people with the requisite experience and exposure are appointed to boards so that there will be better utilisation of the training received. It was established from the survey that organisers of the training programme receive support from government. Directors themselves have hinted that the programmes are effective and supportive of their work, particularly when they assume office. Additionally, a fundamental part of the training programmes given to board members is aimed at enhancing their ethical awareness and the need for boards to comply with the corporate governance guidelines of the country.

Weak Institutions and Poor Leadership

An institution refers to 'a system of rules, beliefs, norms, and organisations that together generate a regularity of (social) behaviour' (Greif 2006, p. 30). This means that institutions are pervasive and affect any behaviour that manifests any semblance of regularity, including ethical and political behaviour among governing boards, political leaders, bureaucrats and the citizenry itself. The pervasiveness of institutions is directly related to the systems of rules, beliefs, norms and organisations that govern behaviour and must be understood as the outcome of institutions. In Ghana, there are institutions and statutory bodies established under a legislative instrument or registered under the code with appropriate legal and regulatory provisions to determine and promote effective corporate governance practice in terms of formulation and enforcement.

Institutions responsible for effective corporate governance regulations are weak in ensuring all appropriate enforcement environments and are incapable of promoting effective corporate governance practices. This is because of their lack of financial independence and appropriate enforcement powers. The Registrar General's department which is responsible for the registration of companies and the enforcement of the Companies Code (1963, Act 179) has experienced challenges in carrying out its functions effectively as a result of inadequate resources, training and support. Even though it has the powers to impose penalties on defaulting companies and persons, this responsibility is not monitored and enforced and is attributable to resource and training constraints. However, there has been an improvement in their enforcement functions over the years, particularly due to the computerisation of their systems which have led to improved access to records of the companies they register and are expected to monitor.

In Ghana, state-owned enterprises and public institutions are governed by the corporate governance guidelines of best practices which are voluntary and under the State Enterprises Commission. The general conclusion was that governance institutions are weak and unable to provide the appropriate monitoring and enforcement environment for effective corporate governance practice. In order to ensure effective practice, it is important that institutions are encouraged to develop and grow to be stronger. Truly, effectiveness of any practice is dependent on strong and effective governance institutions.

Conclusions

This chapter concentrated on the ethical dimensions of corporate governance practice in the Ghanaian public sector in relation to practices in certain parts of the private sector. Through a grounded theory methodology of constant comparison, the study identified eight open categories including board effectiveness, cultural influence, ethical concerns, board accountability, government interference, regulations, training and education, and weak institutions and poor leadership. Upon further analysis, the construction of relationships, verification and validation of data, and the influence of *culture* on governance practices emerged as the core category. Examining the *influence of Ghanaian culture* on corporate governance practices in the country revealed that *Ghanaian cultural values and norms influence* corporate governance practices in the country. However, certain corporate governance regulations and guidelines that corporations within the country are expected to abide by are often influenced by Western paradigms that do not reflect the Ghanaian culture. This is because the regulations are often imported from the developed world and include ideas relating to colonialism. This identified major elements of Ghanaian corporate governance practice that differed significantly from Western models. They included weak institutions, government interventions, political interference, gift giving/receiving and respect for authority. However, the relative elements of corporate governance practice identified were not entirely negative. For example, gift giving and receiving in itself is not negative or unethical in that it assists in establishing or enhancing all types of relationships in the Ghanaian context, including demonstrating gratitude towards stakeholders for good work done, recognising talent and achievements and establishing stronger ties with stakeholders (Ruth et al. 1999). There is no doubt that the current state of corporate governance in Ghana could be improved. However, in attempting to do so, we need to look at how we could use the positive aspects of Ghanaian culture together with best practices from other places to strengthen continually corporate governance practices in Ghana.

References

Abor, A., & Adjasi, C. K. D. (2007). Corporate governance and the small and medium enterprises sector: Theory and implications. *Corporate Governance, 7*(2), 111–122.

Adda, E., & Hinson, R. (2006). Exploring the legal framework for business and ethical practices in Ghana. *Journal of Legal, Ethical and Regulatory Issues, 9*(2), 69–80.

Adegbite, O. G. (2012). Corporate governance developments in Ghana: The past, the present and the future. *Public and Municipal Finance, 1*(2), 74–77.

Amao, O. O., & Amaeshi, K. (2007). Galvanising shareholder activism: A pre-requisite for effective corporate governance and accountability in Nigeria. *Journal of Business Ethics*, 82(1), 119–130.

American Evaluation Association. (2004). *Guiding principles for evaluators* [Online]. http://www.eval.org/Publications/GuidingPrinciples.asp. Accessed 16 Feb 2010.

Ardayfio-Schandorf, E. (1994). *Family and Development in Ghana*. Accra: University Press.

Baah, Y. A. (2007). *Organizing the informal economy: Experience and lessons from Asia and Africa*. Accra: Ghana TUC, LOFTF (Denmark) Project.

Banking Law. (1989). *PNDCL 225*. Official Gazette of the Republic of Ghana. Accra.

Basu, K. (2001). The role of norms and law in economics: An essay in political economy. In J. W. Scott & D. Keates (Eds.), *Schools of thought: TwentyFive years of interpretive social science* (pp. 154–178). California: Princeton University Press.

Boadu, M., & Sorour, M. K. (2015). Utilizing grounded theory in business doctoral research: Guidance on the research design, procedures, and challenges. *International Journal of Doctoral Studies, 10*(9). ISSN: 1556–8881.

Bovens, M. (2007). Analysing and assessing accountability: A conceptual framework. *European Law Journal, 13*(4), 447–468.

Bruner, C. (2011). Corporate governance reform in a time of crisis. *Journal of Corporation Law, 36*, 309–341.

Business Dictionary Online. (2011). http://www.businessdictionary.com/

Carasco, E., & Singh, J. (2003). The content and focus of the codes of ethics of the world's largest transnational corporations. *Business and Society Review, 108*(1), 71–94.

Carcio, W. (2004). Board governance: A social systems perspective. *Academy of Management Executive, 18*(100), 97–100.

Collis, J., & Hussey, R. (2003). *Business research: A practical guide for undergraduate and postgraduate students* (2nd ed.). London: Palgrave Macmillan.

Corbin, J. A. and Strauss, A. (2008) Basics of qualitative research. 3rd edn. Thousand Oaks, CA: Sage Publication.

Companies Code. (1963). *Act 179*. Ghana.

De George, R. T. (2000). *Business ethics*. Upper Saddle River, NJ: Prentice Hall.

De Wit, B., & Meyer, R. (1998). *Strategy: Process, content, context* (2nd ed.). London: Thompson Learning.

De Wit, R., & Meyer, R. (2004). *Strategy: Process, content, context—an international perspective* (3rd ed.). London: Thompson Learning.

Djankov, S., La Porta, R., Lopez de Silanes, F., & Shleifer, A. (2008). The law and economics of self-dealing. *Journal of Financial Economics, 88*(3), 430–465.

Dyck, A., & Zingales, L. (2004). Private benefits of control: An international comparison. *Journal of Finance, 59*(2), 537–600.

Financial Reporting Council. (2011). *Guidance on board effectiveness* [Online]. http://www.frc.org.uk/Our-Work/Publications/Corporate-Governance/Guidance-on-Board-Effectiveness.aspx. Accessed 25 Feb 2013.

Gibson, D. E., & Barsade, S. G. (2003). Managing organizational culture change: The case of long-term care. *Journal of Social Work in Long-Term Care, 2*(1), 11–34 [Online]. doi:10.1300/J181v02n01_02. Accessed 2 Feb 2013.

Giurca, V. L. (2008). *Corporate governance in developing and emerging countries: The case of Romania* (MPRA Paper, No. 10998) [Online]. http://mpra.ub.unimuenchen.de/10998/. Accessed 10 Feb 2012.

Graham, G., & Thomas, K. (2008). *Building knowledge: Developing a grounded theory of knowledge management for construction* (p. 116). Waterford Institute of Technology: Waterford.

Graham, J., Amos, B., & Plumptre, T. (2003, June 30). *Principles for good governance in the 21st century Ottawa*. Institute on Governance, The Fifth World Parks Congress in Durban, South Africa [online]. http://www.iog.ca/publications/pa_governance2.pdf. Accessed 12 Sept 2009.

Green, T. A. (1997). *Folklore: An encyclopedia of beliefs, customs, tales, music, and art* (pp. 80–1210). ABC-CLIO.

Gregory, C. A. (1982). *Gifts and commodities*. London: Academic Press.
Greif, A. (2006). *Institutions and the path to the modern economy: Lessons from medieval trade*. Cambridge University Press. ISBN: 978-0-521-48044-4. Accessed 9 Dec 2012.
Hendrick, J. (2000). *Law and ethics in nursing and health care*. Cheltenham: Nelson Thornes.
Hofstede, G. (2001). *Culture's consequences* (2nd ed.). Thousand Oaks, CA: Sage.
Holme, L., & Watts, R. (2000). *Making good business sense* (pp. 1–4) [Online]. www.Mallenbaker.net/csr/CSRfiles.definition.html. Accessed 15 Nov 2009.
Huse, M. (2005). Accountability and creating accountability: A framework for exploring behavioural perspectives of corporate governance. *British Journal of Management, 16*, 65–79.
Institute of Directors (2010): Guidelines on Corporate Governance Practices in Ghana, Accra.
Internal Revenue (Amendment) (No. 2) Act (2006). (Act 710)6, Ghana.
Jackson, A. C., & Thomas, S. A. (2005). Client's perspectives of, and experiences with, selected Australian problem gambling services. *Journal of Gambling Issues*. www.camh.net/egambling/issue14/pdf/jgi_14_jackson.pdf. Accessed 1 Oct 2010.
Klein, S. B., Astrachan, J. H., & Smyrnios, K. X. (2005). The F-PEC scale of family influence: Construction, validation, and further implication for theory. *Entrepreneurship Theory and Practice, 29*(3), 321–339.
Klomegah, R. (1997). Socio-economic characteristics of Ghanaian women in polygynous marriages. *Journal of Comparative Family Studies, 28*, 73–88.
Kotler, P. (1991). *Marketing management: Analysis, planning, implementation and control* (7th ed.). Englewood Cliffs, NJ: Prentice Hall.
Kotler, P., & Lee, N. (2005). *Corporate social responsibility: Doing the most good for your company and your cause*. Hoboken, NJ: John Wiley.
Kyereboah-Coleman, A., & Biekpe, N. (2005).*Corporate governance and the performance of microfinance institutions (MFIs) in Ghana* (Working paper No. 4330–05). Legon: UGBS.
Li, J., & Harrison, R. (2008). Corporate governance and national culture: A multi-country study. *Corporate Governance, 8*(5), 607–621 [Online]. doi:10.1108/14720700810913278. Accessed 21 Mar 2013.
Licht, A. C., Schmidt, G., & Schwartz, S. H. (2005). Culture, law, and corporate governance. *International Review of Law and Economics, 25*, 229–255.
Mauss, M. (1954). *The gift*. London: Routledge and Kegan Paul.

Mauss, M. (2002). *The gift: The form and reason for exchange in archaic societies.* Abingdon: Routledge.

Muenjohn, N., & Armstrong, A. (2008). Evaluating the structural validity of the Multifactor Leadership questionnaire (MLQ), capturing the leadership factor in transformational-transactional leadership. *Contemporary Management Research, 4*(1), 3–14.

Mysterud, I., Drevon, T., & Slagsvold, T. (2006). An evolutionary interpretation of gift giving behavior in modern Norwegian society. *Evolutionary Psychology, 4*, 406–425.

Nwanji, T. I. (2006). *Ethical implications of corporate governance a deontological and teleological approach: Applying grounded theory.* Cambridge and Chelmsford: Anglia Ruskin University.

Odotei, K., & Aweodoba, A. (Eds.). (2006). *Chieftaincy in Ghana: Culture governance and development* (p. 11). Legon: Sub-Saharan.

OECD. (2004). *Corporate governance principles: OECD—Organisation for Economic Co-operation and Development* [Online]. Paris: OECD. www.oecd.com. Accessed 18 Mar 2010.

Ofori, E. G. (2009). *Taxation of the informal sector in Ghana: A critical examination.* A dissertation presented to the Institute of Distance Learning, Kwame Nkrumah University of Science and Technology, in partial fulfilments for the degree of Commonwealth Executive Master of Business Administration (CEMBA).

Oghojafor, B., George, O., & Owoyemi, O. (2012). Corporate governance and national culture are Siamese twins: The case of Cadbury (Nigeria) Plc. *International Journal of Business and Social Science, 3*(15), 270.

Okike, E. N. M. (2007). Corporate governance in Nigeria: The status quo. *Corporate Governance, 15*(2), 173–193.

Prempeh, H. K. (2002a). *The persistent corporate governance deficit in the Ghanaian public sector: An agenda for reform.* Ghana: Ghana Center for Democratic Development, CDD.

Prempeh, H. K. (2002b). Reforming corporate governance in Ghana - Part 1: The private sector. *CDD Briefing Paper, 3*(4), 1–7.

Report on the Observance of Standards and Codes (ROSC). (2005). *World Bank: Corporate governance country assessment* (pp. 2–8). Ghana: The World Bank.

Ruth, J. A., Cele, C. O., & Frederic, F. B. (1999). Gift receipt and the reformulation of interpersonal relationships. *Journal of Consumer Research, 25*(3), 385–402.

Schein, E. M. (2004). *Organizational culture and leadership* (3rd ed.). San Francisco, CA: Jossy-Bass.

Schmidt, S. L., & Brauer, M. (2006). Strategic governance: How to assess board effectiveness in guiding strategy execution. *Strategic Governance, 14*, 13–22.

Securities and Exchange Commission. (2009). *Corporate Governance, Guidelines on Best Practice*. Ghana.

Securities Industry Law. (1993). *PNDCL 333*.

Shils, E. (1971). Tradition. *Comparative Studies in Society and History, 13*, 122–159.

Stiglitz, J. E. (1985). Credit markets and the Control of Capital. *Journal of Money, Credit, and Banking, 17*(1), 133–152.

Stoker, G. (1998). Governance as theory: Five propositions. *International Social Science Journal, 50*, 17–28.

Strauss, A., & Corbin, J. (1990). *Basics of qualitative research: Grounded theory procedures and techniques* (pp. 12–145). London: Sage.

Strauss, A., & Corbin, J. (1994). Grounded theory methodology: An overview. In Denzin, N.K., & Lincoln, Y. S. (eds). *Handbook of Qualitative Research*. London: Sage Publications.

Strauss, A., & Corbin, J. (1998). *Basics of qualitative research: Techniques and procedures for developing grounded theory* (2nd ed.). Thousand Oaks, CA: Sage.

Takatera, S., & Yamamoto, M. (1987). *The cultural significance of accounting in Japan*. Seminar on Accounting and Culture, European Institute for Advanced Studies in Management, Brussels.

Tsamenyi, M., Enninful-Adu, E., & Onumah, J. (2007). Disclosure and corporate governance in developing countries: Evidence from Ghana. *Managerial Auditing Journal, 22*(3), 319–334.

World Bank. (2004). *Corporate governance country assessment: Nigeria*. Report on the observance of standards and codes (ROSC). Washington, DC: World Bank–IMF.

World Bank. (2005). *Capacity building in Africa: An OED evaluation of World Bank support*. Washington, DC: World Bank Operations Evaluations Department.

Yücel, R., Elibol, H., & Dağdelen, O. (2009). Globalization and international marketing ethics problems. *International Research Journal of Finance and Economics, 26*, 94–104.

6

Corporate Governance in Nigeria

Umar Abbas Ibrahim

Introduction

The post-economic reform programme in the 1990s ushered in a new business environment as well as challenges associated with effective corporate governance, especially for financial institutions such as banks. Analysis of governance occurrences based on several reports indicated that existing codes and government regulations failed to resolve significantly the fundamental causes of corporate governance failures. More so, due to the complex interactions between internal and external factors in the business environment attempts to produce a corporate governance framework that met certain international standard still proved difficult. Although previous studies on corporate governance in Nigeria have reasserted thinking about alternative governance mechanisms (Okike 2007), limited research exists on understanding the underlying social/cultural phenomena and relationships with governance. That said, cer-

U.A. Ibrahim (✉)
A Management Consultant, UK

K.E. Howell, M.K. Sorour (eds.), *Corporate Governance in Africa*,
DOI 10.1057/978-1-137-56700-0_6

tain academics have argued for the evolution and refinement of alternative corporate governance frameworks to reflect issues peculiar to specific environments or organisations (Daily et al. 2003; Sonnenfeld 2002), especially for banks in developing countries (Arun and Turner 2004).

In heeding the call for alternative governance frameworks, in this chapter I concentrate on the exploration of non-economic variables to provide an understanding of the phenomenon that underlies the governance activities in banks in Nigeria. Primarily, I aim to identify why banks in Nigeria continue to fail despite reforms and the introduction of a banking code of corporate governance in 2006. I also develop a substantive theory of corporate governance based on a constructivist grounded theory of methodological approach to determine how culture and leadership can influence governance activities in banks. I also investigate social contract and trust principles as possible strategic approaches for assessing and implementing the identified findings. This alternative mechanism is in response to reported evidence of continued limitations of the conventional dominance of economic and legal/regulatory approaches to corporate governance practice (Young and Thyil 2011; Tomasic 2011; Ibrahim 2013).

The Evolution of Corporate Governance in Nigeria

In his review of corporate governance in the Third World, Yakasai (2001) observed that, prior to the independence of Nigeria in 1960, there were fewer challenges to management's prerogatives in controlling corporate enterprises. This means there was no demand for independent and off-site supervision, nor the need for transparent disclosure of information. It also implies that there was little or no cause for intervention in matters of accountability and corporate power games, except for the compliance with the corporate law that regulated corporate governance. Although there have been arguments that, as salient corporate governance issues emerged, most were resolved through the Company and Allied Matters Act (CAMA) of 1990, or similar legislation. As Okike (2007) pointed out, issues relating to the regulation, control and governance of businesses in Nigeria are largely contained within the provisions of company legislation, which has its roots in the nation's colonial past.

With the emergence of indigenisation[1] of corporations in 1977 and the proliferation of many financial and non-financial corporations in the 1980s and thereafter, corporate governance issues began to emerge. Indeed, the corporate governance discourse in Nigeria has involved issues of ownership and control structure, voting rights, corporate social responsibility and the board of directors' tenure and composition. However, continued corporate failures in the financial sector have renewed interest in the need for corporate governance reform in both private and public corporations, especially in the banking industry. More so, most of the initiatives from institutional and regulatory bodies have only reviewed previous legislations or codes of governance based on legal and economic models of developed economies. For instance, despite the post-consolidation banking reforms in 2006, there is still evidence of bank failures and unresolved corporate governance issues (Nworji et al. 2011). Furthermore, even though it is a settled argument that good corporate governance is essential for corporations and their stakeholders it was not until 2013 that a committee was set up to propose a National Code of Corporate Governance (NCofCG).

Profile of Banks in Nigeria

Modern banking in Nigeria dates back to 1892, when the African Banking Corporation was set up in the then-British colony of Lagos. In 1894, the Bank for British West Africa was established which in the same year acquired the African Banking Corporation (now First Bank of Nigeria). Other banking institutions were subsequently established, such as Barclays Bank DCO in 1925 and the British and French Bank for Commerce and Industry in 1949. Along with this colonial legacy came the establishment of smaller indigenous banking institutions, including

[1] The indigenisation policy was introduced through the Nigerian Enterprises Promotion Act (NEPD) of 1972 and revised in 1977. The main aim was the diffusion of shareholdings through the disinvestment of foreign ownership of corporations to Nigerians.

the National Bank of Nigeria Ltd in 1933, and the Agbonmagbe Bank Ltd (now Wema Bank) in 1945. The Central Bank of Nigeria (CBN), established in 1959, was the sole regulatory body in the country and assumed the responsibility for the supervision, monitoring and regulation of banks. Today's banking sector is therefore a product of several transformations that took place soon after Nigeria gained independence from Britain in 1960.

The first significant transformation took place through the noted indigenisation programme in 1977, which led to the diffusion of shareholdings that provided a basis for state ownership. Until then foreign shareholdings had formed the dominant pattern with some largely fragmented share ownership by Nigerians. The practice during this era was based on weighted voting schemes that allowed control to remain with foreign partners with block share ownership. The second transformation occurred through a series of reforms undertaken after the indigenisation era, as the number and functions of banks increased. For instance, the banking reform carried out through deregulation policy that commenced in 1986 to 2004 was informed by the need first to create the right incentives for banks and to encourage them to empower other private corporations. This resulted in the extensive privatisation of state-owned enterprises as well as the liberalisation of the financial sector. It also limited the government's role in providing the right environment for private-sector-led growth. The second step was to reposition the banks in response to the observed weaknesses that had caused a series of corporate failures that led to the reduction of the number of banks from 114 in 1991 to 23 by 2015. However, despite the reforms and consolidation, there is evidence that corporate governance issues are still unresolved in the banking system. Moreover, it has been argued that the post-consolidation governance mechanism process appears to lack any integration of ideas or the involvement of wider stakeholders (Somoye 2008).

Corporate Governance of Banks in Nigeria

Until 2006, there was little concern from researchers about the need for appropriate corporate governance for banks. As such, observance of the principles of corporate governance of banks has been dependent on a combination of voluntary and mandatory mechanisms. Voluntary mechanisms were based on the 2003 Code of Best Practice for Public Companies, which was designed to ensure good business practices and standards for the board of directors, CEOs and auditors of listed companies, including banks. On the other hand, the mandatory corporate governance provisions are contained in CAMA (1990) and the related regulations that supplement it. The reliance on the ability and willingness of banks to comply with these provisions and of regulators to enforce them explains why there have been continued corporate governance issues with banks, which have also affected the financial industry as a whole.

This implied that the spate of banking failures in the 1990s and beyond was an indication of the absence of more inclusive guidelines for the boards of directors of banks, and a pointer to the ineffectiveness of the Nigerian Deposit Insurance Corporation (NDIC) which was established in 1991 to complement the CBN in terms of monitoring responsibilities. In general, the main governance process in banks consists of three parts: composition in relation to competence, knowledge, experience and business networking; strategy in terms of the board's teamwork, organisation and tenure; and actions which relate to responsibility, commitment and performance. Each of these elements has experienced problems, largely due to human and behavioural issues that the regulatory framework has failed to address. For instance, the ROSC Report (2011)[2] indicated how a number of banks exploit loopholes in the accounting and auditing practices to boost their balance sheets, and the weak capacity of the regulatory bodies in relation to enforcement. In fact, reports of this nature were part of the reason for the consolidation of banks in 2004 and the introduction of the Code of Corporate Governance in 2006 to ensure compliance. With the commencement of the Code of Corporate Governance for Banks, it was hoped that the consolidation of the banks would constitute the first phase of the reform. As Soludo (2004) stated, the reform was designed to 'ensure a diversified, strong and reliable bank-

[2] ROSC (2011) was produced under the remit of the World Bank. In collaboration with the country's stakeholders, it assessed the implementation of Nigeria's accounting and auditing practices, and identified ways of strengthening the institutional framework.

ing sector which will ensure the safety of depositors' money, play active developmental roles in the Nigerian economy, and be competent and competitive players in the African regional and global financial system' (p. 2). Though the initiative is laudable, the mechanism is not inclusive enough to address cultural variables regarding Nigeria and the peculiarities of banking activities.

Banks' Corporate Governance Practice in Nigeria

As with the majority of African countries, there is no clear-cut system or model-based governance for banks in Nigeria, except those obtained from previous legislations. While the lack of an adequate framework, including institutional and political factors and supervisory mechanisms, was identified (Ogunleye 2002), there were also arguments relating to policy environment and management problems (Nworji et al. 2011). Therefore, revisiting corporate governance practice from the perspectives of regulation and a code of governance, internal control and disclosure of information could provide a critical insight into the nature of corporate governance issues in the banking sector.

Regulation and the Code of Governance for Banks

Corporate governance regulation refers to the rules established by law in relation to the management, supervision and control of the activities of the banking industry (Ibrahim 2013). Prior to Nigeria's independence in 1960, issues related to corporate governance of banks were controlled and managed by Company Ordinance of 1922 and later the 1968 Companies Act, which extensively mirrored the UK Companies Act of 1948. Over time, inadequacies were noticed in the 1968 Act that led to the enactment of what is now called CAMA (1990). The central provisions of CAMA were substantially related to the management, supervision and control of the business of companies,[3] which are not that different from those of the previous acts. This implies that as an instrument of corporate governance practice in Nigeria, CAMA (1990) was based on UK corporate law and fashioned along the lines of the Anglo-Saxon model. There have been doubts expressed over whether rules based on UK corporate law can sufficiently resolve corporate issues in Nigeria, or reflect the Nigerian business environment (Okike 2007; Adegbite 2010).

In response to the implementation of global corporate governance standards Okike (2007) advised the need to appreciate the differences in the socio-economic environments in which businesses operate. Moreover, she stated that 'it would be unwise to assume that corporate governance issues would be resolved by a framework that mirrored the legal values of our colonial past, particularly in terms of entrenched principles' (p. 188). As Charkham (1994) concluded, foreign systems of corporate governance reflect those countries' histories, assumptions and value systems, and, as such, countries should be allowed to identify the most appealing mechanisms in which the universal principles can be accepted and applied. To achieve this, global search for corporate governance standards should be aligned with the aspirations of each specific environment.

In addition to CAMA 1990, corporate governance practice in Nigerian banks were also guided by the Banks and Other Financial Institutions Act (BOFIA) of 1991, the Investment and Securities Act (ISA) of 1999, the Securities and Exchange Commission (SEC)'s Code of Corporate Governance (SEC 2003) and, recently, a post-consolidation Code of Corporate Governance (CBN 2006) aimed specifically at addressing governance issues in banks. Both the SEC (2003) and CBN (2006) codes evidently reflect some features of the Organisation for Economic Cooperation and Development (OECD) principles and the Basel Committee on Banking Supervision (BCBS). It is apt to note that corporate governance codes are documents that state the rules and procedures for governing and managing corporations, and as such are instituted by

[3] Under CAMA (1990), a company is defined as including all banks and any other corporations registered and practising in Nigeria.

self-regulating professional bodies with the consent of the relevant government regulatory agencies.

Although compliance with the provisions of all the legislative acts and codes of corporate governance for banks is mandatory in Nigeria, this requirement has not been translated into action. Studies also revealed that good corporate governance goes beyond rules and regulations (Ariely 2009; Barth et al. 2006). There are also views that, in terms of good corporate governance, consolidation of the banks was only the first step towards ensuring stability, though this is not in itself enough to improve significantly the performance of the participating banks (Amel et al. 2003). In addition, Amel et al. (2003) also advanced the notion that, even though the consolidation of banks may exploit economies of scale, 'it does not significantly improve cost and profit efficiently, and on average, does not generate significant shareholder value' (p. 18). It is therefore indicative that practitioners of consolidation often advocate this reform approach without understanding the differences between the econometric factors and bankers' beliefs. Furthermore, it can be argued that, even when consolidation may improve management quality, such gains are often diminished by organisational diseconomies of scale. More worrisome is the fact that the Code of Corporate Governance for Banks introduced by the CBN in 2006 appears to be influenced by a number of internal and external regulatory frameworks as indicated in Fig. 6.1.

The central box represents the Code of Corporate Governance for Banks that was introduced in 2006. The Code primarily was influenced internally by the reports of established committees, regulatory acts and instruments introduced by the government, including CAMA, BOFIA, the SEC Act (SECA), the Corporate Affairs Commission (CAC) and the NDIC. Externally, there are the international agencies, including the BCBS, the ROSC, the OECD, the CACG, the UK's Cadbury Report, the US Sarbanes-Oxley Act and the South African King's Report that have variously influenced the reports and codes of governance for corporations in Nigeria. While the international agencies have been involved in the governance process in an attempt to ensure that global standards of corporate governance are met, the Cadbury Report (UK) and the Sarbanes-Oxley Act (USA) have been used as references in the establishment of

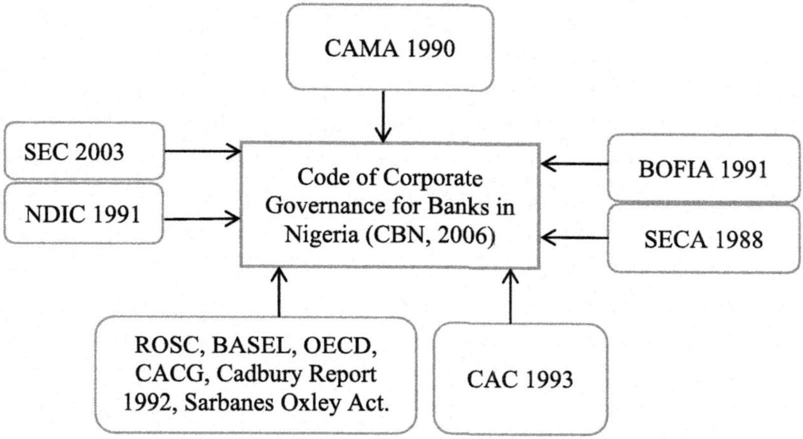

Fig. 6.1 The development of corporate governance for banks in Nigeria

previous and existing corporate governance guides for banks. These amalgamated provisions have evidently proved difficult to enforce or to comply with, due to numerous insufficiencies.

Internal Control Mechanisms

Internal governance mechanisms involve a critical feature of bank management, particularly in ensuring the safeness and soundness of the industry. One of the most important aspects of the internal governance of banks is the supervision and monitoring of activities by boards of directors. Previous studies identified boards of directors as the primary internal control agents and their responsibilities included monitoring management behaviour, formulating strategic decisions that may have a considerable impact on the owners, and ensuring that all involved act in the best interests of the corporation (Waldo 1985; Filatotchev and Nakajima 2010). This implies that they have the legal authority to ratify and monitor managerial initiatives, evaluate the performance of top managers, and reward or penalise their performance where necessary.

According to Tricker (1994), there is an understanding that effective corporate governance rests on the boards of directors, whose roles involve both the conformance and performance of their firms. Tricker (1994) explained that conformance roles refer to 'accountability to the shareholders and stakeholders and the monitoring through questioning, judging and supervising management. Performance roles here refer to the strategy formation—developing plans for interaction with external environment, profit strategy and policy making through establishing rules and norms to meet the strategic goals of the firm' (p. 147). To help boards carry out their responsibilities, the CBN (2006) also considers that boards should be accountable and responsible for the performance and affairs of the bank. This indicates that the entire internal control process is affected by the board of directors through the senior management and the various structures implemented.

It therefore means that good corporate governance practice rests on the compliance with and enforcement of the provisions set out in the rules and guidelines provided by the codes of governance. However, as Sanusi (2010) pointed out, in many cases CEOs of banks were found to have set up 'special purpose vehicles to lend money to themselves for stock price manipulation or the purchases of estates all over the world. In another bank, the management set up 100 fake companies for the purpose of perpetrating fraud' (p. 7). Indeed, it was this concern that led Yakasai (2001) to conclude that key issues in the banks relate to the varied and deceptively intractable activities of boards. This casts further doubt on the ability of the current leadership of the boards of banks to deliver the expected responsibilities that are entrenched in the regulatory framework, despite attempts to address some of these emerging issues by the CBN.

Corporate Information Disclosure

Information disclosure is a statutory requirement under the company law and other provisions relating to the governance of banks. It is also an international standard practice and an essential aspect of accountability and communication of the stewardship of the board of directors. As Tricker (1984) explained, disclosure of information involves 'an ex gratia act, by those with knowledge, to convey information to others … with the intention to orientate, or to motivate, to create a climate of understanding, acceptance, involvement and participation, or to reach a consensus between otherwise conflicting views' (p. 123). In business and accounting terms, disclosure is seen as a motivational tool used by decision makers to stimulate action. Acts of disclosure are also associated with 'transparency', which relates to unfettered access to timely and reliable information on decisions and performance. Moreover, this is also one of the main principles of corporate governance provisions (OECD 1999).

Compelled by corporate governance guidelines through their boards of directors banks are committed to make required disclosures. Above all, information presented should be considered for its relevance, completeness, comparability, comprehensibility and timeliness if it is to be useful for business purposes. In this regard, CBN (2006) specifically encourages banks to make robust disclosures beyond the statutory requirements as provided in BOFIA (1991), CAMA (1990) and other applicable laws. However, Sanusi (2010) observed that 'banks' reports to the CBN and investors were often inaccurate, incomplete and late, thereby depriving the CBN of the right information to effectively supervise the industry and depriving investors of the information required to make informed investment decisions' (p. 8).

Sanusi (2010) further explained that some banks were manipulating their accounts by colluding with other banks to enhance artificially their financial positions and stock prices. In addition, there are reports of converting non-performing loans into commercial papers and bank acceptances, and the setting up of off-balance-sheet special purpose vehicles to hide losses. The array of corporate governance issues in banks clearly demonstrated the need for an alternative corporate governance mechanism that deals with such issues which could be mutually implementable by all those responsible for governance practice. However, due to the shortcoming of traditional corporate governance theories and practices of shareholdership and stakeholdership and its resultant debates around the globe, a theoretical thought on culture and leadership framework is identified to underpin appropriate corporate governance in banks in Nigeria.

Culture and Leadership as a Framework for Corporate Governance

Ibrahim (2013) identified that there have been a number of empirical studies that provided evidence of the link between leadership and culture (Schein 2004; Alvesson 2011). Howell (2009) further explained that both leadership and culture are intrinsic to an institution. For instance, Schein (2004) stated that culture involves the identification of behaviours, attitudes or norms that 'help to explain some of the more seemingly incomprehensible and irrational aspects of what goes on in groups and organisations' (p. 22). On the other hand, leadership is explained as a group process, inducing compliance and executive influence, a particular behaviour or forms of persuasions and instruments to achieve goals (Bass 1990).

The Nigeria banking experience during the global financial crisis and thereafter suggested the need for an alternative corporate governance mechanism which included leadership and culture variables. This is premised on the reasoning that organisations can disseminate behaviours that provide accepted values and norms for new recruits and on-going decision making as well as daily interactions. As Schein (1996) noted, since leadership is about shaping beliefs, desires and priorities, culture is therefore seen as the most important social and contextual factor that can influence a leader's capacity to influence others within an institution. Moreover, corporate governance codes, practices and systems have emanated from diverse cultures. It therefore makes intuitive sense that leadership and culture within a given environment is essential in developing an enforceable framework. More so, they are both essential in balancing between economic and social goals and between individual and community goals.

Methodological Approach

Since corporate governance is socially constructed, it requires an understanding of the dynamic nature of social reality in order to uncover the underlying phenoma (Letza et al. 2008). For this reason a qualitative investigative approach is considered most appropriate in addressing the meanings individuals or groups ascribe to social or human problems regarding notions of corporate governance. In this chapter a constructivist paradigm underpins the methodology and data collection and analysis. As Howell (2013) stated, groups/individuals are changeable and mind *creates* reality, and facts are produced by human consciousness. In addition, the constructivist approach offers a radical and critical alternative inquiry for social science while affording an understanding of the social practices engaged in by people and their interactions with each other.

Based on constructivism this chapter draws on the grounded theory (GT) methodological approach because it allows the construction of substantive theory through qualitative data collection, e.g. interviews and focus group. The data for this study was collected from commercial banks, the Central Bank of Nigeria (CBN), the Nigeria Deposit Insurance Corporation (NDIC), the Security and Exchange Commission (SEC), the Chartered Institute of Bankers in Nigeria (CIBN) and other sample stakeholders.

Data Analysis and Substantive Theory

The data obtained from banks by way of interviews and focus group was analysed through constant comparison of coding procedures—open coding, axial coding and selective coding, through which concepts and categories were developed. These concepts have developed eight open categories and their properties/dimensions, which include corporate transformation, enforcement, code/regulation, improving competence, internal control mechanism, lack of transparency, self-interest, and organisational factors and their properties, as shown in Table 6.1.

The axial and selective coding are the second and final stages of the GT analytic process, and it is through the process of axial coding that the initial eight categories indicated in Table 6.1 were subsumed into six main categories. These six categories are corporate control strategies, human action, enforcement, lack of leadership, competency, and code/regulation. This stage allows for the reassembling of data that were fractured during open coding, which facilitate the developed open categories

Table 6.1 Summary of open categories and their properties

Open coding	
Open category	Properties
Corporate transformation	Board structure, Tenure
Enforcement	Compliance, Monitoring, Trust
Code/regulation	Harmonisation, Regulatory review
Improving competence	Training, Job assessment, Skills development
Internal control mechanism	Whistle-blowing, Risk-taking
Lack of transparency	Lack of accounting, Quality of auditing
Self-interest	Human attitude, Moral value
Organisational factors	Corporate culture, Leadership problem, Public pressure

Source: Ibrahim (2013)

to be linked together to form a more precise and complete explanation about the phenomenon. Moreover, this application of coding has assisted in specifying the terms of the conditions that create the circumstances, the context in which the phenomenon is embedded, the action or interaction strategies by which a group or individual responded, and the consequences of those strategies. Although the axial coding analysis provides higher-level codes when compared to the open codes, in the selective coding stage, the outcomes from the open and axial coding are utilised to identify the core category and develop it in relation to subcategories.

Significance of Selective Coding

Selective coding is the final stage of the analysis and the main stage of theorising that is achieved through connecting the axial categories to the other categories. In other words, it is the process of selecting the core category, systematically relating it to other categories, and validating those relationships. As Goulding (2002) stated, the core category 'pulls together all the strands in order to offer an explanation of the behaviour under study' (p. 88). More importantly, it is at this stage that the major categories are finally integrated to form a larger theoretical scheme, which allows the findings to take the form of a substantive theory. Indeed, the selective coding process focuses on integrating and refining categories at a higher level of abstraction (Strauss and Corbin 1998). Here, the process began when the eight open categories were subsumed into the six main axial coding categories. Hence, it is these categories that are interpreted as affecting the corporate governance practice of banks in Nigeria.

Although grounded theory emerges from the data, by the time integration occurs, it represents an abstract rendition of that raw data, and as such it is important to validate the data that is part of the selective coding process. It is also an essential part of providing credibility of any investigative process, and making the findings trustworthy and transferable. This is achieved by continually making comparisons and asking questions, and in all cases the questions were asked continually as the analysis progressed. These questions relate to the main analytical idea, patterns occurring in the data and what all the action/interaction seems to do. As Charmaz (2006) pointed out, in the initial fieldwork, both open and axial categories are suggestive, but not yet definitive, regarding the happenings. Moreover, obtaining the additional data is intended to help explicate the categories and further reflect qualities of the respondents' experiences that would provide a useful analytical understanding of their views. Indeed, it is the analyses of the responses from the core participants that have helped in refining the abstract nature of the properties identified previously, and which adds to the credibility of the findings.

Furthermore, whilst undertaking selective coding, it is important to identify core categories in terms of properties and dimensions, as well as their relationships to the subcategories in order to build a theory that can explain what the issue is all about. In this instance, the subsumed properties and dimensions of the subcategories, of self-interest and lack of transparency, into the human action category indicates the broader meaning and interpretation of the effects of human action. In other words, it suggests that the various strategic reforms by CBN and other banks were intended to curtail the effects of self-interest behaviours and the lack of transparency that were found to guide corporate actors' decisions. It also explains why enforcing compliance is still a challenge in the banking sector, and the inability of the leadership to develop a corporate culture that can impact on corporate governance practice.

In formulating a broader 'story' of the core categories and the possible conceptual relationships for a future theory, the relationships around the action/interaction strategies, conditions and consequences of the actors are therefore vital. This relationship is synchaptered in order to explicate a framework of alternative corporate governance through the paradigm model that defines the relationship between the core categories and the subcategories as presented diagrammatically in Fig. 6.2.

From the model above, it can be observed that the central forces of corporate governance of banks are human action that occurs through acts of self-interest and lack of transparency on the one hand, and the inability of the leadership to develop a corporate culture to steer enforcement and compliance on the other. The arrows pointing up and down incorporate enforcement, control strategies and code/regulation, which suggest the overall expectations of the consolidation reform and the reforms that are to follow. In contrast, the findings revealed constraining factors related to the broader elements of the core categories of human action—self-interest and transparency as indicated on the left hand side—and lack of leadership in relation to organisational factors and competence, as shown on the right hand side, and this is what forms the developed substantive theory.

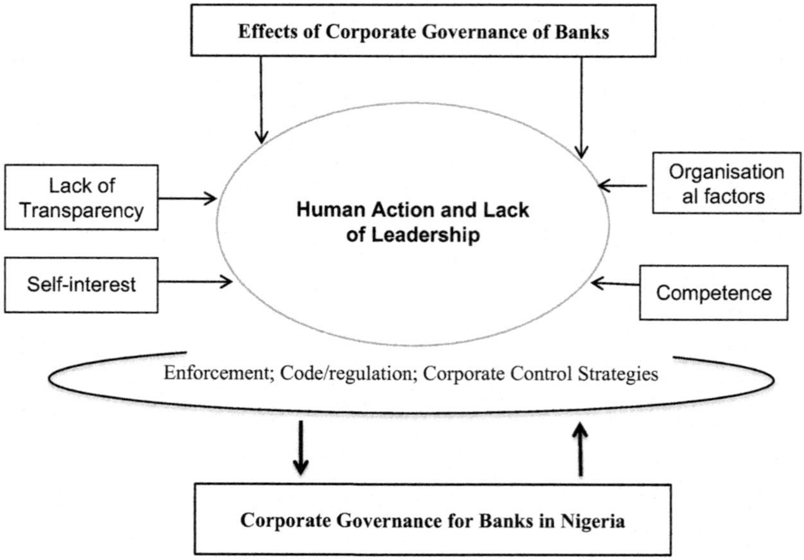

Fig. 6.2 A model integrating the core categories with the subcategories

Culture and Leadership to Corporate Governance Study

Although both culture and leadership may have been used differently and could have their limitations in terms of unusual attributes, it can be argued that their integration within a given context allows for a more powerful explanation of organisational activities. Moreover, there has been evidence that both culture and leadership have been used to create powerful concepts that are also intrinsic to institutions (Howell 2009) and which have variously influenced institutional settings. As Conger (1990) stated, leadership is useful for examining behavioural aspects and their impact on organisations' activities, while culture helps in the task of interpreting matters in hand or shared beliefs that influence actions (Hofstede 2001). In fact, banks' activities like many other organisations is the focus of any corporate governance study, and as such has the quality of being adaptable to the process of change. More importantly, both leadership and culture theories can also be explored through the use of a qualitative research design (Parry 1998; Den Hartog et al. 1999), which this study has employed. Indeed, the qualitative design helps in understanding and uncovering nuances of the corporate governance issues.

The Substantive Theory

The basis of the substantive theory relates to the identification of what banking corporate governance in Nigeria entails, what phenomena are present, how they are related to each other, and what effects they have on corporate governance practice. Even though the findings vary according to the perspectives and understanding of participants, the substantive theory of corporate governance developed recognises human action and lack of leadership as forces that have, in many ways, shaped and refined the activities and achievements of the corporate governance of banks. Indeed, it is the interplay of these forces that provides a description of the causation, consequences and associated processes for the banks and other stakeholders in corporate governance. While the theory acknowledges some of the measures placed by CBN and other banks, it is the developed theory that could give the banks a focus and clarity of purpose, and enable it to attain its corporate governance objectives.

The Substantive Theory as a Cultural Process

The substantive theory holds that self-interest behaviour observed is influenced by three factors: individual greed; desire to protect individual, family or group interests; and organisational self-interest aimed at maximising corporate profits. These underlying elements have continued to motivate some banks and individuals to resort to manipulation of procedures, or to take actions that consequently affect the corporate prospects of banks. The participants' interpretations relates to how scholars (Kangas 1997; Kohn 1990; Miller and Ratner 1996) label self-interest as the cardinal human motive or activity that is carried out in search of personal or group advantage or gain. It is also consistent with what Bourdieu (1977) described as 'Habitus', which he explained as a system of durable transposable disposition learned from everyday practices and experiences. Indeed, it relates to what Hofstede (1991) referred to as the broad tendency to prefer certain states of affairs over others, and that very often lead to the development of new rules of conduct. Often, these tendencies make groups more powerful and consequently impede organisational change (Gorga 2003).

Similarly, even though disclosures are made regularly, for example in banks' annual financial reports, the CBN has found that most of the information did not represent banks' true accounting positions and hence was unreliable. The findings further mirrored the conclusion of Zarzeski (1996), Hope (2003) and Akman (2011) regarding the influence of culture on financial disclosure. It can therefore be argued that resistance or refusal by the bank leaders to comply with or enforce the provisions of the 2006 Code of Corporate Governance for Banks is due to the extent to which human action is embedded in the banking sector. However, as Schwartz and Davis (1981) argued, firms with internal cultures that are supportive of their strategies are more likely to be successful, hence it is desirable to change a bank's internal culture so as to improve its corporate performance.

The Substantive Theory as a Leadership Process

The substantive theory emphasised internal compliance and monitoring of the strategies initiated by the CBN and other banks. It also reveals how banks' leadership through boards of directors failed to steer corporate culture towards meeting the expectations of the regulatory authority, the shareholders and depositors, as well as international standards. This interpretation is consistent with Osborn et al. (2002) who identified the dominance of senior executive self-interest in decision-making processes. Again, since the board represents an organisation's owners and is responsible for ensuring that the organisation is managed effectively through the adoption of control mechanisms aimed at ensuring that management behaviour is consistent with the interests of the owners (Filatotchev and Nakajima 2010), they are considered to be 'the apex of the internal control system' (Jensen 1993, p. 862). This means boards of directors are essentially important in the process of monitoring and directing compliance with regulatory provisions and other directives. More significantly, since leadership is a culture-influencing activity (Alvesson 2011), leaders are expected to embody the norms of their positions and persuade others in ways that are consistent with their normative obligations.

Implications of the Substantive Theory to Practice

A substantive theory is a single-area theory developed for a substantive or situational context (Strauss 1987) and stating its implications for practice forms an important aspect of GT methodological application. Therefore the findings of the substantive GT can have several implications in the achievement of good corporate governance practice for banks in Nigeria. Hence, it is recommended that policy makers for corporate governance in banks and other stakeholders, including the CBN, the boards of directors and management of banks, are required to consider the following:

a) To utilise the principle of social contract. In this case, the boards of directors of banks along with the regulators should develop the idea of rational agreement, which would work simultaneously in two directions. Firstly, it would give moral reasons for perceiving the institution from an impartial and impersonal standpoint. Secondly, it would show the direct implications of personal incentives and motivations that could be implemented in practice.
b) The regulatory body should encourage individual boards to take a moral perspective; this could be ensured through codes of practice specific to individual banks, as well as more generic ones relating to the whole of Nigeria.
c) The boards of directors/management and the regulatory agency (CBN) should also create a stimulating and high-trust environment that will restore trust within the hierarchy and between the banks and their stakeholders. It is important that the boards of directors and indeed the stakeholders involved in the corporate governance process are willing to accept the challenges of change and improve their commitment to banking organisations.
d) The board members/management should be encouraged to be continually aware of and sensitive to the impact their self-interest and lack of transparency has on the banking system. This will be possible if they are constantly made aware of and more knowledgeable about the need for integrity. As Hung and Huang (2010) contended, 'the concept of integrity is closely bound to morality' (p. 81).
e) In addition, the boards of directors, the regulatory body and the bank employees should convert their own perceptions into beliefs and attitudes among the bank employees through cooperation and trust so as to forge greater commitment towards good governance practice. This step would ensure long-term corporate performance and the rebuilding of business confidence in the banking sector.
f) The substantive theory findings offer suggestions about the underlying motives behind the current culture that is unreceptive to leadership, and ruled by self-interested attitudes and a lack of transparency. To improve the situation, the boards of directors and the management should exhibit a spirit of transparency and the desire for common

good. This can be achieved through the entrenchment of trusting elements and mutual cooperation in the corporate culture of banks.

g) In order to achieve leader transparency, boards of directors should ensure that they share relevant information during their interactions with their followers and are open to giving and receiving feedback, and that they are forthright about the reasons behind their decisions.
h) Finally, without overlooking the legal and economic efficiency requirements of the existing framework, it is indicative that the desired corporate governance for banks should consider the broader social products of corporate governance by incorporating an understanding of the continually changing cultural and leadership dynamics that impact on the effectiveness of corporate governance practice in Nigerian banks.

The Strategic Approach for Implementation

Since culture and leadership have an influence on the decision-making process and institutional performance, especially in balancing between economic and social goals and between individual and communal goals (Iskander and Chamlou 2000), there is the need to incorporate to the economic and legal aspects an acceptable social arrangement between people and institutions. This can be achieved through a social contract and trust principles between and within institutions and actors, which is expected to provide the essential mechanism required to resolve the institutional and governance impasse.

A Social Contract Strategy

A precise definition of social contract theory is unavailable as the idea varies; however, contemporary ideas of social contract theory are associated with modern moral and political theories, which can be traced back to the political philosophers of the seventeenth and eighteenth centuries. Thus, the full exposition of social contract theory is credited to Hobbes (1996), Locke (1980) and Rousseau (1987), whose work has been continued by generations that have followed. In fact, the traditional concept of social contract theory is implicit in the work of these political philosophers and is grounded on basic logic that a given human nature determines how people would live in the 'state of nature' (that is if there were no social institutions). This in turn determines the terms of an acceptable social arrangement, a contract among the people or between people and a social institution.

Although early philosophers' conceptions of social contract theory focused on the origin and legitimacy of political institutions, subsequent developments have moved the theory towards its application into various spheres of human activity (Donaldson and Dunfee 1999). For instance, in organisations, it is intended to curtail the free-rider syndrome that primarily underlies institutional agency problems, especially in business activities where it should be seen as processes in which a person's immediate surroundings are constantly adapting, revolving and evolving (Hung and Huang 2010). Moreover, such forms of association will defend and protect, with the common (community), the person (individual) and goods of each associate.

Trust as a Strategy

There has been considerable increase of late in the interest among researchers in the concept of trust, and in its application to a variety of important social and organisational issues. Often, trust is defined in relation to (1) individual expectations, (2) interpersonal relationships, (3) economic exchanges, and (4) social structures (Chiles and McMakin 1996). These broad and evolving concepts are used in honouring moral obligations inherent in the social norms and ultimately constraint opportunistic behaviours. Although trust itself is based on the assumption that one person can and wants to meet the other's needs, and this depends on the situation, attitudes and dispositions of those involved in the potentially trusting relationship, a considerable number of theoretical perspectives of trust have been taken in a number of disciplines, including management and wider economic and social organisations. For instance, in the wake of social excesses and business abuses of the 1980s, a move was made to conceptualise these issues within law and economics and hence its significance to different managerial settings, collaborations and alliances and their governance structures (Beccerra and Gupta 1999).

Moreover, trust in leadership harnesses the followers' efforts towards achieving a common goal or strategy. There are evidences suggesting that it was the breakdown of trust and trustworthiness that led to the collapse of corporations such as Enron, Tyco and Arthur Anderson (Kramer and Cook 2004), all of which have been referred to in research on corporate governance failures. Although, in some cases, there could be difficulties in creating and maintaining trust between leaders and their constituents even under the best circumstances, such difficulties can be overcome by designing more effective governance processes that can foster greater transparency and accountability.

Conclusions

Continued corporate governance failures in Nigeria (despite the economic and government regulatory reform initiatives through privatisation and consolidation) identified the need for an alternative mechanism. Although some attributed the failures to the inability of the legal and economic mechanisms that are perceived to have mirrored Nigeria's colonial past to address corporate issues, others believed the failures required a more thoroughgoing review of existing corporate governance mechanisms and the inclusion of social factors. This chapter has undertaken an empirical investigation of the effects of existing corporate governance frameworks, especially the recent code of governance for banks and its methodological constraints in achieving effective objectives. Using constructivist grounded theory methodology and qualitative method, the findings have highlighted the centrality of corporate governance issues and identified human agency and leadership as main factors in governance processes. The findings were based on the leadership and culture theoretical framework which is found to have significant influence in the study of corporate governance issues.

The data also revealed that effective corporate governance is a process that cannot be addressed sufficiently through codes or government regulations alone, and as such the governance system must continue to incorporate other lenses relating to human nature and its behavioural elements if it is to ensure corporate accountability. In order to implement the developed substantive grounded theory, there is the need to employ a strategic approach to the refined corporate mechanism. In this instance, the adoption of the principles of social contract and trust within banks and their stakeholders are suggested. This moral reasoning and motivation is intended to collectively strengthen the leadership and other stakeholders to overcome the embedded self-interests of decision-makers and lack of transparency in the activities of banks.

References

Adegbite, E. (2010). Corporate governance and responsibility in Nigeria. *International Journal of Disclosure and Governance, 8*(3), 253–271.

Akman, H. N. (2011). The effects of IFRS adoption on financial disclosure: Does culture still play a role? *American International Journal of Contemporary Research, 1*(1), 6–17.

Alvesson, M. (2011). Leadership and organisational culture. In A. Bryman, D. Collinson, K. Grint, B. Jackson, & M. Uhl-Brien (Eds.), *The handbook of leadership* (pp. 151–164). London: Sage.

Amel, D., Barnes, C., Panette, F., & Selleo, C. (2003, June). *Consolidation and efficiency in the financial sector: A review of international evidence* (Working Paper No. 20). Tor Vergata: Centre for International Studies on Economic Growth.

Ariely, D. (2009, July–August). The end of rational economics: The new economies in the new world. *Harvard Business Review.*

Arun, T. G., & Turner, D. J. (2004). Corporate governance of banks in developing economies: Concepts and issues. *Corporate Governance: An International Review, 12*(3), 371–377.

Barth, J. R., Caprio, G., Jr., & Levine, R. (2006). *Rethinking bank regulation: Till angels govern.* Cambridge: Cambridge University Press.

Bass, B. M. (1990). *Bass and Stogdill's handbook of leadership: Theory, research, and managerial applications* (3rd ed.). New York: Free Press.
Beccerra, M., & Gupta, A. K. (1999). Integrating the trust literature with agency theory and transaction costs economics. *Public Administrative Quarterly, 23*(2), 177–203.
Banks and Other Financial Institutions Act (1991). Government of Nigeria.
Bourdieu, P. (1977). *Outline of a theory of practice* (Cambridge Studies in Social and Cultural Anthropology). Cambridge: Cambridge University Press.
CAMA. (1990). *Companies and Allied Matters Act*, Federal Government of Nigeria, Lagos, FGN Publications.
CBN: Central Bank of Nigeria. (2006, April). *Code of Corporate Governance for Banks in Nigeria Post Consolidation*, CBN Publication.
Charkham, P. J. (1994). *Keeping good company: A study of corporate governance in five countries*. Oxford: Clarendon Press.
Charmaz, K. (2006). *Constructing grounded theory: A practical guide through qualitative analysis*. London: Sage.
Chiles, T. H., & McMakin, J. F. (1996). Integrating variable risk preferences, trust, and transaction cost economics. *Academy of Management Review, 21*(1), 73–99.
Conger, J. A. (1990). The dark side of leadership. *Organisation Dynamics, 19*(2), 44–55.
Daily, C. M., Dalton, D. R., & Cannella, A. A., Jr. (2003). Corporate governance: Decades of dialogue and data. *Academy of Management Review, 28*(3), 371–382.
Den Hartog, D. N., House, R. J., Hanges, P. J., & Ruiz-Quintanilla, A. S. (1999). Culture specific and cross-culturally generalizable implicit leadership theories: Are attributes of charismatic/transformational leadership universally endorsed? *Leadership Quarterly, 10*(2), 219–256.
Donaldson, T., & Dunfee, T. (1999). *Ties that bind: A social contracts approach to business ethics*. Cambridge, MA: Harvard Business School Press.
Filatotchev, I., & Nakajima, C. (2010). Internal and external corporate governance: An interface between an organisation and its environment. *British Journal of Management, 21*(3), 591–606.
Gorga, E. (2003). *Does culture matter for corporate governance? A case study of Brazil* (Working Paper). Stanford Law School. Available at: www.ssrn.com/. Accessed 11 Aug 2010.
Goulding, C. (2002). *Grounded theory: A practical guide for management, business and market researchers*. London: Sage.

Hobbes, T. [1651](1996). Leviathan. In T. Richard (Ed.), *Cambridge texts in the history of political thought* (revised edition). Cambridge: Cambridge University Press.
Hofstede, G. H. (1991). *Cultures and organizations: Software of the mind, intercultural cooperation and its importance for survival.* London: McGraw-Hill.
Hofstede, G. H. (2001). *Culture's consequences: Comparing values, behaviours, institutions and organisations across nations* (2nd ed.). Thousand Oaks, CA: Sage.
Hope, O. K. (2003). Firm-level disclosures and the relative roles of culture and legal origin. *Journal of International Financial Management and Accounting, 14*(3), 218–248.
Howell, K. E. (2009). Devolution and institutional culture: Path-dependency and the Welsh Assembly. *Policy Studies, 30*(2), 221–235.
Howell, K. E. (2013). *An introduction to the philosophy of methodology*. London: Sage.
Hung, Y., & Huang, J. H. (2010). Contexts, social contract, and leader integrity. *International Conference on Economics, Business and Management*, Manila, Philippines.
Ibrahim, A. U. (2013). *Investigating the effects of corporate governance of banks in Nigeria: A grounded theory approach*. Plymouth, UK: University of Plymouth.
Iskander, M. R., & Chamlou, N. (2000). *Corporate governance: A framework for implementation* (Report). Washington, DC: World Bank Group.
Jensen, M. C. (1993). The modern industrial revolution, exit, and the failure of internal control systems. *Journal of Finance, 48*(3), 831–880.
Kangas, O. E. (1997). Self-interest and the common good: The impact of norms. *Journal of Socio-Economics, 26*(5), 475–494.
Kohn, A. (1990). *The brighter side of human nature*. New York: Basic Books.
Kramer, R. M., & Cook, S. K. (2004). Trust and distrust in organisations: Dilemmas and approaches. In R. M. Kramer & K. S. Cook (Eds.), *Trust and distrust in organisations: Dilemmas and approaches* (pp. 18–20). New York: The Russell Sage Foundation.
Letza, S., Kirkbride, J., Sun, X., & Smallman, C. (2008). Corporate governance theorising: Limits, critics and alternatives. *International Journal of Law and Management, 50*(1), 17–32.
Locke, J. (1980). *Second treatise of government*. Indianapolis: Hackett.

Miller, D. T., & Ratner, R. K. (1996). The power of the myth of self-interest. In L. Montada & M. J. Lerner (Eds.), *Current societal issues about justice* (pp. 25–48). New York: Plenum Press.

Nworji, D. I., Adebayo, O., & David, O. A. (2011). Corporate governance and bank failure in Nigeria: Issues, challenges and opportunities. *Research Journal of Finance and Accounting, 2*(2), 1–19.

OECD: Organization for Economic Cooperation and Development. (1999). *Principles of corporate governance.* Paris: OECD.

Ogunleye, G. A. (2002). The causes of bank failures and persistent distress in the banking industry. *NDIC Quarterly, 2*(2), 19–36.

Okike, E. N. M. (2007). Corporate governance in Nigeria: The status quo. *Corporate Governance: An International Review, 15*(2), 173–193.

Osborn, N. R., Hunt, G. J., & Jauch, R. L. (2002). Toward a contextual theory of leadership. *The Leadership Quarterly, 13*(6), 797–837.

Parry, W. K. (1998). Grounded theory and social process: A new direction for leadership research. *Leadership Quarterly, 9*(1), 85–105.

ROSC Report. (2011). Accounting and auditing. *Report on the Observance of Standards and Codes in Nigeria.* Washington, DC: World Bank.

Rousseau, J. J. (1762/1987). In D. A. Cress (Ed.), *The social contract.* Indianapolis: Hackett.

Sanusi, L. S. (2010, 26 February). *The Nigerian banking industry: What went wrong and the way forward* (Convocation Paper). Kano: Bayero University.

Schein, E. (1996). Three cultures of management: The key to organisational learning. *Sloan Management Review, 37*(3), 9–20.

Schein, E. (2004). *Organisational culture and leadership* (3rd ed.). San Francisco, CA: Jossey-Bass.

Schwartz, H., & Davis, S. M. (1981). Matching corporate culture and business strategy. *Organisational Dynamics, 10*, 30–48.

SEC: Securities and Exchange Commission. (2003, October). *Code of Best Practice on Corporate Governance for Public Quoted Companies in Nigeria.*

Soludo, C. (2004, 6 July). Consolidating the Nigerian banking industry to meet the development challenges of the 21st century. *Paper at Bankers' Committee Forum*, Abuja.

Somoye, C. O. R. (2008). The performances of commercial banks in the post-consolidation period in Nigeria: An empirical review. *European Journal of Economics, Finance and Administrative Sciences, 14*, 62–72.

Sonnenfeld, J. (2002, September). What makes great boards great: Best practice. *Harvard Business Review*, pp. 1–10.

Strauss, A. (1987). *Qualitative analysis for social scientists*. Cambridge: Cambridge University Press.

Strauss, A., & Corbin, J. (1998). *Basics of qualitative research: Techniques and procedures for developing grounded theory* (2nd ed.). Thousand Oaks, CA: Sage.

Tomasic, R. (2011). The failure of corporate governance and the limits of law: British banks and the global financial crisis. In W. Sun, J. Stewart, & D. Pollard (Eds.), *Corporate governance and the global financial crisis: International perspectives* (pp. 28–49). Cambridge: Cambridge University Press.

Tricker, R. I. (1984). *Corporate governance: Practice, procedures and powers in British companies and their boards of directors*. Aldershot, Hants: Gower.

Tricker, R. I. (1994). *International corporate governance*. Singapore: Simon & Schuster.

Waldo, C. N. (1985). *Boards of directors: Their changing roles, structures, and information needs*. Westport: Quorum Books.

Yakasai, A. G. A. (2001). Corporate governance in a third world country with particular reference to Nigeria. *Corporate Governance: An International Review, 9*(3), 152–166.

Young, S., & Thyil, V. (2011). A holistic approach to corporate governance: Lessons from the financial crisis and the way forward. In W. Sun, J. Stewart, & D. Pollard (Eds.), *Corporate governance and the global financial crisis: International perspectives* (pp. 28–49). Cambridge: Cambridge University Press.

Zarzeski, M. T. (1996). Spontaneous harmonisation effects of culture and market forces on accounting disclosure practice. *Accounting Horizons, 10*(1), 18–37.

7

An Examination and Analysis of Bank Corporate Governance Regulation in The Gambia: A Grounded Theory Approach

Sainey Faye

Introduction

It is easy to see why there is an absence of literature on corporate governance in The Gambia. The Gambia is a small under-developed African economy with a GDP of £510.1 million ($807.1 million), a population of 1.9 million (World Bank 2014), and a workforce of over half a million. Only 5% of people are employed in organisations of more than 50 employees. Fifty-five percent of these organisations are found in two industries: (1) finance and insurance and (2) electricity and gas. These two industries, however, have an overall workforce of a mere 2500 employees (GBoS 2013). 'Most of the smaller private sector companies [are] operating in the informal sector' (Nshimyumuremy and Workie 2015). In The Gambia the corporate sector is small and no stock exchange currently exists. Indeed, one might wonder whether anything meaningful can be learnt from studying corporate governance in The Gambia. For those

S. Faye (✉)
Buckinghamshire Business School, Buckinghamshire New University, High Wycombe, UK

K.E. Howell, M.K. Sorour (eds.), *Corporate Governance in Africa*,
DOI 10.1057/978-1-137-56700-0_7

living in the country, a case can be made. But can a case be made to help understand corporate governance in general and Africa in particular? Can this study benefit those living in Africa? In this chapter, I put forward an argument that responds to the question with an affirmative.

To do this, one should closely examine the reasons why there is so little literature available about the subject, a situation that it shares with other African countries. An overview of corporate governance will be based upon official sources from The Gambia and reports and statistics produced by international bodies, such as the African Development Bank and the World Bank. The limitations of this approach will be examined.

This will be followed by a review of corporate governance and an examination of reliance upon abductive reasoning (abductive reasoning involves providing the likeliest possible explanation for an incomplete set of observations (Douven 2011)) to make conclusions about corporate governance within The Gambia. An evaluation of the legislative and regulatory framework relating to corporate governance in The Gambia will also be carried out and the benefits of using a constructivist approach will be discussed.

The main aim of this chapter is to outline a substantive theory of bank corporate governance regulation within the context of The Gambian banking system using grounded theory methodology. The case for primary research and theoretical perspectives will be made. I will draw upon Faye's (2014) study of corporate governance and regulation in The Gambian banking sector. The justification for the study is outlined and the methodology examined. This will be kept as simple as practicable since grounded theory is an unfamiliar approach to many of those in the field of banking and finance yet is a vital part of the chapter.

Suggestions for government regarding ethical values and principles for the banking sector are outlined. The ethical values and principles are designed to be compatible with The Gambia's dual Western and Islamic banking system and draws upon extant literature. Findings will then be presented, as well as the resulting substantive theory, the human factor model and how this can be used to develop an understanding of corporate governance in The Gambia. There is also a reflexive account regarding the limitations of the study. This includes adopting a more Afrocentric and multidisciplinary approach to corporate governance. It is necessary, at this point, to provide a more detailed overview of The Gambia to help contextualise later discussion.

About The Gambia

The Gambia is Africa's smallest and most densely populated mainland country (1.9 million) and has high rates of population growth and urbanisation. It is a former British colony with a legal and institutional legacy. Over 90 % of the population is Muslim and 8 % Christian. The literacy rate is 55 %. It is ranked as the third poorest country in the world with a GDP per capita of £275.03, and a GDP of £525 million (World Bank 2015). Foreign direct investment in 2014 was $76 million (£48 million), a 25 % decline from 2013. It has a large fiscal deficit and a heavy debt burden (8.7 % and 100 % of GDP, respectively) (Nshimyumuremy and Workie 2015). Its economy has recently been hit by poor harvests, drought and a decline in tourist revenues because of the Ebola crisis. As with many less developed countries, it lacks robust financial and economic institutions. Key information and up-to-date statistics about the country are absent or difficult to obtain.

Regarding ease of credit, The Gambia is 160th out of 189 countries in terms of ease of credit (Doing Business 2015). The rule of law in terms of property rights and freedom from corruption is significantly below the world average and is deteriorating (Nshimyumuremy and Workie 2015).

The financial sector is a small yet significant part of the economy, contributing 10.5 % of the GDP, but it only has 1500 or more employees (out of a total national workforce of 520,788 (GBoS 2013)) and has the largest share of companies with over 50 employees in the country. There are 12 banks in the country whose combined assets were £385 million, and commercial lending totalled £9.64 million. Real interest rates at 28.8 % were the fourth highest in the world in 2014 (World Bank 2015; CBG 2016). The financial and banking sector is underdeveloped with few financial products. The banks serve 25 % of the urban and 5 % of the rural population (World Bank 2015) (Tables 7.1 and 7.2).

Table 7.1 Share of GDP and work force per sector in The Gambia

	% GDP	% Workforce
Agriculture	24.0	31.5
Manufacturing & Construction	11.0	13.5
All Services	65.0	55.0
Breakdown of services		
Wholesale and retail trade	*27.7*	*32.0*
Transport, storage and communication	*16.9*	*4.8*
Finance, real estate, and business services	*10.5*	*0.2*
Others	*9.9*	*8.0*

Source: Nshimyumuremy and Workie (2015) & GBoS (2013)

Table 7.2 Employment by size of organisation

Number employees in the organisation	% of organisations
50+	5.2 %
20–49	4.0 %
10–19	7.9 %
2–9	39.6 %
1	43.3 %

Source: GBoS (2013)

This chapter seeks to justify the importance of looking into corporate governance in a seemingly peripheral and unimportant country, the challenges in studying it, and the lessons that result.

In the context of this research, it is essential to examine the paucity of literature and the strategies to combat this challenge.

The Paucity of Literature

Corporate governance regulation in The Gambia is an area that is not well researched. The country lacks the academic and financial resources with which to support such research. A brief review of the literature on business related to The Gambia over the past 25 years produced few journal articles on the effects of tourism (Dieke 1993; Baum 1996), the economic efficiency of commercial banking (Agu 2004), privatisation (Forster and Nilakant 2005; Forster and Mouly 2006) and the illusion of capitalism

(Sallah and Williams 2011). The bulk of academic literature is linked with funded projects that include malaria, tropical medicine and health issues and is carried out by academics from foreign institutions. There were articles related to corporate governance that focused on Africa, sub-Saharan Africa and West Africa but not specifically The Gambia.

The paucity of literature on corporate governance regulation led to the consideration of three strategies for undertaking the research. First, reliance on literature that focused on the same topics but at different levels of analysis. Inferences can be made by looking at countries with similar levels of development, at other sub-Saharan or West African countries with a British colonial legacy, at countries with a dual Western-Islamic banking system, at those countries that are small and cannot benefit from economies of scale, and so on and so forth. It is likely that meaningful results could be yielded from such an enterprise.

Second, one can conduct secondary analysis using reports from sources such as the Central Bank of The Gambia (CBG), The Gambia Bureau of Statistics (GBoS), and the African Development Bank (ADB). Relying on secondary sources means dealing with issues relating to rigour, data collection techniques and the nature of the information sought/required.

Third, one can conduct primary research. This is time consuming and resource hungry, and the number of researchers able to study corporate governance in The Gambia is small. As with the study of corporate governance in other African countries, a decade ago, a key reason for the dearth of literature—primary or secondary—can be accounted for by the low priority given to them because of the lack of development in these economies.

> Corporate governance was long ignored as a matter of importance for developing countries. It remained virtually invisible in those countries until the East Asian financial crisis of 1997–8 . . . Little attention was given to corporate governance in other developing countries, especially the smaller ones. (Oman 2004, p. 2)

Some African countries have progressed, sizable corporations have emerged, and the need for corporate governance has been recognised as domestic corporations grow in number and expand, and foreign-owned corporations become more established. Governments and businesses perceive a need to develop these activities within the corporations (Budhwar and Debrah 2006).

> Relatively very little has been written about . . . developing nations. This was probably due to the limited number of researchable topics in mainly small economies and small wage employment sector. However, over the past two decades, foreign direct investment … and multinational companies have [arrived]. As a result of such developments, there is now a sudden research interest in management in developing countries. (Budhwar and Debrah 2001, p. 7)

The lack of development in The Gambia and its small size mean that market growth potential is more limited, arguably placing it decades behind other countries, such as Nigeria, Kenya and South Africa.

Review of Corporate Governance in The Gambia

It is important to avoid committing an ecological fallacy, i.e. 'the attempt to conclude information, concerning an individual from related characteristics observed at an aggregated level' (ZDS 2014). To avoid this, it is necessary to be familiar with aspects of The Gambia that distinguishes it from other members of a larger aggregate group. This means being aware of the country's geography, its modest resources, and its history, culture and institutions. Therefore, it is important to be aware of the country's path dependency, especially in relation to banking and the regulation of corporate governance. Path dependency refers to a dynamic process whose evolution is governed by its own history (David 2007). The Gambia has a distinct historical legacy.

The Gambia's banking sector is relatively healthy; non-performing loans as a percentage of banks' total loan portfolio remain high despite a drop from 14 % in March 2011 to 12.7 % in June 2011 (Making Finance Work for Africa 2015). This is mainly because there are no official limits to the level of interest commercial banks can charge customers. However, Agu (2004) found that commercial banks in The Gambia have not performed as efficiently as they could because of the heavy regulatory framework. Vittas (1991) added that high interest rate spreads in developing countries may be a consequence of monetary regulations, such as reserve requirements, high inflation, high loan losses, and high cost and profit because of operation inefficiency and uncompetitive behaviour. Worrell (1996) contended that the wide spreads can be due to small volumes of business, which necessitate a higher mark-up because of diseconomies of scale. Howard and Haynes (2001) suggested that reserve requirements impose an implicit tax on financial intermediation since they constrain the bank's ability to extend credit and may reduce their profitability.

A feature of sub-Saharan African development in the last four decades has been the rather limited role played by the financial market in the mobilisation of essential resources to facilitate growth-enhancing investments (Aryeetey and Nissanke 2004). Crosse and Hampel (1980) contended that both big and relatively small banks have demonstrated that the greatest savings in cost are to be found not in machines alone but also in a more efficient organisation of management. However, Heffernan (2005) stated that banking in poor countries is more labour intensive and much less computerised. Banks and branches are small, so economies of scale are not as high as they might be elsewhere. Furthermore, government restrictions and regulations tend to raise bank-operating costs. The World Bank argued that Africa is making progress in cutting red tape and improving business regulations (Guha 2006).

The most informative account of governance in The Gambia is the 2006 Country Governance Profile (African Development Bank 2007). The African Development Bank research is a rich source of information about corporate governance in The Gambia. It was produced after consulting: 77 Gambians, mostly government officials; 12 civil society organisations and 18 representatives from international development partners from the UNDP; the WFP; Unicef; the UNFPA; US, French and Taiwanese embassies; the European community; the Department for International Development; and the World Bank. The report utilises a five-point framework in its analysis of governance in The Gambia, i.e. 'accountability, transparency, stakeholder participation, legal and judicial framework, and the fight against corruption' (African Development Bank 2007, p. vi). These points underpin 'good governance' promoted by the World Bank and other international banks and development agencies. The agenda calls for

> the strengthening of public sector management, promoting rules and institutions to provide a predictable and transparent framework for public and private business and promoting accountability for economic and financial performance . . . Good governance also implied promoting a suite of essentially Western institutions: a separation of powers, free press, independent judiciary, pluralistic civil society, and respect for the rule of law, and . . . multiparty elections (Kelsall 2008, p.1).

The ADB (2007) profile focuses on country governance, government, legislation and state organisations. It is also linked with the provision of financial aid and exercises and some leverage over the government to promote reforms designed to support development according to the ADB's perspective on progress and governance. Apart from a brief review of the relevant legislation, the report has very little to say about the corporate governance of business, adopting as it does a top-down approach to corporate governance. It provides few real insights into the nature of corporate governance in the commercial sector. It does, however, provide a fair snapshot of country governance and the institutional environment of corporate governance. See Table 7.3 for a summary of its key findings.

Kelsall (2008, p. 1) argued that the good-governance agenda 'met with disappointing results'. A major reason for this is that Western concepts are ill-suited to African societies. Kelsall identifies that

> a core set of beliefs and values concerning power, accountability and social morality [which] are widely observed across sub-Saharan Africa, [has] proven extremely durable and remain powerful drivers of behaviour. . . . The institutions that work well in solving collective action problems and providing public goods are those that harness the motivating forces of family, ethnicity and religion. This confirms the relevance of the question of how might development efforts be redirected so that they stop working against and start to build upon the extant notions of moral obligation and accountability in the region.

Table 7.3 Key points in the ADB profile of Gambian governance

Accountability
• *Government effectiveness* is a proxy for political interference and has deteriorated since 2007.
• *Financial stability* is significant progress made mainly because of technical assistance by development partners in the area of preparing and auditing a backlog of national accounts.
• *Resource constraints* are notably in terms of senior level staff.
• *The budget process* as a whole needs to be improved. Annual off-budget expenditures undermine budget transparency.
• *Internal audit*, as a recognised discipline, is hard to come by international audit standards, for public and private firms have yet to formally adopt it.
• *The Bank of Gambia* has been radically reformed since 2003 and presents a fine example of *what can be achieved in a short period when incentives loom*.
Transparency
• The Gambia ranks 149th out of 168 countries according to Reporters without Borders.
• Transparency in public budget spending or local decision making seems to be out of reach for most civil society organisations.
• There is some progress in the area of public procurement framework, but it continues to experience operational shortcomings with respect to data processing and adequately skilled staff.
Stakeholder participation
Much of the report is focused on the electoral system and the local government. However, identification of key intervention areas for the promotion of a private sector, socio-economic development in a participatory and democratic environment are mentioned.
As regards gender issues, 'despite the adoption of policies to promote gender equality, significant gender disparities continue to exist' (p. 9).
Legal and judicial system
• There continues to be many challenges for The Gambia judiciary to exercise and uphold its independence.
• Most of the regional and international instruments have been signed and ratified.
Anticorruption and money laundering
• When it comes to corruption, The Gambia ranks 123rd out of 163 countries according to Transparency International. Corruption appears to be increasing.
• Anticorruption measures are weak and have not been formalised and made legally explicit, except what is found in the 1997 constitution.
• Money-Laundering Act of 2003 marked notable progress, but there is no enforcement agency; however, the bank is in the process of creating the financial intelligence unit in charge with investigating and reporting suspicious transactions.

(*continued*)

Table 7.3 (continued)

Priority governance areas
The question of leadership and how seriously the executive is committed to sound public financial management and political accountability is crucial. The dominance of the executive over the legislature and the judiciary must be sharply curtailed and a true and genuine system of checks and balances be established. The capacity of key governance oversight institutions must be enhanced in order to perform as expected.
Conclusion and recommendations
• With a few exceptions, the institutions visited during the preparation mission were characterised by serious resource and capacity constraints aggravated by excessive turnover of staff, posing a challenge to any capacity development program.
• The importance of continuity in policy and program design and implementation cannot be overemphasised in all aspects of sustainability and governance.

Source: ADB (2007)

Others also speak of the need to develop African theories of corporate responsibility and CSR based on notions such as African renaissance, Ubuntu and the Omoluwabi (Dartey-Baah and Amponsah-Tawiah 2011). African renaissance originated with the Senagalese philosopher and politician, Cheikh Anta Diop in 1946 and developed and was popularized by Thabo Mbeki in South Africa in the late 1990s. Dartey-Baaah and Amponsah-Taiwah (pp 112–3) see this concept as "an emerging, ideal type which provides a view of what Africa can offer global management". They also note that Ubuntu (which is discussed in the next chapter) is "the belief in a universal bond of sharing that connects humanity" and see Omulawabi as a developing concept based on the Yoruba notion of character.

Kelsall (2008) provides a rich analysis of such traditions drawing upon a rich body of literature. He argues that Western institutions are incompatible with African tradition, culture and institutions. Where the two have interacted two main problems have emerged. First an externalisation of accountability which reduces traditional imperatives of accountability. Second "a parallelization and obscurantization of political and economic activity, meaning that there exist parallel worlds of politics, with the real world obscured behind a screen and to some extent inverted." Kelsall (p10, 2008) These issues need to be addressed and development and modes of corporate governance need to be developed so that go with the grain of the African way of doing things.

Currently, there is no specific Gambian banking sector corporate governance code or requirement. Thus, financial institutions in The Gambia do not have to comply with any corporate governance rules and regulations. Financial institutions are therefore compelled to adopt corporate governance regulatory policies and requirements that are mainly internally generated or imposed on them by their parent companies. As a result, there are no consistent or standardised corporate governance frameworks across the financial sector.

A largely descriptive review relying on government sources reveals that in The Gambia there is a fairly rudimentary system of corporate governance. As noted this research has been undertaken by employing grounded theory (GT) methodology which demands qualitative data and analysis using open, axial and selective coding. This is not the same as letting the facts speak for themselves (Durkheim) but methodically and systematically sifting through data to produce core categories to identify the meanings and understanding (induced) from the actors themselves.

Positivists consider that the purpose of research is to create theories that help us identify and describe relationships between variables to make predictions and that the scientific enterprise is value free. Others would add that another role of research is to explore and generate further research questions. Marx said that philosophers interpret the world, but 'the point is to change it'. I also subscribe to this viewpoint, and this is a key tenet of a constructivist paradigm of inquiry.

Studies mainly utilise sources such as country-specific information and studies by international institutions, such as the World Bank, which collects a relatively limited amount of information about The Gambia. While such information enables comparisons with other countries, such information is limited, superficial and lacking contextual nuances.

Legislative and Regulatory Framework Relating to Corporate Governance in The Gambia

In developed countries, there is a wealth of data that analyses the practical implications of legislation to business. In The Gambia there are no voluminous annual reports with sections on corporate governance, CSR and risk management. There is not a major market for this information, given the small number of large businesses, the low level of education, a limited number of skilled professionals, and comparatively low levels of literacy. This severely constrains what can be said about the legal framework. The gap in the literature is wide. Much time and effort will be required to find out which parts of this legislative framework are legally applicable to which type of business. A provisional list of relevant legislation is in Table 7.3 to illustrate this point.

Table 7.4 Legislation affecting corporate governance and regulation

- Business Registration Act 2005
- The Partnership Act 2005
- Companies Act 1955 and 2013
- Finance and Audit Act 1996
- The Accountants' Act 2005
- Insolvency Act 1992, Amendment Act 1997, and Insolvency Bill 2003
- Gambia Investment and Promotion Act 2001
- Anti-Terrorism Act 2002
- Money Laundering Act 2003
- Financial institutions Act 2003
- Insurance Act 2003
- Gambia Revenue Authority Act 2005
- The Central Bank of The Gambia Act 2005
- Banking Act 2009
- International Convention of the Elimination of All forms of Racial Discrimination 1969
- International Convention of the Elimination of All forms of Discrimination Against Women 1981
- Labour Act 1990
- The Copyright Act 2003

Source: Based on information from CBG (2016) and Nshimyumuremy and Workie (2015)

Both the ADB (2007) and the CBG (2016) refer to some of this legislation in terms of their relevance to the banking and finance sectors. The current regulatory framework consists of the Banking Act 2009, Money Laundering Act 2003, Central Bank Act 2005, Anti-Terrorism Act 2002, Insurance Act 2003, Financial Institutions Act 2003, and Companies Act 2013 (CBG 2016). These acts are designed to improve the regulation and monitoring of financial institutions. The Money Laundering Act 2003 guarantees the confidentiality of companies' reporting suspect transactions. It is hoped that these acts will lay the required foundation for a legitimate and transparent system of regulation and corporate governance. This, in turn, boosts foreign-investor confidence in The Gambia's regulatory environment because the majority of banks are foreign owned. Guha (2006) also added that The Gambia has improved property rights and made it easier to form companies, start businesses and simplify business regulations. However, on a practical level weak institutional capacity and corruption still posed problems (OECD 2015). The Central Bank of The Gambia [CBG] (regulator) increased the capital adequacy requirements for commercial banks operating in the country in an attempt to bolster the stability and quality of the banking system. All commercial banks are now required to adhere to the new minimum capital requirement of D200 million (£3.21 million) (Table 7.4).

Constructivism and Its Contribution in Understanding This Research

This research will focus on the little information we have about corporate governance in The Gambia. Much of this is based upon abduction, making reasoned but tentative conclusions based on partial information. Referring to studies of other countries that may share some similar characteristics to The Gambia can provide useful insights for understanding corporate governance and directing future research. One of the few in-depth studies on corporate governance in The Gambia is Faye (2014), which uses a grounded theory approach to study it and regulation in the banking and finance sector.

Commenting on the constructivists paradigm, Guba and Lincoln (1989, p. 12) posited that 'for the constructivist paradigm, the core assumption is that realities are not objectively "out there" but constructed by people, often under the influence of a variety of social and cultural factors that lead to shared construction'. Hence, for constructivism, 'humanity alone is responsible for knowledge development and understanding is a matter of interpretive construction on the part of the active subject' (Howell 2013, p. 90).

Greene (2000, p. 986) suggested that 'constructivist inquirers seek to understand contextualised meaning . . . the meaningfulness of human actions and interactions—as experienced and construed in a given context'. Furthermore, Charmaz (2006) argued that a constructivist approach places priority on the phenomena of the study and sees both data and analysis as created from shared experiences and relationships with participants (see Charmaz 1990, 1995, 2000, 2001; Charmaz and Mitchell 1996). Constructivist grounded theory therefore assumes that both data and analysis are social constructions that reflect what their production entailed (see Bryant 2002, 2003; Charmaz 2000; Hall and Callery 2001; Thorne et al. 2004). Thus, any analysis is therefore contextually situated in time, place, culture and situation. Furthermore, Charmaz (2000) argued that constructivist grounded theory lies squarely in the interpretative tradition, contrary to objectivist grounded theory, which is derived from positivism. Thus, we do not exist in a social vacuum but instead interact with data and create theories about it. This may also suggest that in the process of conducting research using the constructivist approach, research participants may live in the researcher's mind and influence how the researcher conducts research long after immediate contact with them. Hence, constructivism understands reality as being locally constructed and based on shared experiences.

Epistemologically, constructivist research results are created through consensus and individual constructions, including the constructions of the investigator (Howell 2013). Furthermore, Guba and Lincoln (1989, p. 13) concurred that such 'socially constructed realities are not independent of the "observer" (constructor) but are absolutely dependent on him or her for whatever existence they have'. Constructivists therefore focus on how and occasionally why participants construct meanings and actions in specific situations. Charmaz (2006, p. 130) suggested that a constructivist approach means more than looking at 'how individuals view their situations. It not only theorises the interpretive work that research participants do, but also acknowledges that the resulting theory is an interpretation' (Bryant 2002; Charmaz 2000, 2002).

Social constructivists assume that individuals seek understanding of the world in which they live and work. It is argued that individuals develop subjective meanings (varied and multiple) of their experiences—meanings directed at certain objects or things (Creswell 2009). As a result of multiple and varied meanings, the researcher is able to look at the complexity of views rather than narrowing meaning into a few categories or ideas. The subjective meanings are therefore negotiated socially and historically, not imprinted on individuals but formed through interaction with others (hence, social constructivism) and through historical and cultural norms that operate in individuals' lives (Creswell 2009).

Therefore, the objective of a constructivist approach to research is to make sense of (or interpret) the meanings others have; inquirers therefore generate or inductively develop a theory or pattern of meaning. Thus, constructivism fosters researchers' reflexivity about their own interpretations, as well as those of their research participants. However, critics of constructivism point out that 'researchers recognise that their own backgrounds shape their interpretation, and they position themselves in the research to acknowledge how their interpretation flows from their personal, cultural and historical experiences' (Creswell 2009, p. 8). Other researches, such as Charmaz (2006), suggested that grounded theorists can import preconceived ideas into their work if they remain unaware of their starting assumptions. According to Howell (2013), the main criticism of constructivism involves the relativist reduction and self-refutation; reality is constructed, so all constructions are realities. This would suggest that truth in one construction can be true for all or even another, separate construction. This would be difficult to uphold if not impossible because social structures are totally different; each has an incommensurable worldview, and comparative judgement between them is impossible. Therefore, prediction and causality are unlikely outcomes of constructivist research, although with different levels of understanding (Verstehen) they can be achieved (Guba and Lincoln 1985).

Social constructivism (often combined with interpretivism; see Mertens 1998) is typically seen as an approach to qualitative research. The ideas came from Mannheim and from works such as Berger and Luckmann's (1967) and Lincoln and Guba's (1985). Recently, further academics have summarised social constructivism, including Crotty (1998), Lincoln and Guba (1985), Neuman (2000), and Schwandt (2007). The qualitative research, which generally uses the case study technique, is the most suitable one for conducting research inside an interpretivist paradigm (Corbetta 1999; Thietart 2001). Qualitative research therefore may not necessarily lead to general rules, but the qualitative approach helps to read reality in a wider range of circumstances, if the authors conceptualise (Ciao 2011).

Grounded Theory Research Methodology

Grounded theory was initially developed by sociologists Barney G. Glaser and Anselm L. Strauss. They published a seminal work entitled *The Discovery of Grounded Theory* in 1967. This work was a result of a successful collaboration during their studies of the dying (see Glaser and Strauss 1965, 1968; Strauss and Glaser 1970). Despite this successful collaboration, grounded theory appears to marry two rather contrasting and competing traditions in sociology as represented by Glaser and Strauss: Columbia University positivism and Chicago school pragmatism and field research. Glaser's rigorous quantitative training is demonstrated in his epistemological assumptions, logic and systematic approach to grounded theory. In contrast, Strauss brought notions of human agency, emergent processes, social and subjective meanings, problem solving practices, and open-ended study of action to grounded theory (Charmaz 2006). Stern (1994) claimed that the differences between the two researchers had always been apparent, but it was not until Strauss published a detailed guidance to the grounded theory process (Strauss 1987; Strauss and Corbin 1990) that the divergence was more widely recognised.

Glaser and Strauss (1967, p. 1) defined grounded theory as 'the discovery of theory from data—systematically obtained and analysed in social research'. As a result, Martin and Turner (1986) and Jones and

Noble (2007) concluded that grounded theory was an inductive, theory-discovery methodology that allows the researcher to develop a theoretical account of the general features of a topic while grounding the account in empirical observations or data (see Chenitz and Swanson 1986; Locke 2001; Goulding 2002).

Alternatively, Charmaz (2006) defined grounded theory methods as systematic yet flexible guidelines for collecting and analysing qualitative data to construct theories 'grounded' in the data themselves. Grounded theory methodology is therefore aimed at systematically deriving theories of human behaviour from empirical data. At this point, it is important to note that there is a difference between grounded theory method and grounded theory itself. A grounded substantive or formal theory is the possible outcome of using the grounded theory method. Therefore, it is possible that one might use the method without producing a grounded theory.

There are some who claim to use the method as part of an approach that does not seek to develop grounded theories (Bryant 2002). Myers (2006) argued that to ensure that the concepts indeed emerge from the data, as a general rule, the researcher should make sure that he or she has no preconceived theoretical ideas before starting the research. Therefore, grounded theory researchers should ensure that reading prior literature does not contaminate or stifle creativity (Urquhart et al. 2006).

One notable distinction between grounded theory and other qualitative research is its specific approach to theory development. Grounded theory suggests that there should be a continuous interplay between data collection and analysis (Myers 1997). Thus, 'the purpose of grounded theory research in business and management is to develop new concepts and theories of business related phenomena, where these concepts are firmly grounded in qualitative data' (Myers 2006, p. 107). Since its introduction in 1967, grounded theory has been used in qualitative studies within organisations and managements (Nwanji 2006), as well as social sciences, nursing, and many other fields (Glaser 1978; Strauss 1987; Dey 1993; Annells 1996).

As a methodology for qualitative research, grounded theory has spread across a number of domains—economics, education, nursing, and psychology just to name a few (Nwanji 2006). Grounded theory methodology has also been used in the study of European integration and political science and recently on European financial services (Howell 2000, 2002). There are few methodological references on grounded theory approaches (Strauss 1987; Strauss and Corbin 1990; Howell 2000). Grounded theory has been used in many qualitative researches in the past, but few methodological references used grounded theory for the study of corporate governance issues.

This research approach is therefore aimed at providing new insights and understanding between business ethics and corporate objectives. Grounded theory can also provide the basis for a mix of inductive and deductive approaches (Howell et al. 2007).

Grounded theory is a research methodology that offers a comprehensive and systematic framework for inductively building of theory. A grounded theory is one that is discovered and provisionally verified through systematic data collection and analysis of data pertaining to a particular phenomenon (Strauss and Corbin 1990). The careful and precise application of this method will ensure that the theory that emerges from this study meets the criteria of good science: generalisability, reproducibility, precision, rigour, and verification (Corbin and Strauss 1990).

Grounded theory suggests that there is an overemphasis on verification theory and wishes to demote the idea that discovery of relevant concepts and hypotheses are a priority to research (Howell 2000, p. 4). The purpose of grounded theory is to build theory that is faithful to and illuminates the area under study. Glaser and Strauss (1967) considered that grounded theory was concerned with two types of theories: substantive and formal (conceptual). The theory allows hypotheses and substantive concepts to emerge from the data, so analysis may identify concepts relevant to understanding the data. This view is also supported by Howell (2000, p. 7), suggesting that

> in discovering theory, one generates conceptual categories or their properties from evidence; then the evidence from which the categories emerged is used to illustrate the concept. The evidence may not . . . be accurate beyond doubt . . . but the concept is undoubtedly a relevant theoretical abstraction about what is going on in the area studied.

According to Howell (2000, p. 7), generating a theory was accomplished through the collection, coding and analysis of data. Therefore, these three operations should be undertaken together as much as possible. These areas should interact continually, from the beginning of the investigation to its end. The separation of these areas hinders theory generation, whereas set ideas stifle it.

A number of the basic features of grounded theory make it an appropriate method for this research:

1. Grounded theory methodology includes analysis of process. Within grounded theory methodology, the term *process* is used to describe 'the linking of sequences of action/interaction as they pertain to the management of, control over or response to, a phenomenon' (Strauss and Corbin 1990, p. 143). Process is the analyst's way of accounting for or explaining change.
2. Grounded theory methodology directly links macroscopic issues to the phenomenon under investigation. This mode of research requires that broader, contextual issues that influence the phenomenon under study be given appropriate recognition in the development of a theory.
3. Grounded theory makes its greatest contribution in areas in which minimal research has been undertaken. There is little or no research on corporate governance using grounded theory that focuses on corporate governance regulations on financial organisations in developing countries, such as The Gambia. Most of the research that used grounded theory has been in the area of politics, government and economics (Howell 2000).
4. Grounded theory is very useful in developing context-based, process-oriented descriptions and explanations of organisational phenomena (Myers 1997).
5. Grounded theory offers relatively well-signposted procedures for data analysis (Urquhart 1997, 2001) and potentially allows for the emergence of original and rich findings that are closely tied to the data (Orlikowski 1993). This, according to Urquhart et al. (2006), provides researchers with a great deal of confidence because, for each

concept produced, the researcher can point to many instances in the data that relate to it.

6. By adopting the grounded theory method, the researcher can direct, manage and streamline their data collection and, moreover, construct an original analysis of data (Charmaz 2006). It also lets the researcher analyse the data early. Furthermore, it encourages a constant interplay between data collection and analysis.
7. Grounded theory encourages a systematic, detailed analysis of the data and provides a method for doing so. For the novice researcher in particular, the detailed guidance provides a certain level of confidence that the data is being analysed in a systematic and rigorous manner. Grounded theory is a 'bottom-up' approach to coding data (Dey 1993). It also permits investigation into new areas of significance as they emerge from the data (Simpson et al. 2004).
8. A key strength, and one still central to grounded theory method, is that it offers a foundation for rendering the process and procedures of qualitative investigation visible, comprehensible and replicable (Bryman and Charmaz 2007), thereby fulfilling the need to justify qualitative approaches (justification process).
9. Grounded theory method offers a rationale for researchers as they begin their research; the method eliminates and precludes the need for hypotheses and conjectures (justification of methodological flexibility and indeterminacy) (Bryman and Charmaz 2007).
10. Grounded theory is also useful for developing new theory or fresh insights into old theory, it generates theory of direct interest and relevance for practitioners, and it can uncover micromanagement processes in complex and unfolding scenarios (Locke 2001).

Grounded theory is the most appropriate methodology for this research because an empirical investigation of governance systems within the financial organisations and its impact on the society as the stakeholder is a research phenomenon that can be studied using grounded theory methods (Hussey and Hussey 1997). Furthermore, the impact of corporate governance regulation on the performance of banks in developing countries has been relatively ignored in the literature or has been given superficial attention. Consequently, this researcher's mission is to build his own theory from the ground. The nature of grounded theory is to enable the emerging theory to 'be abstract enough and include sufficient variation to make it applicable to a variety of contexts related to that phenomenon' (Strauss and Corbin 1990, p. 23). Thus, the theory developed from this research will be of used by other researchers interested in studying the issue of corporate governance in the financial sector in developing countries.

Proposed Ethical Codes for The Gambian Banking Sector

Most developing countries have no effective governance system based on law and regulations. The minimal financial sector mechanisms available are riddled with corruption, mismanagement and ineffective provisions of services/delivery to the public (World Bank 1997). The issue of corruption and mismanagement of financial sector financial systems could be viewed from ethical theory, as well as regulatory theory.

I will use the Kantian ethical perspective focusing on categorical imperative (CI) as an alternative theoretical underpinning. The focus of the management of financial organisations is the provision of services to society as stakeholders; therefore, stakeholder theory has ethical issues, which require a relevant ethical theory. Artigas (2006) suggested that philosophical ontologism based on the concept of good as opposed to evil helps us define the banking business from the point of view of ethics. Davies (2001) added that the internal audit of the bank's operations should conform to the operating principles and business ethics code pertaining to internal auditors. Codes of ethics are now prevalent in large corporations around the world (Schwartz 2002). This development is likely to continue and even accelerate as governments, industry associations and special interest groups increasingly call for the establishment of corporate codes of ethics (Schwartz 2002).

Currently, there is no specific or generic ethical code of conduct in The Gambian banking sector from a regulatory point of view (CBG 2016). As a result, some banks have developed their own ethical banking code as part of their internal governance mechanisms. The Arab Gambia Islamic Bank (the only Islamic bank), for example, is likely to follow the Accounting and Auditing Organisation for Islamic Finance Institutions (AAOIFI) ethical framework. AAOIFI was established to provide industry-wide standards for accounting, auditing, governance and ethics for central banks, Islamic financial institutions and others from the international Islamic banking and finance industry (Mathenge 2013). All Islamic banks are encouraged to adopt the AAOIFI ethical framework, but it is not mandatory (Mathenge 2013).

Given that the economy cannot successfully function in the absence of ethics and morals, the necessity of introducing an ethical code is frequently advocated (Hazard 1995). Thus, the application of the code of ethical principles would establish a defensive mechanism in the area of ethical values because the code requires more stringent moral standards and involves sanctions for the breach of principles (Mathenge 2013). However, given The Gambia's dualistic banking model because of the British colonial legacy, cultural diversity and ties with the Islamic and Western world (World Bank 1997), any proposed code of conduct will

Table 7.5 Proposed ethical values and principles and expected behaviour

Values	Principles	Examples of how this will influence behaviour in The Gambian banking sector
Honesty	Be honest with stakeholders	Avoid misleading advertising and falsifying statements
Integrity	Stick to values despite financial loss	Avoid bribery despite contract loss
Reliability	Fulfil commitments	Fulfil all contractual obligations
Loyalty	Avoid conflicts of interest	Don't accept gifts
Respect	Respect the rights of others	Do not engage in sexual and religious harassment
Responsibility	Take responsibility for actions	When misconduct takes place, take steps to ensure it is not repeated
Fairness	Treat stakeholders fairly	Avoid anti-competitive activities
Caring	Avoid unnecessary harm	Employee community involvement
Citizenship	Obey the law and protect the environment	Follow the law of the country

Source: Adapted from Schwartz (2002, p. 32)

therefore need to recognise the different ethical practices amongst banks and how the codes will influence behaviour. Muhammad and Jolis (2001) suggested 13 basic ethical principles in banking. Schwartz (1998) came up with six universal moral standards, which take into account global codes of ethics and the interfaith declaration.

An evaluation of the basic ethical principles in banking and the universal moral standards suggests that there are commonalities between the two (Schwartz 2002), which are as follows:

- Trustworthiness (including notions of honesty, integrity, reliability and loyalty);
- Respect (including notions of respect for human rights);
- Responsibility (including notions of accountability);
- Fairness (including notions of process, impartiality and equity);
- Caring (including the notion of avoiding unnecessary harm);
- Citizenship (including notions of obeying laws and protecting the environment).

The six standards, based on their universal nature and fundamental importance, would necessarily be required to take priority over other values (Schwartz 2002). Thus, an argument can be raised that these standards are universal in nature 'in that they can be considered of fundamental importance regardless of time, circumstance, cultural beliefs, or religious convictions' (Schwartz 2002, p. 30). In this respect, these core moral standards are suggested as forming a normative basis by which to construct a corporate code of ethics (Schwartz 1998, 2002). I am proposing that The Gambian banking sector adopt this universal code of ethics as part of the regulatory framework. Table 7.5 focuses on proposed ethical values and principles and how this will influence changes in behaviour.

The proposed universal code of ethics for The Gambia would recognise different ethical practices, cultural beliefs and religious convictions amongst banks (Schwartz 1998, 2002). The following is an evaluation of the substantive theory of bank corporate governance regulation.

Jones and Noble (2007) concluded that grounded theory in management research is in danger of losing its integrity and that the methodology has become so pliant that management researchers appear to have accepted it as a situation of 'anything goes'. 'Grounded theory' is now loosely used as a generic term to refer to any qualitative approach in which inductive analysis is grounded in data. Bryant (2002) added that many researchers often use grounded theory unsystematically to mask their own or their discipline's methodological confusion. Other grounded theorists also found the Strauss and Corbin (1990) book rather formulaic and overburdened with many rules (Melia 1996; Kendall 1999). Wasserman et al. (2009, p. 355) argued that while grounded theory 'provides no such systematic or transparent way for gaining insight into the conceptual relationship between the codes. And that various works on grounded theory have failed to provide any systematic way of using data specific levels of scale (the codes) to gain insight into more macro levels of the scale (concepts and themes)'.

This makes it difficult and at times daunting for first-time users of grounded theory to understand the concept and process and often find themselves overwhelmed at the coding level and 'scale up' to larger concepts or themes. The net result is often lower-level theories. In fact, the use of grounded theory never leads to grand social theory, nor should it be expected to do so, but this can be frustrating for some people (Myers 2009). The use of grounded theory does not guarantee original and interesting results. As Strauss and Corbin (1998) point out, creativity is essential, and grounded theory procedures should not be followed dogmatically and in an inflexible manner. Therefore, grounded theory procedures should be followed carefully, while trying to foster your own critical and creative inspiration (Myers 2009). There are some who claim to use grounded theory method as part of an approach that does not seek to develop grounded theories, highlighting the confusion between grounded theory itself and grounded theory methodology (Bryant 2002).

Bryman (2008) suggested that it is somewhat doubtful whether grounded theory, in many instances, really results in theory. Most grounded theories are substantive in character, thus suggesting that they pertain to the specific social phenomenon being researched and not the broader range of phenomena (though, of course, it may have such broader applicability) (ibid.). Grounded theory is associated with an approach to data analysis that invites researchers to fragment their data by coding them into discrete chunks. To others, this kind of activity results in loss of a sense of context and of narrative flow (Coffey and Atkinson 1996).

Another constraint on the use of grounded theory is the presence of competing accounts of the ingredients. This does not make it easy to characterise or to establish its use. This point is further compounded by Charmaz's (2000) suggestion that most grounded theories are objectivist and that an alternative, constructivist approach is preferable. Furthermore, she argued that grounded theory associated with

> Glaser, Strauss, and Corbin is objectivist in that it aims to uncover a reality that is external to the social actors. She subsequently offered an alternative (constructionist) version that assumes that people create and maintain meaningful worlds through dialectical processes of conferring meaning on their realities and acting within them. (Bryman 2008, p. 549)

Thus, it implies that social reality is dependent on human action (Charmaz 2000). This view contradicts earlier grounded theory texts that say categories and concepts can be found within the data, while constructivists suggest that categories and concepts at the theoretical level emerge as a result of the researcher's interaction within the field and of the questions about the data (Charmaz 2000).

Grounded theory method has also been criticised as being empiricist; that is, it relies too heavily on the empirical data, considers the fieldwork data as the source of its theories, and sets itself against the use of preceding theories (Parker and Roffey 1997). Other critics, such as Bryant (2003), argued that conceptualisation of data at the methodological level can degenerate into methodological indifference, resulting in superficial and ambiguous conclusions.

Furthermore, grounded theory's central practice of overlapping data collection and analysis poses other problems. In a grounded theory analysis, generalisability and reliability may be a problem as well. Critics of grounded theory also point out that grounded theory methodology is still so intimately linked to its founders that it might be taken as evidence for its failure to move far beyond its origin (Bryant 2002). Bulmer (1979) has questioned whether, as prescribed by the advocates of grounded theory,

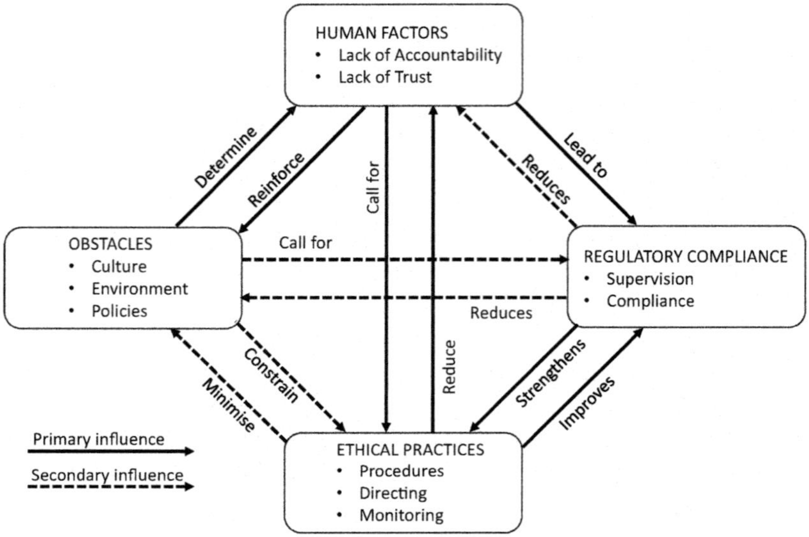

Fig. 7.1 The human factor model

researchers can suspend their awareness of relevant theories or concepts until a quite late stage in the process of analysis.

It is generally agreed that 'what we "see" when we conduct research is conditioned by many factors, one of which is what we already know about the social world being studied (in terms of both social scientific conceptualisations and as members of society)' (Bryman 2008, p. 549). Furthermore, there are practical difficulties with grounded theory. The time taken to transcribe interviews can make it difficult for researchers, especially when they have tight deadlines, to carry out a genuine grounded theory analysis with its constant interplay of data collection and conceptualisation (Bryman 2008).

In the absence of robust corporate governance codes and framework in the banking sector in The Gambia, ethical values become quite important. Here the stewardship of these vital institutions, serves as the moral compass.

A Substantive Theory of Bank Corporate Governance Regulation

The main aim of this chapter was to outline a substantive theory of bank corporate governance regulation within the context of The Gambian banking system using grounded theory methodology. The substantive theory developed in this research achieved this objective by establishing the causes that led to the existence of the phenomenon, context, intervening conditions, causal conditions, action/interactional strategies and consequences. As a result, the substantive theory has enabled me to develop a thorough understanding and balanced view of bank corporate governance in The Gambia.

A model of bank corporate governance regulation in The Gambia (Fig. 7.1) is the substantive theory integrating the core categories with subcategories based on Faye (2014).

Using grounded theory, the human factor model based on Faye (2014) explains the current corporate governance phenomenon that exists in The Gambian banking system. This substantive theory can be summarised as follows.

The substantive theory shows there that is no consistency between banks in The Gambia when it comes to general banking issues, corporate governance mechanisms, ethics and codes. In the context of this research, the lack of accountability and trust is because of environmental, cultural and policy obstacles. Enhanced accountability and trust will lead to improved regulatory compliance and therefore minimise the conflict of interest between key stakeholders in the banking sector (depositors, regulators and shareholders). Regulatory compliance aims to control, monitor and enforce corporate governance rules and regulations in The Gambian banking system.

This will eventually protect and enhance shareholder wealth and profit. Human factors and regulatory compliance are therefore central to the development and implementation of any meaningful corporate governance rules and regulations in The Gambian banking system. Efforts are now on the way to the regulatory level to develop corporate governance policies for the system, which would benefit the human factor as the core category. Banks have now developed their own internal corporate governance policies, most of which were adopted from their parent company. The interplay between human factor, regulatory compliance and ethics will eventually lead to a more transparent, accountable and trustworthy banking system in The Gambia.

The establishment of substantive theory will enable banks to develop strategies aimed at maximising shareholder profit and wealth. Furthermore, this will also protect depositors and enhance corporate governance regulation and thus minimise corporate governance-related bank failures. The development of a substantive theory is the final stage following coding, categorising and analysis of data, systematically collected for this research through semi-structured interviews and focus group discussions. The substantive theory reflects the opinions of regulators, commercial bank executives, legal and compliance officers, employees and customers. This substantive theory is therefore grounded in the data obtained in The Gambia, thus enabling the researcher to ascertain and understand the human factor phenomenon that exists within the banking system and how this phenomenon interacts with obstacles, regulatory compliance and ethics. As such, from a CI point of view, ethics, in one form or another, is grafted onto the corporate body as a preventative or remedial measure to help combat corruption, promote obedience to laws and procedures, and increase trust between citizens and institutions (Garofalo and Geuras 1999; Garofalo 2003).

This chapter has also demonstrated that it is possible to use non-traditional theoretical frameworks, such as CI, in understanding corporate governance within a banking system. Primary data for this research were collected in two main stages, namely, semi-structured interviews and focus group discussions, in addition to secondary data. I adopted Strauss and Corbin's (1998) method of grounded theory development, which focuses on open coding and axial and selective coding. Using the CI theoretical framework, I constructed a formal grounded theory, summarised below:

- The substantive theory has indicated that the human factor calls for regulatory compliance and ethical practices to restore public confidence in the banking system in the absence of mandatory corporate governance regulatory framework. However, human factors are indeed obstructed by culture, environment and policies that exist in The Gambian banking system. Thus, ethics is grafted onto the corporate body as a preventative or remedial measure to help combat corruption, promote obedience to laws and procedures, and increase trust between citizens and institutions (Garofalo and Geuras 1999; Garofalo 2003).

- It is about how human behaviour is motivated by principles of right and wrong and the concern for consequences. Therefore, profit, stock price, size or power alone cannot serve as the criteria for a well-run organisation. Thus, organisations come to gain public respect and community approval. They have accomplished far more than a return on their investment (Brady 1999).
- The substantive theory is about bank managements designing internal control systems and risk management practices that seek to achieve an optimal level of protection for stakeholders and enhance accountability and confidence in the banking system.
- It is about the need for accountability, responsibility, transparency and trust if the financial institutions are to regain public trust and investor confidence (Fakuyama 1995; Monks and Minow 1996; Wolfensohn 1999; Holland 2002; OECD 2004; Forster and Nilakant 2005; Chalhoub 2009; Labelle 2009; Griffin 2010; Kaur and Mishra 2010; Yandle 2010).
- The substantive theory is about ensuring the principles of transparency, sound banking, responsibility, integrity, global standards and supervision in bank corporate governance.

Conclusion

An evaluation of corporate governance literature highlights the weakness of the shareholder and stakeholder theories in understanding corporate governance phenomena. The use of a CI framework to address The Gambia's corporate governance phenomena serves as an alternative theoretical attempt to address this weakness. The development of a substantive theory within The Gambian banking system using the CI also serves as an alternative theoretical underpinning to create research purely designed to focus on the banking context. Furthermore, the study outlines a proposed ethical code of conduct. The proposed code of conduct will influence future behaviour and subsequently improve the robustness of the banking system. The chapter has explained the construction of tighter control procedures in the oversight and supervision level, which will be useful for board members, managers and regulators. Thus, the findings of this research can be considered a starting point for future researchers within the banking industry.

The combination of interpretative and social constructivist paradigms enabled me to achieve the research objectives. This research therefore extended grounded theory research by utilising it as a methodology relevant to exploring the phenomena of corporate governance regulation within an unexplored area of The Gambian banking system. The collection of data through semi-structured interviews and focus group discussions and analysis using grounded theory methodology enabled the development and identification of human factors as the substantive theory using the CI theoretical framework. This research can therefore serve as a contribution for regulators and stakeholders in The Gambian banking industry.

The bank corporate governance regulatory framework currently existing in The Gambia is inconsistent and not standardised. Hence, it can be best described as a 'fractured independent corporate governance regulatory framework'. As a result, most banks have developed voluntary corporate governance codes and frameworks for internal use. In some cases, these practices have been imposed on them by their parent body as part of their internal control mechanisms. As a consequence of these strategies, banks are likely to be accountable and ethical, thereby enhancing supervision, compliance and trust. These will ultimately protect the interest of shareholders.

Corporate governance regulation of countries and organisations are uniquely affected by a number of factors, including legal, regulatory, human, organisational and cultural factors. Therefore, this research, in unveiling the human factor model as the core phenomenon with emphasis on corporate governance regulation, is in line with empirical corporate governance studies such as Berle and Means (1932); Aguilera and Cuervo-Cazuraa (2004); Enrione et al. (2006); Deo et al. (2007); Khadaroo and Shaikh (2007); Zattoni and Cuomo (2008); and Yandle (2010).

Combining corporate governance, grounded theory and CI to explore a phenomenon in an unexplored context makes this research the first to combine all three areas together, thus providing a new approach to corporate governance understanding, which will benefit key stakeholders and improve the overall efficiency of The Gambian banking system. This will ultimately explain and improve corporate governance practices. The research will also provide some practical contributions to regulators, bank managers and other stakeholders in the banking system. The identification of the substantive theory will help key stakeholders—such as investors, management and regulators—to address challenges, including obstacles that are impeding the development of corporate governance as part of the regulatory framework, thus minimising the risk of bank failures and improving the corporate governance regulation framework.

The purpose of this research was to carry out an empirical investigation of bank corporate governance regulation in The Gambia and, through the application of grounded theory methodology, build a substantive theory of it. Therefore, the substantive theory developed in this research only reflects the corporate governance phenomenon in The Gambian banking context, underpinned by the opinions of those included in the research. As a result, the substantive theory of human factors does not necessarily constitute an upgrade of the theory into a formal theory.

This can only be achieved by conducting research based on human factors within many substantive areas. Therefore, future researchers can explore the human factor model further in different banking jurisdictions to explore how credibly it offers explanations of bank corporate governance and possibly to develop a formal theory. One can conclude that this research does offer useful directions for regulators, bank executives and investors to minimise the effects of human factors and develop strategies addressing obstacles faced when developing corporate governance regulations as part of The Gambia's regulatory framework.

References

African Development Bank. (2007). *Republic of The Gambia country governance profile*. Washington, DC: World Bank.

Agu, C. C. (2004). Efficiency of the commercial banking in The Gambia. *African Review of the Money, Finance and Banking* (pp. 31–50).

Aguilera, R. V., & Cuervo-Cazuraa, A. (2004). Codes of good governance worldwide: What is the trigger? *Organization Studies, 25*(3), 415–443.

Annells, M. (1996). Grounded theory method: Philosophical perspectives, paradigm of inquiry and postmodernism. *Qualitative Health Research, 6*(3), 379–393.

Artigas, M. (2006). *Philosophy: An introduction*. Manila: Sinag-Tala Publications.

Aryeetey, E., & Nissanke, M. (2004). *Financing Africa's future growth and development: Some innovations*. Accra: Institute of Statistical, Social and Economic Research, University of Ghana.

Baum, T. (1996). Images of tourism past and present. *International Journal of Contemporary Hospitality Management, 8*(4), 25–30. doi:10.1108/09596119610119958.

Berger, P., & Luckmann, T. (1967). *The social construction of reality: A treatise in the sociology of knowledge*. Harmandsworth: Penguin.

Berle, A. A., & Means, G. (1932). *The modern corporation and private property*. New York: Macmillan.

Brady, F. N. (1999). A systematic approach to teaching ethics in business. *Journal of Business Ethics, 19*(3), 309–318.

Bryant, A. (2002). Grounded system research: Re-establishing grounded theory. *The Journal of Information Technology, Theory and Application, 4*(1), 25–42.

Bryant, A. (2003). A constructivist response to Glaser. *Forum: Qualitative Social Research, 4*(1). Available from http://www.csa.com/factsheets/socialabs-set-c.php. Accessed 23 Mar 2013.

Bryman, A. (2008). *Social research methods* (3rd ed.). Oxford: Oxford University Press.

Bryman, A., & Charmaz, K. (2007). *The SAGE handbook of grounded theory*. London: Sage.

Budhwar, P., & Debrah, Y. (2001). *Human resource management in developing countries*. Abingdon: Routledge.

Budhwar, P., & Debrah, Y. (2006). *Human resource management in developing countries*. Abingdon: Routledge.

Bulmer, M. (1979). Concepts in the analysis of qualitative data. *Sociological Review, 27*, 651–677.

Central Bank of The Gambia (CBG). (2014). *Financial systems.* Available from http://www.cbg.gm/finance_systems/banking.html. Accessed 3 May 2016.

Chalhoub, M. S. (2009). Relations between dimensions of corporate governance and corporate performance: An empirical study among banks in Lebanon. *International Journal of Management, 26*(3), 476–488.

Charmaz, K. (1990). Discovering chronic illness: Using grounded theory. *Social Science and Medicine, 30*, 1161–1172.

Charmaz, K. (1995). Grounded theory. In J. A. Smith, R. Harre, & L. Van Langonhere (Eds.), *Rethinking methods in psychology* (pp. 27–49). London: Sage.

Charmaz, K. (2000). Grounded theory: Objectives and constructive methods. In N. K. Denzin & Y. S. Lincoln (Eds.), *Handbook of qualitative research* (2nd ed.). Thousand Oaks, CA: Sage.

Charmaz, K. (2001). Qualitative interviewing and grounded theory analysis. In J. F. Gubrium & J. A. Holstein (Eds.), *Handbook of interview lessons* (pp. 675–694). Thousand Oaks, CA: Sage.

Charmaz, K. (2002). Grounded theory: Methodology and theory construction. In N. J. Smelser & P. B. Baltes (Eds.), *International encyclopaedia of the social and behavioural sciences* (pp. 6396–6399). Amsterdam: Pergamon.

Charmaz, K. (2006). *Constructing grounded theory: A practical guide through qualitative analysis.* Thousand Oaks, CA: Sage.

Charmaz, K., & Mitchell, R. G. (1996). The myth of silent authorship: Self, substance and style in ethnographic writing. *Symbolic Interaction, 19*(4), 285–302.

Chenitz, W. C., & Swanson, J. M. (Eds.). (1986). *From practice to grounded theory: Qualitative research in nursing.* Reading, MA: Addison-Wesley.

Ciao, B. (2011). Management studies through qualitative analysis: Epistemological justification, verification of originality and efforts of conceptualization. *International Journal of GSTF Business Review, 1*(1), 106–115.

Coffey, A., & Atkinson, P. (1996). *Making sense of qualitative data: Complementary research strategies.* Thousand Oaks, CA: Sage.

Corbetta, P. (1999). *Methodologies and tools for the social sciences.* London: Sage.

Corbin, J., & Strauss, A. L. (1990). Grounded theory methods: Procedures, canons and evaluation criteria. *Qualitative Sociology, 13*, 3–21.

Creswell, J. W. (2009). *Research design, quantitative, qualitative and mixed methods approaches* (3rd ed.). Thousand Oaks, CA: Sage.

Crosse, H. D., & Hampel, G. H. (1980). *Management policies for commercial banks*. Englewood Cliffs, NJ: Prentice Hall.

Crotty, M. (1998). *The foundations of social research: Meaning and perspective in the research process*. Thousand Oaks, CA: Sage.

Dartey-Baah, K., & Amponsah-Tawiah, K. (2011). Exploring the limits of western corporate social responsibility theories in Africa. *International Journal of Business and Social Science, 2*(18).

David, P. (2007). Path dependence: A foundational concept for historical social science. *Cliometrica, The Journal of Historical Economics and Economic History, 1*(2), 91–114. Available from http://www-siepr.stanford.edu/workp/swp06005.pdf. Accessed 23 Feb 2013.

Davies, H. (2001). Ethics in regulation. *Business Ethics: A European Review, 10*(4), 280–287.

Deo, H., Irvine, H., & Abraham, A. (2007). *The legitimising power of regulation for Australian banks: An institutional approach in proceedings of accounting and finance*. Gold Coast: Association of Australia and New Zealand (AFAANZ).

Dey, I. (1993). *Qualitative data analysis*. Thousand Oaks, CA: Sage.

Dieke, P. (1993). Tourism policy and employment in The Gambia. *Employee Relations, 15*(2), 71–80. doi:10.1108/01425459310031868.

Douven, I. (2011). Abduction. In E. N. Zalta (Ed.), *The Stanford Encyclopedia of Philosophy*. Spring. Available from: http://plato.stanford.edu/archives/spr2011/entries/abduction/. Accessed: 3 May 2016.

Enrione, A., Mazza, C., & Zerbini, F. (2006). Institutionalizing codes of governance. *American Behavioural Scientist, 49*(7), 961–973.

Fakuyama, F. (1995). *Trust: Social virtues and the creation of prosperity*. New York: Free Press.

Faye, S. (2014). *An examination and analysis of bank corporate governance regulation in the Gambia: A grounded theory approach* (Master's thesis). University of Plymouth, Plymouth, England.

Forster, T. H., & Nilakant, V. (2005). Role of trust in privatization: Transformation of the electricity utility in The Gambia. *The Journal of Applied Behavioural Science, 41*(3), 348–366.

Forster, T. M., & Mouly, V. S. (2006). Privatisation in a developing country: Insights from the Gambia. *Journal of Organizational Change Management, 19*(2), 250–265. doi:10.1108/09534810610648942.

Gambia Bureau of Statistics (GBoS) & Gamjobs, & Ministry of Trade, Industry, Regional Integration and Employment (MOTIE) (2012). *Labour Force Survey Report*. Banjul, Gambia.

Garofalo, C. (2003). Toward a global ethic: Perspectives on values, training and moral agency. *The International Journal of Public Sector Management, 16*(7), 490–501.

Garofalo, C., & Geuras, D. (1999). *Ethics in the public service: The moral mind at work*. Washington, DC: Georgetown University Press.

Glaser, B. G., & Strauss, A. (1965). *Awareness of dying*. Chicago: Aldine.

Glaser, B. G., & Strauss, A. (1967). *The discovery of grounded theory*. New York: Aldine de Gruyter.

Glaser, B. G., & Strauss, A. (1968). *Time for dying*. Chicago: Aldine.

Goulding, C. (2002). *Grounded theory: A practical guide for management business and marketing research*. London: Sage.

Greene, J. C. (2000). Understanding social programs through evaluation. In N. K. Denzin & Y. Lincoln (Eds.), *Handbook of qualitative research* (pp. 981–990). Thousand Oaks, CA: Sage.

Griffin, L. (2010). The limits to good governance and the state of exception: A case study of North Sea fisheries. *Geo Forum, 41*(2), 282–292.

Guba, E. G., & Lincoln, Y. S. (1985). *Naturalistic inquiry*. London: Sage.

Guba, E. G., & Lincoln, Y. S. (1989). *Fourth generation evaluation*. Newbury Park, CA: Sage.

Guha, K. (2006). World Bank praises pro-business reforms in many African countries, doing business report. *Financial Times, 6–7*.

Hall, W. A., & Callery, P. (2001). Enhancing the rigor of grounded theory incorporating reflexivity and rationality. *Qualitative Health Research, 11*(2), 257–272.

Hazard, G. C. (1995). Law, morals and ethics. *Southern Illinois Law Journal, 19*(1), 447–458.

Heffernan, S. A. (2005). *Modern banking*. London: Wiley.

Holland, J. B. (2002). *A dynamic model of corporate disclosure: Choices, intangibles use of story, benchmarks and continuous interaction* (Working paper). Department of Accounting and Finance, University of Glasgow.

Howard, M., & Haynes, C. (2001). Commercial bank efficiency in Barbados. *Savings and Development, 3*(25), 31–50.

Howell, K. E. (2000). *Discovering the limits of European integrations: Applying grounded theory*. Huntington, NY: Nova Science Publishers.

Howell, K. E. (2002). *Integrating European financial services: A grounded theory approach*. Ashcroft International Business School, Research Paper Series.

Howell, K. E. (2013). *An introduction to the philosophy of methodology*. London: Sage.

Howell, K. E., Nwanji, T., Hardwick, P., & Ozuem, W. (2007). *BAM developmental paper proposal: Telling the truth and ethical perspectives in corporate decision making*. The British Academy of Management Conference at the University of Warwick.

Hussey, J., & Hussey, R. (1997). *Business research: A practical guide for undergraduates and postgraduate students*. Basingstoke: Palgrave.

Jones, R., & Noble, G. (2007). Grounded theory and management research: A lack of integrity? *Qualitative Research in Organizations and Management, An International Journal, 2*(2), 84–103.

Kaur, G., & Mishra, R. (2010). Corporate governance failure in India: A study of academician perception. *The IUP Journal of Corporate Governance, 9*(1 & 2), 99–112.

Kelsall, T. (2008). *Going with the grain in African development?* (Discussion paper). London: Oversees Development Institute.

Kendall, J. (1999). Axial coding and the grounded theory controversy. *Western Journal of Nursing Research, 21*(6), 743–757.

Khadaroo, I., & Shaikh, J. (2007). Corporate governance reforms in Malaysia: Insights for institutional theory. *World Review of Entrepreneurship, Management and Sustainable Development, 3*(1), 37–49.

Labelle, H. (2009). A transparent road to recovery: Organizations for economic corporation and development. *The OECD Observer, 273*, 18–19.

Lincoln, Y., & Guba, E. (1985). Paradigmatic controversies, contradictions, and emerging confluences. In N. K. Denzin & Y. S. Lincoln (Eds.), *The handbook of qualitative research* (2nd ed., pp. 163–188). London: Sage.

Locke, K. (2001). *Grounded theory in management research*. London: Sage Publications.

Making Finance Work for Africa. (2015). *Gambia: Financial Sector Profile*. Retrieved from Making Finance Work for Africa: https://www.mfw4a.org/gambia/financial-sector-profile.html. Accessed Oct 2015.

Martin, P. Y., & Turner, B. A. (1986). Grounded theory and organizational research. *Journal of Applied Behavioural Science, 22*(2), 141–157.

Mathenge, G. D. (2013). The value system of commercial banking in Kenya: An ethical perspective. *Journal of Business and Social Sciences, 4*(1), 153–163.

Melia, K. M. (1996). Rediscovering Glaser. *Qualitative Health Research, 6*(3), 368–378.

Mertens, D. M. (1998). *Research methods in education and psychology: Integrating diversity with quantitative and qualitative approaches*. London: Sage.

Monks, R. A., & Minow, N. (1996). *Watching the watchers: Corporate governance in the 21st century*. New York, NY: Blackwell.
Muhammad, Y., & Jolis, A. (2001). *Banker to the poor: An autobiography of M. Younas, the founder of Grameen Bank*. Oxford: Oxford University Press.
Myers, M. D. (1997). Qualitative research in information systems. *MIS Quarterly, 21*(2), 241–242.
Myers, M. D. (2006). *Psychology* (8th ed.). Basingstoke: Worth Publishers.
Myers, M. D. (2009). *Qualitative research in business and management*. London: Sage.
Neuman, W. L. (2000). *Social research methods: Qualitative and quantitative approaches*. Boston: Allyn and Bacon.
Nshimyumuremy, A., & Workie, A. Y. (2015). Gambia 2015. *African Economic Outlook*. Available from http://www.africaneconomicoutlook.com
Nwanji, T. I. (2006). *Ethical implications of corporate governance, a deontological and teleological approach: Applying grounded theory* (Unpublished master's thesis). Angelia Ruskin University, UK.
OECD. (2004). *Principles of corporate governance*. Paris: Author.
OECD. (2015). *The Gambia*. Retrieved from OECD: http://www.oecd.org/dac/effectiveness/49320393.pdf. Accessed Oct 2015.
Oman, C. P. (2004). *Organization for economic co-operation and development*. Paris: OECD.
Orlikowski, W. J. (1993). CASE tools as organizational change: Investigating incremental and radical changes in systems development. *MIS Quarterly, 17*(3), 309–340.
Parker, L. D., & Roffey, B. H. (1997). Back to the drawing board: Revisiting grounded theory and the everyday accountant's reality. *Accounting, Auditing and Accountability, 10*, 212–247.
Sallah, A., & Williams, C. C. (2011). The illusion of capitalism in contemporary sub-Saharan Africa: A case study of the Gambia. *Foresight, 13*(3), 50–63. doi:10.1108/14636681111138767.
Schwandt, T. A. (2007). *Dictionary of qualitative inquiry* (3rd ed.). Thousand Oaks, CA: Sage.
Schwartz, M. S. (1998). *The relationship between corporate code of ethics and behaviour: A descriptive exploration and narrative evaluation*. Toronto: York University.
Schwartz, M. S. (2002). A code of ethics for corporate code of ethics. *Journal of Business Ethics, 41*(1–2), 27–43.

Simpson, M., Tuck, N., & Bellamy, S. (2004). Small business success factors: The role of education and training. *Education & Training, 46*(8/9), 481–491.

Stern, P. N. (1994). Eroding grounded theory. In J. Bryant (Ed.), *Critical issues in qualitative research* (pp. 212–223). London: Sage.

Strauss, A. (1987). *Qualitative analysis for social scientists*. Cambridge: Cambridge University Press.

Strauss, A., & Corbin, J. (1990). *Basics of qualitative research grounded theory procedures and techniques*. London: Sage.

Strauss, A., & Corbin, J. (1998). *Basics of qualitative research: Techniques and procedures for developing ground theory* (2nd ed.). Thousand, Oaks CA: Sage.

Strauss, A., & Glaser, B. G. (1970). *Anguish*. San Francisco, CA: Sociology Press.

Thietart, R. A. (2001). *Doing management research: A comprehensive guide*. Thousand Oaks, CA: Sage.

Thorne, S., Jensen, L., Kearney, M. H., Noblit, G., & Sandelowski, M. (2004). Qualitatitive meta synthesis: Reflections on methodological orientation and ideological agenda. *Qualitative Health Research, 14*(10), 1342–1365.

Urquhart, C. (1997). Exploring analyst client communication: Using grounded theory techniques to investigate interaction in informal requirements gathering. In A. S. Lee, J. Liebenau, & J. I. DeGrass (Eds.), *Information research and qualitative research* (pp. 149–181). London: Chapman and Hall.

Urquhart, C. (2001). An encounter with grounded theory: Tackling the practices and philosophical issues. In E. Trauth (Ed.), *Qualitative research in IS: Issues and trends* (pp. 104–140). Hershey, PA: Idea Group Publishing.

Urquhart, C., Lehmann, H., & Myers, M. D. (2006). *Putting the theory back into grounded theory: A framework for grounded theory studies in information system* (Unpublished).

Vittas, D. (1991). Measuring commercial bank efficiency. *Policy Research Working Paper Series, Country Economic Development*. Washington, DC: World Bank.

Wasserman, J. A., Clair, J. M., & Wilson, K. L. (2009). Problematics of grounded theory: Innovations for developing an increasing rigorous qualitative method. *Qualitative Research, 9*(3), 355–381.

Wolfensohn, J. (1999). Corporate governance is about promoting corporate fairness transparency and accountability. *Financial Times*.

World Bank. (1997). *Helping countries combat corruption: The role of the World Bank*. Washington, DC: World Bank.

World Bank. (2014). *The Gambia sub-Saharan Africa (developing only)*. Available from http://www.data.worldbank.org/country/gambia. Accessed 2 Sept 2014.

World Bank. (2015). *The Gambia country report*. Available from http://www.worldbank.org/en/country/gambia. Accessed Sept 2015.

Worrell, D. (1996). Bank behaviour in small open economies (*Working Papers*). Central Bank of Barbados.

Yandle, B. (2010). Lost trust: The real cause of the financial meltdown. *The Independent Review, 14*(3), 341–361.

Zattoni, A., & Cuomo, F. (2008). Why adopt codes of good governance? A comparison of institutional and efficiency perspectives. *Corporate Governance: An International Review, 16*(1), 1–15.

ZDS. (2014). Fallacy effects: The realisation of ecological and other fallacies. Available from http://www.zonedesignsystems.com/intro3. Accessed 25 Mar 2014.

8

The King Reports on Corporate Governance in South Africa: An *Ubuntu* African Philosophy Analysis

Zenzo L. Dube

Introduction

In 1994, South Africa opened its doors to democracy. It was a utilitarian effort; the previously disadvantaged/marginalised sections of its society could now participate in the economic and political sphere of the South African landscape (Stewart 2010). In that same year the first King Report on corporate governance was introduced and which sought to educate and align the newly democratic South Africa to the machinations of the capitalist market system. A revised King Report culminated into King (ii) in 2002, then King (iii) in 2009. King (iii) came into effect in 2010 and sought to emulate the United Kingdom Combined Code of 2010. One can posit that the King Reports reflected the changes in the socio-economic and political sphere apparent in South Africa and the ideal corporate governance frameworks at particular times in history

Z.L. Dube (✉)
National University of Science and Technology-Institute of Development Studies, Bulawayo, Zimbabwe

K.E. Howell, M.K. Sorour (eds.), *Corporate Governance in Africa*,
DOI 10.1057/978-1-137-56700-0_8

(1994, 2002 and 2009). King (i) was meant to address the face of a new corporate governance and laid the foundations of an institutionalised corporate governance. King (ii) identified the changes in the economic environment and global corporate world. King (iii) argued that the harsh and inflexible Sarbanes Oxley Act, failed to prevent the collapse of many of the leading corporate entities in the USA.

In this chapter the changes between King (i), (ii) and (iii) are analysed through *ubuntu* ethics. The changes are interpreted through their logic of social appropriateness within the African socio-economic and cultural sphere. This bridges an understanding of the Reports from the Western mind-set (a universal perspective) to that of the locale or relative position. Mapping out and dissecting these changes necessitates a critical theory epistemology and methodology; the relationship between the researcher and the researched is transactional and subjective. (Howell 2006). A person with *ubuntu* is

> open and available to others, affirming of others, does not feel threatened that others are able and good, for he or she has a proper self-assurance that comes from knowing that he or she belongs in a greater whole and is diminished when others are humiliated or diminished, when others are tortured or oppressed. The cardinal belief of Ubuntu is that a man can only be a man through others. In its most fundamental sense it stands for personhood and morality (Darty-Baah and Tawiah 2011, pp. 133–134)

Darty-Baah and Tawiah (2011) noted the key values of *ubuntu* as follows, namely group solidarity, conformity, compassion, respect, human dignity and collective unity. Individuals who pursue individualism and selfishness are described as '*akanabuntu*' (lacking *ubuntu*) or '*akongomtu hase motho*' (not a person, not human) (Munyaka and Motlabi 2009). An '*ubuntu* world view is the basis, centre and end of everything; *izinto* (all other things) only make sense in relation to persons. Regardless of their social status, gender or race, persons are recognised, accepted, valued and respected for their own sake' (Munyaka and Motlabi 2009, p. 60).

According to Turyahikayo (2014) '*ubuntu* is based on the realization that the humanness that I share with others makes me conscious of the reality that in my essential being I depend on the essential beingness of the other. Therefore, "being for - other" appears to be a necessary condition for being for myself' (p. 66).

Khomba et al. (2013) posit that an inclusive corporate governance framework, under the African *ubuntu*, implies that the organisation foremost and above all sees its commitment in a holistic way, a commitment which encompasses the interests of both shareholders and non-shareholding stakeholders. They argue that Africa's socio-cultural framework (*ubuntu*) has a direct bearing on corporate governance approaches and overall performance of corporate entities operating in Africa. The next section is the empirical literature review and is in two parts. The first covers corporate governance in South Africa and the second the *ubuntu* philosophy doctrine.

Literature Review

Corporate Governance in South Africa

The Cadbury Report (1992) defined corporate governance as the system by which companies are directed and controlled. The OECD Principles of Corporate Governance (2004) viewed corporate governance as involving 'a set of relationships between a company's management, its board, its shareholders and other stakeholders' (p. 11). Corporate governance concerns the relationships among the management, board of directors, controlling shareholders, minority shareholders and other stakeholders. Good corporate governance contributes to sustainable economic development by enhancing the performance of companies and increasing their access to outside capital. Daily et al. (2003) define corporate governance in the context of exploitation and use of organizational resources as well as the resolution of conflicts between parties within the corporation. Traditional corporate governance theory has focused more on protecting shareholders and controlling executive self-interest (Daily et al. 2003).

In order to placate shareholders, internal and external corporate governance mechanisms are implemented to keep management's interests in line with those of the shareholders. Examples of internal mechanisms are effectively structured boards, incentive schemes and intense ownership holdings that encourage monitoring of executives. Lanoo (1999) further identified the shareholder–manager relationship as the most essential framework in corporate governance and suggested that a good corporate governance system is one which is able to tackle the conflicts of interest between managers and owners of a corporation and resolve them (p. 27). Letza et al. (2004) argued that 'corporate governance is about the understanding and institutional arrangements for relationships among various economic actors and corporate participants who may have direct or indirect interests in a corporation, such as shareholders, directors/managers, employees, creditors, suppliers, customers, local communities, government, and the general public' (p. 242).

Howell and Letza (2000) argued that corporate governance usually involves a reactive approach that is executed without taking into account different historical interpretations and that the current corporate governance debate lacked philosophical underpinnings. Corporate governance benefits involve long-term objectives (Letza and Sun 2004) rather than the short-termism described by Robinson (2002). 'The capacity of investors to sell their shares has led to charges that the market for the shares is characterized by "short-termism" and yet an excess loyalty from the shareholders may mean that they remain supine while their agents destroy long-term shareholder through inappropriate decision making and poor management' (pp. 463–485).

In essence it can be argued that the imperfect balance between shareholders and management as well as 'short-termism' can be addressed through arguments that the prime benefit of corporate governance leads to good management and improved long-term performance (Letza and Sun 2004). Arguments regarding long run benefits of good corporate governance blend with Steinberg's (2000) view that the business's specific objectives are to maximise owner value over long term (p. 79). According to Steinberg (2000) for long term value to be realised, two prerequisites need to be included: 'distributive justice' and 'ordinary decency'. Collectively, 'ordinary decency' requires respect for property ownership, trust, honesty, fairness and legality in conducting business. 'Distributive justice' refers to the just distribution of rewards according to individual efforts and performance. Thus, according to Sternberg 'distributive justice' and 'ordinary decency' when fused with the business's objectives of maximising owner value over the long term is the key to good corporate governance and ethical activity. Effectively, Sternberg seemed to accept the nature of business as a stakeholder entity on the condition that the stakeholder entity acknowledged the maximisation of owner value as a long term objective.

Okeahalam and Akinboade (2003) argued that African business is highly influenced by mismanagement and corruption. An effective corporate governance system can create transparency and accountability as safeguards against such corporate malfeasances. South Africa's corporate structure is modelled along the lines of the Anglo-American model (West 2006). This model is a legacy of its historical path and reflects the polarisation of the realities since the realisation of democracy. Opening the doors to democracy incorporated a new multi-racial corporate South Africa. The previously disadvantaged minorities could now equally participate in political decision-making as well as the economy. This meant that the Anglo-American corporate structure had to adjust, accommodate the changes in the polity and the emerging cultures that came with it. Hence the South African form of corporate governance had to adopt some elements of the *ubuntu* African philosophy as part of the new multi-racial corporate South Africa.

The Johannesburg Stock Exchange is rated as 'advanced emerging' (West 2006, p. 435). The King Report (iii), Shleifer and Vishny (1997) and Tricker (2012) reveal that corporate governance involved the following:

(a) Governance guidelines: include systems of governance, structures, by-laws, policies, direction, regulations and conformance to ethics, standards and codes of best practices, codes of conduct; compliance with relevant laws and regulations; socially defined constraints; it relates to public policy; legal regulatory framework; fairness and transparency, sustainability.

(b) Stakeholder dynamics and accountability processes: including constitution of the organization, board accountability and responsibility to stakeholders, relationships among legitimate stakeholders who may include shareholders or donors, managers, employees, creditors, customers, members, beneficiaries and other stakeholders.
(c) Authority and power: including how organizations and stakeholders are directed, controlled and held to account; how they perform; how authority in firms is exercised and the way power is exercised over corporate entities.

As noted, the King Codes of Corporate Governance have informed public companies since 1994. These codes in unison require that inter alia shareholders approve remuneration, an annual remuneration report needs to be published, the audit committee be appointed by shareholders, sustainability reporting should be an ongoing process and the majority of the board should be non-executive. South Africa has a Westernised approach to corporate governance which places emphasis on the market-based model underlined by dominant shareholders. This emanates from its historically linked Anglo-Saxon mode of capitalism (Gstrauntlhaler 2010). King (ii) recommends high levels of non-executive representation on their boards as well as the committees of listed companies. The thinking is that non-executives are relatively impartial; they bring different expertise and strategic input as they are not involved in operational activities and they should be in the majority on the remuneration and audit committees in order to represent shareholder interests.

Gstrauntlhaler (2010) noted that the steps that South Africa embarks upon in pursuit of its economic policy are often assimilated throughout the rest of Africa. King (iii) strives to balance between international developments and African 'peculiarities' (ibid., p. 146). According to the King (iii) (2009)

> in the African context these moral duties (of stakeholders) find expression in the concept of *Ubuntu* which is captured in the expression '*umuntu ngumuntu ngabantu*', 'I am because you are; you are because we are'. Simply put, *Ubuntu* means humaneness and the philosophy of *Ubuntu* includes

> mutual support and respect, interdependence, unity, collective work and responsibility and it involves a common purpose in all human endeavour and is based on service to humanity (servant leadership). (p. 23)

This provides for the possibility of collective stakeholder goodwill. King (iii) (2009) indicated that good corporate governance was essentially about effective leadership which includes responsibility, accountability, fairness and transparency. Furthermore, good corporate governance requires that all deliberation, actions and decisions of the board and executive management should be based on these four ethical principles:

- *Responsibility*: The board should assume responsibility for the assets and actions of the company and be willing to take corrective actions to keep the company on a strategic path that is ethical and sustainable.
- *Accountability*: The board should be able to justify its decisions and actions to the shareholders and other stakeholders.
- *Fairness*: The board should ensure that it gives fair consideration to the legitimate interests and expectations of all stakeholders of the company.
- *Transparency*: Transparency is the ease with which an outsider is able to make meaningful analysis of a company's actions, its economic fundamentals and non-financial aspects pertinent to that business.

King (iii) (2009) and the Institute of Directors (2009) posited that 'good governance refers to effective leadership that is characterised by the ethical values of Responsibility, Accountability, Fairness and Transparency (RAFT), that is based on moral duties that are that are embedded in *Ubuntu*' (Mukusha 2012, p. 17). This also entails a long-term view of the corporate entity. In a sense, sound ethics plus good corporate governance provides fair sustainable business practices. Corporate entities which do not practice good corporate governance are not sustainable especially in the highly competitive global markets of the twenty-first century (Mukusha 2012).

The Report went on to outline the duties that the director, as a steward of the company, is required to discharge:

- *Conscience*: A director should act with intellectual honesty and independence of mind in the best interests of the company and all its stakeholders; in accordance with the inclusive stakeholders approach to corporate governance, conflicts of interest should be avoided.
- *Inclusivity of stakeholders*: Inclusivity of stakeholders is essential to achieving sustainability and the legitimate interests and expectations of stakeholders must be taken into account in decision-making strategy.
- *Competence*: A director should have the knowledge and skills required for governing a company effectively and competence should be continually developed.
- *Commitment*: A director should be diligent in performing his duties and devote sufficient time to company affairs.
- *Courage*: A director should have the courage to take the risks associated with directing and controlling a successful and sustainable enterprise and act with integrity in all board decisions and activities.

King (iii) (2009) stated that the board is responsible for risk management and must decide on the company's appetite for risk and ability to bear the consequences of risk. Risk should be evaluated in terms of high and low probability and in terms of severity. The board should ensure that a comprehensive risk assessment is undertaken on a regular basis. The board's responsibility for risk management should be expressed in the board charter and be supported by training and induction processes. The board should ensure that there is adequate disclosure of risk tolerance and risk management processes in the annual report. King (iii) (2009) stated that the board may delegate authority to management but, in doing so, the boards do not abdicate their duties and responsibilities. In delegating authority, the board should establish benchmarks and performance indicators to hold management accountable for decisions and actions delegated to them (ibid.).

Ubuntu

The demise of apartheid in South Africa in 1994 and the nation building that followed saw the concept of *ubuntu* becoming a key notion in the circles of the new elite (McAllister 2009). South Africa's transition to democracy, including the process of reconciliation and nation building through the Truth and Reconciliation Commission (TRC), has been attributed to *ubuntu*. It is seen as a return to African roots and 'the African way of life' (ibid.). Nussbaum (2003) posits that *ubuntu* and other dimensions of culture could become a positive source for catalysing socio and economic transformation in South Africa. South Africa's corporate culture and business models are heavily influenced by the Anglo-Saxon approaches. Nussbaum (2003) notes that 'after the political changes resulting in the 1994 election of President Mandela, it became increasingly evident that the South African business community needed to transform as well. New paradigms were needed to inform thinking, about management and leadership development' (p. 1).

As noted above, the key values of *ubuntu* are group solidarity, conformity, compassion, respect, human dignity, and collective unity (Darty-Baah, & Tawiah, 2011). It seeks to conceptualise African values so that they can be applied to South African businesses. *Ubuntu* is built on the values of sharing, community, harmony with the past and present (ibid.). Sibanda (2014) posits that discipline, morality, altruism, self and social consciousness, responsibility and duty are the cardinals of *ubuntu* as it forms the foundation of the African concept of humanism. A person with *ubuntu* should at least strive to meet the standards required of a reasonable citizen and 'uphold the norms and values of the family, the community … abide by the country's laws and statutes, respect, him/herself … and also respect the leadership of the community, state and the world at large' (ibid., p. 27). It can be argued that *ubuntu* informs corporate practices and influences perceptions on what constitutes 'good' corporate governance and ethical practices in the region of Southern Africa. Africa is a continent deeply entrenched in traditional values and yet there is a mismatch between corporate governance and traditional values (Turyahikayo 2014). This mismatch is evidenced by the rampant corporate scandals. Corporate governance in Africa has remained vulnerable (Mukusha 2012). As such '*Umuntu ngumuntu ngabantu* means a person is a person through other people or a thing is a thing through other things. This means that all things know each other in relationship to each other' (Mucina 2013, p. 24). *Ubuntu* can be considered to be a human quality, African humanism, a philosophy, an ethic, or a worldview (Gade 2011). According to Nelson Mandela, in an interview with Tim Modise (a South African journalist): 'a traveller through a country would stop at a village and he didn't have to ask for food or for water. Once he stops, the people give him food, entertain him. That is one aspect of *Ubuntu*, but it will have various aspects. *Ubuntu* does not mean that people should not enrich themselves. The question therefore is: Are you going to do so in order to enable the community around you to be able to improve?' (Oppenheim 2012, p. 369).

Turyahikayo (2014) draws upon public service works as an example of the traditional *ubuntu* methodology. When a job was at hand, the community turned up with supplies and music. Through music and collective effort each phase of the job would be executed collectively, with song and dance in rhythm, such that the job becomes a productive, pleasurable time. In a sense this can be viewed as what Okari et al. (2012) calls 'the principle of participation', where for Africans 'the 'whole', which is the community, takes priority over the part and the individual can best be understood and be defined in the context of participation in the community' (p. 24). The principles negate individualism and embraces the notion that 'I' joins the 'other' to form 'we', a cultural interdependent identity. They posit that the principle of participation should be embraced if Africa is to propel itself to sustainable social economic development. They argue this principle is everyday reality in African life and as such should form the basis of an African orientated form of corporate governance. The culture of reciprocity within a work and community is deeply entrenched in the African culture (Nussbaum 2003; Brubaker 2013). This is known as '*ilima*' in IsiNdebele, '*umsebenzi*' in the Nguni language. As such '*ubuntu*' would mean embracing in the business context. Business did not begin by having as its goal increasing shareholder value, but used to be interconnected with society and was there to serve the local community. 'The original focus of business, which was about helping a local community to grow and prosper, has shifted to helping a few prosper' (Nussbaum 2003, p. 23). Ndondo & Mhlanga (2014) argued that 'the African communitarian way of life, the success of the individual is shared among all he or she relates with. Similarly the misfortune of the individual is the misfortune of many through relational ties. Thus sharing is not only sharing the good things of life' (p. 3).

The *ubuntu* philosophy implies that if people are treated well, they are more likely to improve and increase performance. The belief in *ubuntu* is as authentic as it is a discourse about human behaviour and social practice. McAllister (2009) noted that it is rarely mentioned in practice but it is ingrained within the traditional humanistic African settings. However, McAllister (2009) calls for caution as the *ubuntu* philosophy evoked sweeping generalisation of the social settings within the African landscape 'as it seems, [*ubuntu*] has become all things to all people, a magical elixir invoked to promote almost any form of human development, and to explain success and failure in many spheres of life' (p. 4). However, that said, it is a construction, a part of an identity-making process (ibid.).

King (i) (1994) points out how the African worldview can have a positive influence on corporate culture and governance. According to Nussbaum (2003) corporate systems reflect the values and traditions of their jurisdictions. This means that it would be pertinent to take into account the values and customs of the African worldview in the context of governance of companies in South Africa. These include the following as highlighted by Nussbaum (2003) drawn from The King Report on Corporate Governance in South Africa:

- Spiritual collectiveness is prized over individualism. This determines the communal nature of life where households live as an interdependent neighbourhood.
- An inclination towards consensus rather than dissension helps to explain the loyalty of Africans to their leadership.
- Humility and helpfulness to others is more important than criticism of them.
- In the main, African culture is non-discriminatory and does not promote prejudice. This explains the readiness with which Africans embrace reconciliation at political and business levels.
- Co-existence with other people is highly valued. The essence of ubuntu (humanity) that cuts across Africa is based on the premise that you can be respected only because of your cordial co-existence with others.

There is also an inherent trust and belief in the fairness of all human beings. This manifests itself in the predisposition towards universal brotherhood, even shared by African-Americans.

- High standards of morality are based on historical precedent. These are bolstered by the close kinship observed through totem or clan names and the extended family system.
- A hierarchical political ideology is based on an inclusive system of consultation at various levels.
- The tradition of consultation as practised by the chiefs since time immemorial should form the basis of modern labour relations and people and management practices.
- Perpetual optimism is due to strong belief in the existence of an omniscient, omnipotent and omnipresent superior being in the form of the creator of mankind. (p. 26)

Nussbaum (2003) posits that research on South Africa has unequivocally demonstrated how and why Africans, guided by *ubuntu*, are masterful in the skills, knowledge, consciousness and processes required for building and maintaining communal relationships (in the spirit of togetherness). According to Nussbaum (2003) '*ubuntu*, applied to business and corporate responsibility, would be ultimately about sharing wealth and making (at the very least) basic services, such as food, housing and access to health and education accessible and visible to all members of our global family' (p. 3).

The next section covers the critical theory paradigm whose methodology is dialogic, in the ways of interpreting the changes in the King Reports through *ubuntu*. Perhaps this infusion of dialogue can help us to understand corporate governance within entities operating in Africa and improve the corporate governance processes. For corporate governance is not an event but a continuous process which seeks to change in tandem with socio-economic and polity changes.

Critical Theory

The view of reality has progressed from the Aristotelian concept of observing the phenomena under investigation without either altering or getting involved with the subject matter. In this context, undertaking research involved the passive observation of the subject under investigation. Paradigms of inquiry identify different interpretations both in terms of theory as well as the methodological approaches (Howell and Preston 2001, p. 4). Guba and Lincoln (1994) argued that

> a paradigm may be viewed as a set of basic beliefs or metaphysics that deals with ultimates or principles. It represents a worldview that defines, for its holder, the nature of the 'world', the individual's place in it, and the range of possible relationships to that world and its parts. The beliefs are basic in the sense they must be accepted on faith and there is nowhere to establish their ultimate legitimacy. Inquiry paradigms define for the enquirers what they are about and what falls within and outside the limits of legitimate inquiry. (p. 200)

The critical theory paradigm's epistemology has the dual advantage of being eclectic and dialectic in the sense that the researcher and researched become intrinsically interlinked (Howell 2006). A paradigm involves a set of metaphysical or basic beliefs that allows an understanding of the world and their place within it. In the critical theory paradigm of inquiry, the ontology is 'historical realism' where 'reality is shaped by the social, economic, political, ethnic and gender values crystallised over time' (Denzin and Lincoln 1998, p. 203). The epistemology is transactional and subjectivist. The researcher and the researched interact and the values of the researcher inevitably influence the enquiry and are value mediated and therefore subjective. The critical theorist's methodology is dialogic; dialogue is needed between the researcher and the researched and entails covering the past and the present. In the critical theory paradigm 'reality is shaped by social, political, cultural, and economic, ethnic, and gender values; crystallised over time' (Guba and Lincoln 1994, p. 165). Critical theory insists that 'one needs a theory of society grounded in a theory of capitalism to make sense of socio-historical processes and developments because the dynamics of capitalism play such a constitutive role in social life. Furthermore, to understand and explain social phenomena, one needs to contextualize one's topic of inquiry within a comprehensive theoretical framework for social analysis and critique' (Kellner 1990, p. 23).

For the critical theory paradigm the nature of knowledge is structural and offers historical insights, is historically situated, allows erosion of ignorance and misapprehensions and is an action stimulus (Guba and Lincoln 1994). The critical theory ontology (*historical realism*) changes with time which incorporates meaning, dialectics or historical movement. Kellner (1990) posits that 'critical theory is thus intrinsically global and historical, and attempts to provide the "Big Picture" that sketches the fundamental outlines of socio-economic development and the ways in which capitalism structures social life' (p. 23). Critical theory endeavours to understand and change or develop society. Critical theory 'advances the conception of a critical and normative theory which is committed to emancipation from all forms of oppression, as well as to freedom, happiness, and a rational ordering of society … seeks a connection with empirical analysis of the contemporary world and social movements which are attempting to transform society in progressive ways' (Kellner 1990, p. 12).

Methodology

The dialectic and dialogic methodology of critical theory enables interpretation of the changes in the King Reports through *ubuntu*. Popper (1994) held that historians start with questions that are decisive. These questions are in fact 'historical problems'. A historical document, like a scientific observation, is only relative to a historical problem and like an observation it has to be interpreted. The historian's attempt to analyse and describe the situation is nothing else than his historical conjecture, that is his historical theory. Popper (1994) considered 'what were the important or operative elements in the situation? – it is the central problem that the historian tries to solve. To the extent that he solves it, he has understood the historical situation and the piece of history that he tries to capture. What he has to do qua historian is not to re-enact what has happened, but to give objective arguments in support of his situational analysis [through *ubuntu*]. For the act may be in many ways beyond him' (p. 147).

As it was qualitative in nature *ubuntu* was the interpretive means for this analysis. It was inductive, noting the key changes between King (i) and King (ii), between King (ii) and King (iii). King (ii) served as the constant as it lay at the centre of the study. Meaning meant interpreting these changes from *ubuntu* African philosophy. This in a sense meant understanding the key changes from an African worldview of what was essentially, and is to a certain extent, an Anglo-American model of corporate structure. In 1994, corporate governance became institutionalised in the South Africa through King (i). The Anglo-American model had to accommodate the new face of corporate South Africa. This new face was inclusive of the previously disadvantaged minorities. Hence the need to interpret the changes in the King Reports from an *ubuntu* African world view and not from an Anglo-American world view alone. An inclusive approach is needed.

Analysis

It is the key changes in the Reports that were analysed as these were fundamental shifts in corporate governance. King (i) was applicable to all companies listed on the Johannesburg Stock Exchange, banks, financial institutions, the insurance sector and large public entities with shareholders' equity of R50 million. As early as 1992, the private sector saw the need for a new system of governance as South Africa was embarking on sweeping reforms towards democracy (Stewart 2010). King formed his committee 'just when the majority of our citizens needed guidance on how to operate in the economy because they'd never been in the economy. We couldn't just cookie-cut what the UK or America had done. Instead we developed an inclusive approach to governance, taking into account the legitimate interests and expectations of stakeholders … that was the basis of King (i) in 1994' (cited in Stewart 2010).

Unlike its predecessors King (iii) is applicable to all entities. The key changes between King (i) and King (ii) include the responsibility of directors, internal audit, risk management, integrated sustainability reporting, accounting and auditing. These key changes can be seen identified with *ubuntu* tenets such as collectivism and solidarity, sharing of opportunities, responsibilities and challenges, participatory decision making and consultation, across the boardroom. For *ubuntu* 'co-existence with other people is highly valued. The essence of Ubuntu (humanity) that cuts across South Africa is based on the premise that you can be only be respected because of your cordial co-existence with others' (King ii, 2002, p. 18). King (ii) focussed specifically on the South African situation and attempted to take on board the local business culture (Gstrauntlhaler 2010). King (ii) was realised into being due to the changes in the international corporate governance arena and also after taking on board the political and economic uncertainty in South Africa when King (i) was issued (West 2006).

King (ii) moved away from the shareholder approach in favour of the stakeholder approach to corporate governance. It places emphasis on the need 'to observe and to take account of the African worldview and culture in the context of governance of companies in South Africa, some aspects of which are set out as follows, Spiritual Collectiveness, is prized over individualism. This determines the communal nature of life, where households live as an interdependent neighbourhood' (King ii, 2002, p. 17). This augments the stakeholder approach as 'co-existence with other people is highly valued … the essence of *ubuntu* (humanity) that cuts across Africa is based on the premise that you can be respected only because of your cordial co-existence with others … there is also an inherent trust and belief in fairness of all human beings. This manifests itself in the predisposition towards universal brotherhood' (King ii, 2002, p. 18). *Ubuntu* has similar undertones to Kant's (1969) notion of goodwill and the 'kingdom of ends'. Kant argued that, in nature, rational beings are the very end in themselves as 'rational nature exists as an end itself' (p. 56). According to Kant (1969) the 'kingdom of ends' is only possible if all rational beings are subject to the common universal laws and where each and every rational being exists as a sovereign and regards others as ends and not means. In the 'kingdom of ends', rational beings give laws and are not subject to the will of any other. Kant (1969) defined the 'kingdom of ends' as 'the union of different rational beings in a system by common laws' (p. 100). *Ubuntu* implies truth and righteousness of being, treating other human beings more as ends in themselves. King (ii) does acknowledge the African context. However, 'the fact that the introduction to the report opens with a quote from Adrian Cadbury (from the UK) and closes with a brief consideration of the African context, which appears to be little more than a postscript, as well as the attribution of the African values to an external source, suggests that the report's writers consider the African context to be secondary to the global context' (West 2006, p. 438).

West (2006) therefore notes the incompatibility between the current corporate environment in South Africa and the given exposition of African values of *ubuntu*. First, decision making processes under *ubuntu* are realised through the consensus where the leader plays the role of facilitator. It is the views of the community that predominate as the leader's decision is largely influenced by these views. Second, the communitarian aspects of *ubuntu* are in a sense incompatible with the Anglo-American model of corporate governance which places emphasis on ownership through the shareholder system. It is argued that because of the communitarian nature of African society, duties take precedence over rights.

The need to include sustainability was realised by King (i) in 2002 when the Earth Summit took place in Johannesburg (Stewart 2010). Sustainability was included in King (ii); however, King indicated that the report incorporated 'a separate chapter on sustainability reporting and in consequence, companies started reporting on sustainability in a silo, rather than integrating it. In King (iii) we corrected that mistake. I directed my committee on the basis that the cornerstone has got to be that governance, strategy and sustainability are inseparable; companies have to integrate them into the very fabric, the very rhythm or DNA of their business' (Stewart 2010).

In *ubuntu* terms, sustainability means that companies are part and parcel of the community in which they operate in. Their existence comes into being through the very environment in which they operate in. They do not operate in a vacuum and should be seen to be responsible citizens. As such King (iii) (2009):

placed great emphasis on an integrated report, which will evaluate the company's impact on the economic life of the community in which it operates, as well as many other matters. Sustainability reporting is also emphasised in the need to utilise suppliers from amongst previously disadvantaged people. The importance of the concepts of integrated sustainability and social transformation is highlighted. This leads to a lasting concentration on the effects of business on society and the environment. The concept of sustainability is linked with the evaluation of ethics and the improvement of ethical standards in business and in the community. (pp. 3–4)

In a sense this echoes the trusteeship stakeholder approach to corporate governance. The trusteeship model acknowledges the separate legal personae of corporate entities and holds managers as trustees of the company acting in the interests of the broader stakeholder community and not solely on the shareholders' behalf. This model further argues in favour of the long-term perspective rather than short-term shareholder returns (Letza and Sun 2004). The long-term perspective and broader stakeholder community promotes sustainability and accountability for corporate entities. West (2006) notes that King (ii) advocated an inclusive approach to corporate governance despite the fact that South Africa's corporate environment is largely Anglo-American in nature, controlled and dominated by the few. It is a:

modified form of the Anglo-American model (modified by some attempts to incorporate stakeholder theory, notably in King II), with its prominence given to shareholders and the consistent primacy of economic objectives. This stands in contrast to the normative prescriptions from the African intellectuals who espouse communitarian values including communal rights, consensual decision-making and a priority of ethical over economic concerns. (p. 445)

The key changes between King (ii) and King (iii) were inter alia shareholder approval of remuneration policies, directors' performance evaluation, business rescue proceedings, alternative dispute resolution and the composition of the board (whose majority should be independent). In King (iii) the chairman of the board should not be the CEO. The chairman should be an independent non-executive director whereas King (ii) stated that the chairperson should preferably be an independent non-executive director and the role of the chairperson and the CEO should preferably be kept separate. King (iii) uses the term 'should' regarding the separate roles of the chairman and the CEO, whereas King (ii) uses the term 'preferably'. All the key changes include checks and balances to ensure board independence and integrity and to avoid having one person with unfettered power. This is to minimise the possibilities of the agents (directors) defecting. In a sense the drive is to ensure that the agent acts in the best interests of the principal (shareholders). Indeed, Dartey-Baah & Tawiah (2011) indicated that 'the cardinal belief of Ubuntu is that a man can only be a man through others. In its most fundamental sense it stands for personhood and morality' (p. 132). The community is more important than an individual under the *ubuntu* philosophy. 'People should be aware that individualism and greed, and profit achieved by sacrificing other community members, contravenes the true foundations of humanity (Ubuntu). The notion of Ubuntu or humanity teaches the community solidarity, caring, and sharing amongst the members of a community or organisation' (Khomba and Ulaya 2013, pp. 672–689).

Unlike both King (i) and (ii), King (iii) is applicable to all entities be they public, private or non-profit making entities. Gstrauntlhaler (2010) noted that 'King (iii) takes an interesting route and tries to balance between international developments and African peculiarities' (p. 146). King (iii) places emphasis on leadership, sustainability and corporate citizenship. These are the ideals of *ubuntu* life in the corporate world as 'the King Report (iii) has placed great emphasis on an integrated report, which will evaluate the company's impact on the economic life of the community in which it operates, as well as many other matters' (King iii 2009, p. 5). This in turn leads to a lasting concentration on the effects of business on society and the environment. Indeed the concept of sustainability is linked with the evaluation of ethics and the improvement of ethical standards in the corporate world and in the community. It is therefore defined and conceived from a community worldview. As West (2010) noted 'King (iii)'s interpretation of these values … shows its denial of a one-size-fits-all approach and its focus on two South African issues: the changes in the economic situation and the principle of *ubuntu*' (p. 148).

King (iii) places great emphasis on an integrated report, which evaluates the company's impact on the economic life of the community in which it operates. It also highlights the need for business rescue when it becomes evident that a company is distressed. 'The financial crisis absolutely brought sustainability forward. It reinforced the idea that corporations are the greatest pool of human and monetary capital, and when a corporation fails, there is a huge impact on society. On other side of the coin, when you have great corporate success, it impacts positively on society' (Stewart 2010).

The concept of business rescue proceedings is emphasised in King (iii). King (iii) posited the 'need for the Board to follow the business rescue procedures, when it becomes evident that a company is distressed' (King iii, 2009, p. 4). *Ubuntu* is inclusive in nature as it views all members of the community (organisation) as one entity aiming at achieving one common goal/purpose or objective (Khomba et al. 2013). It is an inclusive framework which supports the stakeholder approach to corporate governance. This is in the spirit of the Reports. *Ubuntu* is a holistic approach which places emphasis on the respect for the environment, the society and above all, respect for oneself, through the community. The checks and balances found in the King Reports are meant to ensure that the directors, be it the chairman, CEO or the individual directors, respect their positions as agents of the company. Their positions are those of trust, having been given the mandate by the principal. Lack of respect of this position means abuse of office. This means loss of *ubuntu*. A person who has lost *ubuntu* is said to be '*kala Buntu*' meaning he or she has no *ubuntu*. In the eyes of the community that person has fallen from grace.

Ubuntu and the Reports are social constructions. They reflect the social patterns within South Africa's landscape. The King Reports emanated from the changing socio-polity landscape. They are a product of those changes emanating over time. Each revision to the Reports signified a change in history. A change in history implies movement, a shift in the socio-economic patterns. Indeed Letza and Sun (2004) hold that corporate governance is 'a social construct which represents or reflects the periodic patterns of continuously shifting ideas, paradigms, social norms, codes of behaviour, modes of thinking … Significantly to understand the social product of corporate governance is to place it into wider social, economic and political systems and historical and societal contexts, which themselves are also continuously constructive processes' (pp. 12–14).

Conclusion

The ontology for the critical theory paradigm of inquiry perceives 'reality as shaped by the social, economic, political, ethnic and gender values crystallised over time' (Denzin and Lincoln 1998, p. 203). Indeed, the critical theory paradigm enables the dialogic interpretation of the changes in the corporate governance reports through the means of *ubuntu*. In 1994 South Africa found itself on the road to democracy. King (i) came into being when a cloud of economic and political uncertainty hung over South Africa. Sweeping reforms to democracy meant radical change and it was out of this developing socio-economic and political landscape that the need for a new form of governance arose. King (i) was meant to harmonise the emerging face of corporate South Africa with that of the old. A new corporate South Africa emerged and an inclusive corporate landscape required guidance on how to operate in a new harmonised economy which now included sections of society previously barred.

King (ii) came eight years later by which time South Africa had acclimatised to the post-1994 situation. The concept of *ubuntu* was more pronounced in King (ii) which posited that 'governance in any context reflects the value system of the society in which it operates … It would be pertinent to observe and to take account of the African worldview and culture in the context of governance of companies in South Africa' (p. 17). The changes in the King Reports largely arose from changes in the external and internal socio-economic environments. Inclusivity, stakeholdership and sustainability are some of the themes which are echoed in King (iii). These are some of the key tenets of *ubuntu*. However, it should be noted that these three Reports are by their nature Anglo-American. Corporate South Africa in reality is still largely based on the shareholder approach. The Reports seeks to harmonise these glaring realities through the spirit of inclusivity. Fundamentally, 'corporate governance systems are culturally influenced and existing theories in the realm of contemporary corporate governance systems are alien to the African culture and therefore might not offer sufficient solutions to challenges facing organizations operating in the African environment' (Okari et al. 2012, p. 24).

References

Brubaker, T. A. (2013). Servant leadership, Ubuntu, and leader effectiveness in Rwanda. *Emerging Leadership Journeys, 6*(1), 95–131 (© 2013 Regent University School of Business & Leadership).

Daily, C., Dalton, D., & Cannella, A. (2003). Corporate governance: Decades of dialogue and data. *Academy of Management Review, 28*(3), 371–382.

Darty-Baah, K., & Tawiah, K. A. (2011). Exploring the limits of Western Corporate Social Responsibility theories in Africa. *International Journal of Business and Social Science, 2*(18), 126–137.

Denzin, N. K., & Lincoln, Y. S. (1998). The Landscape of Qualitative Research. Theories and Issues. London: Sage Publications.

Gade, B. N. (2011). The historical development of the written discourses on Ubuntu. *South African Journal of Philosophy, 30*(3), 304–329.

Gstrauntlhaler, T. (2010). Corporate governance in South Africa: The introduction of King III and reporting practices at the JSE ALT-X. *Corporate Ownership and Control, 7*(3), 146–155.

Guba, E. G., & Lincoln, Y. S. (1994). *Naturalistic inquiry*. London: Sage.

Howell, K. E. (2006). Worldviews, moral templates, scripts, symbols & norms: Welsh culture & the role of the National Assembly for Wales. *Public Policy & Administration Autumn.*

Howell, K. E., & Letza, S. (2000). Virtue, Virtu, categorical imperative and the civic constitution: Defining corporate governance. *Journal of Interdisciplinary Economics*, 11, 95-104.

Howell, K. E., & Preston, J. (2001). The state of the Union in 2001. The UACES 31st Annual Conference and 6th Research Conference on *Historical Institutionalism, Europeanization and the National Assembly of Wales; A Preliminary Study*, University of Bristol, 3–5 September 2001.

Kant, I. (1969). *Fundamental principles of the metaphysic of ethics*. London, UK: Longmans Green and Co Ltd.

Kellner, D. (1990). Critical theory and the crisis of social theory. *Sociological Perspectives, 33*(1), 11–33.

McAllister, P. (2009). Ubuntu – Beyond belief in Southern Africa. *Sites: New Series, 6*(1), 15–25.

Ndondo, S., & Mhlanga, D (2014). Philosophy for children: A model for Unhu/Ubuntu philosophy. *International Journal of Scientific and Research Publications, 4*(2), 1–5.

Khomba, J. K., Bakuwa, R. C., & Kangaude-Ulaya, E. C. (2013). Shaping business ethics and corporate governance: An inclusive African Ubuntu Philosophy. *Global Journal of Management and Business Research and Administration, 13*(5).

Khomba, J. K., & Ulaya, C. K. (2013). Indigenisation of corporate strategies in Africa: Lessons from the African Ubuntu Philosophy. *China-USA Business Review, 12*(7), 672–689.

King Report on Corporate Governance in South Africa. (2002). Institute of Directors. Johannesburg, South Africa (March 2002). http://www.iodsa.co.za/?kingIII. Accessed 3 June 2015.

King Report iii. (2009). King code of governance for South Africa 2009. (Online) Available from: http://www.ecgi.org/codes/documents/king3.pdf. Accessed 3 June 2015.

Lanoo, K. (1999). A European perspective on corporate governance. *Journal of Common Market Studies, 37*(2), 269–294.

Letza, S., & Sun, X. (2004). Shareholding versus stakeholding: A critical review of corporate governance. *Corporate Governance: An International Review, 12*(3), 242–262.

Letza, S., & Sun, X. (2004). Philosophical and paradoxical issues in corporate governance. *International Journal Business Governance and Ethics,* X(Y), 1–14.

Mukusha, J. (2012). Business nakedness in the absence of good corporate governance: A case for sustainability in the 21st century and beyond. *Journal of Sustainable Development in Africa, 14*(2).

Munyaka, M., & Motlabi, M. (2009). Ubuntu and its socio-moral significance. In M. F. Murove (Ed.), *African ethic: An anthology of comparative and applied ethics*. Scottsville: University of Kwazulu-Natal Press.

Mudashiru, A., Bakare, A. O. I., Babatunde, Y., & Ishmael, O. (2014). Good corporate governance and organisational performance: An empirical analysis. *International Journal of Humanities and Social Science, 4, 7*(1).

Mucina, D. D. (2013). Ubuntu orality as a living philosophy. *The Journal of Pan African Studies, 6*(4).

Nussbaum, B. (2003). Ubuntu and business: Reflections and questions. *World Business Academy, 17*(3), 2–16.

OECD. (2004). *Principles of Corporate Governance*. Paris: OECD.

Oppenheim, C. E. (2012). Nelson Mandela and the power of Ubuntu. *Religions, 2012*(3), 369–388.

Okari, H., Keraro, V., & Kiambati, H. (2012). The principle of participation in corporate governance; An African perspective. *IJMBS, 2*(3), 24–28.

Okeahalam, C., & Akinboade, O. A. (2003). *A review of corporate governance in Africa: Literature, issues and challenge*. Global Corporate Governance Forum.

Popper, K. R. (1994). *The myth of the framework: In Defence of Science and Rationality*. London: Routledge.

Robinson, A. (2002). Is Corporate Governance The Solution or The Problem? Corporate Board, 07468652, March/April 2002, Volume 23, Issue 133.

Shleifer, A., & Vishny, R. W. (1997). A survey of corporate governance. *The Journal of Finance, LII*(2).

Shepherd, N., & Mhlanga, D. (2012). Philosophy for children: A model for Unhu/Ubuntu Philosophy. *International Journal of Scientific and Research Publications, 4*(2), 1–5.

Sibanda, P. (2014). The dimensions of 'Hunhu/Ubuntu. (Humanism in the African Sense): The Zimbabwe Conception'. *IOSR Journal of Engineering, 04*(01), 26–29.

Steinberg, E. (2000). *Just business: Business ethics in action* (2nd ed.). Oxford, UK: Oxford University Press.

Stewart, N. (2010). An audience with the 'GRI's Mervin King'. *IR Magazine*. Cross Border Ltd. http://www.irmagazine.com. Accessed 20 June 2015.

Tricker, B. (2012). *Corporate governance: Principles, policies and practices* (2nd ed.). Oxford: Oxford University Press.

Turyahikayo, E. (2014). Corporate governance vulnerability in Africa: Do African values matter? *International Journal of Capacity Building in Education and Management, 2*(2), 62–70.

West, A. (2006). Theorising South Africa's corporate governance. *Journal of Business Ethics, 2006*(68), 433–448.

9

The Corporate Governance of the Kenyan Public Sector

D.G. Barako and A.M. Brown

Introduction

As a former British colony, Kenya has inherited comparable Westminster institutional settings, generating both statutory and customary laws since independence in 1963 and maintaining a reasonable degree of macro-economic stability (Nolte and Väth 2015). The governance of the Kenyan government with respect to public financial management oversight falls under the Office of the Auditor General of Kenya (OAGK), which is described in its service charter as 'the lead agency in promoting good governance and accountability in the management of public resources' (OAGK 2014, p. i).

Its independence is constituted under Article 248(3) of the Kenya Constitution of the Republic of Kenya and its statutory duties and responsibilities are laid down in Article 229(4) (5) (6) and (7) of the Constitution and Public Audit Act, 2003. The OAGK states that it is guided by the

D.G. Barako (✉)
Kenya School of Monetary Studies, Nairobi, Kenya

A.M. Brown
Curtin University, Bentley, Australia

K.E. Howell, M.K. Sorour (eds.), *Corporate Governance in Africa*,
DOI 10.1057/978-1-137-56700-0_9

International Standards on Auditing, and Government Financial Regulations and Procedures and Public Finance Management Act, 2012. Therefore, it can obtain reasonable assurance about whether financial statements of public sector entities are free from material misstatement or not (OAGK 2014). Management is responsible for the submission of the financial statements to the Auditor General in accordance with the provisions of Sections 4, 5, 6 and 7 of the Public Audit Act, 2003. In contrast to some jurisdictions (such as the Solomon Islands) which do not legislate for the Auditor General's office (Brown 2013), the OAGK enjoys legislated independence.

This study is important for a number of reasons. As Kenya is a low to middle income economy with a relatively short period of time as an independent country (K'akumu 2004) governance and ethical issues are of critical importance to Kenyans. Moreover, sound governance and ethics helps stamp out absenteeism, bribery, corruption, embezzlement, nepotism, partisanship, patronage and peddling, especially when considering that Kenya is a state characterised by high levels of inequality, insecurity, corruption, factionalism, instrumentalisation of violence and ethnicity (Katumanaga 2013, p. 7). Furthermore, sound governance is essential for the Kenyan public sector to attract foreign direct investment (Hynes 2010).

Despite being a democratic country with free media, parliamentarians have not been responsive to public pressure to deal with scandals (Hassid and Brass 2015) or address the plight of the electorate (Osman et al. 2011). A study which focuses on accountability and audit reports is required because it reveals the type of legitimacy that is shaped and implemented by state auditors in their reports to parliament. Therefore, this study attempts to unpack the motivations that inform the reports. This enhances our understanding of the economic, social and political accountability of an auditing leadership group, as leaders can be seen as moral agents answerable to canons of social responsibility (Parker 2014). The unpacking of audit reports is particularly apt in an African context because the reports represent a unique mode of independent communication as they render an account of intent, action and reflection.

The reasons for identifying aspects of legitimacy in the reports of the OAGK are manifold. If legitimacy is defined as 'an action or usage which is dominant but not recognized as such, that is to say, which is tacitly accepted' use this circulation in order to make informed decisions based on sound governance." (Andon et al. 2014). It may also be seen as a form of cultural reproduction (Shore and Wright 1990) and a scarce symbolic resource that is subject to struggle and negotiation and renegotiation (Brown 2011). It is also of interest to societies to understand how local audit reporting models circulate within local contexts of the African region and how leaders use this circulation.

Nevertheless, there are a number of limitations that this study needs to acknowledge. First, it has assumed that audit work is important for heightening both accountability and governance of auditee entities. There is limited literature that argues that the work of auditors is highly suspect (Taplin et al. 2014) and that they are financially bound up in the work of the International Accounting Standards Board (IASB) and its funders (Porter et al. 2006). However, at the state level, there is some evidence that the work of state auditors is very useful in raising accountability and governance of public sector entities. Brown (2014), for example, found that the Office of the Auditor General of Papua New Guinea raised many examples of improvements in internal controls and documentation to help public sector entities improve fiscal accountability in a developing country setting. Second, this study also assumes that reporting compliance and governance may be achieved through a process of putting in place correct procedures. However, there may be different traditions and cultural values which might inhibit the institution of these procedures in different ways. Examining these traditions and cultural values is outside the remit of this study. However, it is assumed that governance reporting and compliance are considered important across many sectors of the Kenyan economy, including the private (Barako and Brown 2008) and public sectors (Barako and Brown 2009; Barako 2014) and that possible solutions (however procedural) for the improvement of reporting make an important contribution to Kenyan corporate governance. Indeed, this is contextualised later in the study in terms of globalised and local-level corporate governance. It is also assumed that governance has a broad definition, covering both corporate and non-corporate. This is particularly apt in Kenya where the work of the growing public sector (particularly through the expanding Nairobi Stock Exchange) and relatively large public sector (with over 200 departments and state corporations as well 47 county governments) often overlaps (Barako et al. 2010). As such, the study looks at the corporate governance of the whole of Kenyan government from a critical perspective of public auditing.

Lienert and Modi (1997) argue that the public sector in Africa is faced with a number of challenges such as shortage of competent personnel. Like other African countries, since independence, Kenya's public sector has been undergoing various reforms with the primary purpose of improving service delivery to citizens while optimising resources utilisation (Hope 2012; Kobia and Mohamed 2006). According to the former head, the progress in Kenya's public sector is informed by a document titled 'Result Based Management and Performance Contracts and Integrated Financial Management Information System (IFMIS)' (Muthaura 2010). IFMIS is an essential budgetary tool as well as a critical accountability mechanism at both levels of government: national and county. The IFMIS is a department in the National Treasury, which is the ministry in-charge of government budgetary and expenditure management. The National Treasury created the IFMIS Academy and in less than two years trained over 5000 public servants. This is meant to streamline government financial management in all government departments and agencies as well as county governments.

According to the Institute of Internal Auditors, auditing is a cornerstone of good public sector governance (Institute of Internal Auditors 2012). The institute further argues that:

> An effective public sector audit activity strengthens governance by materially increasing citizens' ability to hold their public sector entity accountable. Auditors perform an especially important function in those aspects of governance that are crucial for promoting credibility, equity, and appropriate behaviour of public sector officials. (Institute of Internal Auditors 2012, p. 5)

That said, Diamond (2002) provides a comprehensive review of the role of internal audit in government financial management and raises fundamental questions as to the relevance of International Auditing Standards to developing and transition countries, and the practicality of implementation of such a unified standard by these economies. The Public Audit Act 2003 established the Kenya National Audit Office (OAGK) as a supreme organ. In addition, the independence and supremacy of OAGK is well acknowledged in articles 226, 229, 248 and 249 of the new Constitution of Kenya. Moreover, management of public finance in Kenya is well laid down in the Public Finance Act, 2012. The Act set outs the responsibilities of various stakeholders such as the National Treasury, the County Government Treasury, and the National Assembly in public financial management. The Act also states in great detail the budget process, and specifies the role of Cabinet Secretary for the National Treasury.

The OAGK is established as an independent office for having overarching financial oversight on the executive, legislature and other independent office and commissions. The public audit by the Auditor General is focused on giving assurance on fiscal responsibility, managerial accountability, and service delivery to Kenyans. The OAGK audit is entirely based on International Auditing Standards and strongly embedded in the International Financial Reporting Standards. It is against this background that this chapter presents critical perspectives on public auditing by the Office of the Auditor General of Kenya with emphasis on the role of indigenous knowledge. The contributions of this chapter are as follows. It examines corporate governance practices and ethical issues in Kenya, looks at specific attempts at implementation of accountability and contextualises this work through the theory of indigenous alternatives.

Corporate Governance Practices and Ethical Issues in Kenya

Ouma (2010) argues that governance through externally audited standards attempts to normalise compliance on actors according to prescriptive models of governance but may ultimately open up space for non-compliance. This is because different locales may evaluate the legitimacy of introduced compliance models differently because of unique conventions, institutions, organisational arrangements, practices, and rationalities. This would make the embeddedness of introduced formal systems of governance problematic. Thus, while notions of governance may be defined, politicised and refined over a long period of time in Western societies, this Western understanding of governance may be contested in other geographic regions. Essentially, the export of the International Accounting Standards Board of mainstream codified forms of authoritative knowledge of accounting and auditing practices through self-regulation has an uncertain history in those countries possessing very different cultural, institutional and environmental contexts. As such, it would be difficult to impose prescriptive templates of governance into countries which may enjoy an 'accountability of undecided space' (Brown 2014 p. 5).

Commentators' views of the governance practices of Kenyan public sector entities are favourable. Brass (2012, p. 211) notes that although governance of public sector entities has become 'stronger and more democratic in Kenya ... [it] remains a far cry from being fully democratic or accountable'. This is because it has a relatively limited public administration capacity and is influenced by its hierarchical, authoritarian past (Brass 2012). Odhiambo-Mbai (2003) argues that despite the establishment of watchdog institutions—such as Parliament, Police, Anti-Corruption Unit, Monitoring Unit and the Judiciary to scrutinize the ethical conduct of public officials—accountability of public affairs has declined since independence. Nyamori and Nyamori (2015, p. 275) suggest that the Kenyan parliament has become 'more assertive' but that its ability to scrutinise the executive 'is limited by the effectiveness of the other institutions of government'.

Specific State Attempts at Implementation of Accountability

In Kenya, consistent with the processes of a Westminster parliamentary system, a completed Auditor General's audit report is handed to the Parliamentary Accounts Committee and Parliamentary Investment Committee for scrutiny and ultimately for parliamentary debate and action. However, since 1963, parliament has taken little action to prosecute officers for misuse of public resources (Odhiambo-Mbai 2003). Under a Westminster parliamentary system, a PAC is supposed to review the audit report prepared by the Auditor General as part of its watchdog function (Jacobs and Jones 2009; Jones 2006; Jones and Jacobs 2006). However, in a developing country setting, many difficulties often arise including a lack of preparedness by the Auditor General to report (Brown 2011), a lack of interest by PACs in fulfilling their functions (Pelizzo 2010; Samsuddin and Mohamed 2009; Montano 2009). At the local level,

Nyamori and Gekara (in press, p. 1) state that the 24-year-old regime of President Daniel Arap Moi was 'widely considered corrupt, inept and oppressive'. In an attempt to lift governance of the Kenyan public sector entities, a number of reforms were established including The Kenya Civil Service Reform Programme in 1993 and the Economic Recovery Strategy for Wealth and Employment Creation (2003–2007) in 2002.

In a Westminster parliamentary system, accountability may mean scrutinising public income and expenditure in order to protect public monies from embezzlement, performing a legislative oversight function to improve transparency and compliance, maintaining a record of misappropriation or mismanagement, or to report on economies and efficiencies through corporate governance principles (Hoque and Thiagarajah 2015). Here, formal accountability measures were introduced to Kenya by the British colonial government. Formed in 1906 by the colonial governor, the Legislative Council represented Kenya's first parliament. The Director of Audit presented its audit report to the Director of Colonial Audit in London which was then tabled before the Legislative Council (Nyamori and Nyamori 2015). Later, the Director of Audit report was submitted to the Minister of Finance, who then tabled it before the National Assembly. If the Minister failed to do this, the Director of Audit forwarded the report to the Speaker of the National Assembly. The Kenya Constitution Act 2010 now requires the audit report to be submitted to parliament. Moreover, in accordance with section 8 of the Public Audit Act, 2003, the audit attempts to accord with International Standards on Auditing. Those standards require compliance with ethical requirements and that the audit be planned and performed to obtain reasonable assurance about whether the financial statements are free from material misstatement.

Before Kenya's independence in 1963, expatriate British accountants introduced Western-narrow reporting to colonial Kenya to the exclusion of indigenous African Kenyans (Sian 2007a). Societal structure in colonial Kenya had distinct hierarchical divisions between Europeans, Asians and indigenous Africans with white minority rule (Sian 2010). Indigenous Kenyan Africans 'constituted subsistence farmers, those employed on European farms and those holding menial jobs in the urban areas' (Sian 2010, p. 369). In 1921, the passing of the Companies Ordinance required accounts and audits of Kenyan colonial companies. In 1933, the passing of a further Companies Ordinance strengthened these accounting and auditing requirements. In 1949 the Association of Accountants in East Africa was formed as a company limited by guarantee. Its specific qualifications for admission which effectively excluded indigenous African Kenyans from admission brought about what Sian calls 'closure on the basis of race' (2010, p. 374). From 1970 to 1978, a new professional body called the Institute of Certified Practising Accountants of Kenya attempted to break down this closure through the reworking of admission requirements (Sian 2006) (Table 9.1).

After independence the indigenous African Kenyan Government brought in initiatives to encourage majority indigenous African Kenyans to take on senior roles in the accounting profession body that were previously occupied by minority expatriate European accountants. This was to reverse colonial exclusion policies (Sian 2007b). While the Kenyan accounting profession has become an indigenous-led profession, Sian (2010) notes there is limited professional independence in Kenya. These flows met the demands of what Ossewaarde, Nijhof and Heyse (2008) term regulatory (abiding rules and laws), normative (collective accounting of responsibility), cognitive (conformity of mission through knowledge and expertise) and output (transparent accounts and evidence) legitimacy.

Table 9.1 Summary of events surrounding the emergence of ICPAK

Year	Event
1895	Creation of the British East Africa Protectorate
1907	First-known English Chartered Accountant, E.B. Gill established practice in Nairobi
1920	Establishment of Colony and Protectorate of Kenya
1921	Companies Ordinance 1921 established requirements for accounts and audits for companies operating in the colony
1949	Formation of the Association of Accountants in East Africa (AAEE)
1963	Independence of Kenya
1969	Establishment of Kenyan Accountants and Secretaries National Examination Board (KASNEB)
1977	Establishment of Institute of Certified Public Accountants of Kenya (ICPAK)

Theory and Methods

The specific paradigm of inquiry and methodological approach of the chapter centres on textual analysis, specifically on critical theory of indigenous alternatives, which is informed by a constructivist paradigm of inquiry that involves notions relating to indigenous people's empowerment in local situations. Research is not only about the accumulation of knowledge but political activity and social transformation.

The critical theory of indigenous alternatives challenges globalised perspectives of corporate governance in relation to the needs of indigenous-run states and the contradictions that arise when local circumstances are not taken into consideration. The theory of indigenous alternatives generates a grounded understanding of compliance by taking into account economic, institutional, sociocultural, and socio-environment practices of local circumstances. Kenya's standard-setting processes and the ideas of governance invoked by them offer a contested terrain of competing principles of globalism and local Kenyan African localism. Global governance invokes a Western-narrow or Western-broad reporting model of self-regulation, with attempted normalisation of governance practices through auditing judgements based on structuralist interpretations of 'market' practices, modernity, self-reliance and the deterministic nature of the economy. Local governance invokes standards from specific local settings that are informed by local expert knowledge and draws upon local agency rather than 'market' practices. Moreover, global governance also invokes notions of functionalist forms of development, whereas local governance embraces the idea of peoples' capacity to shape development where governance practice might be informed by indigenous sociocultural meanings of development (Curry 2003).

In contrast, hybridisation draws on a mixture of economic assumptions that give rise to hybrid socio-economies. Hybridisation may entreat indigenous pre-colonial and pre-modern values in forming contemporary understandings of governance. A criticism of the theory of hybridisation is that it still gives primacy to the Western-centric viewpoint of development in the sense that subordinate local contexts will one day give way to the dominant Western sense of development suppressing possible alternative practices for tackling development (Curry 2003). Still, development practice might pay attention to location-based conceptions of economy and community and identity.

The study looked at the audits of many ministries and departments which are listed in Table 9.2.

The study also takes into account the OAGK's audit of county governments (listed in Table 9.3) as part of its remit for auditing the whole of the government of Kenya.

The study period straddled the passing of the Government Financial Regulations and Procedures and Public Finance Management Act, 2012 and thus included the broad reflections of the OAGK from year ending 2011 to 2013. The broad reflections were framed around four technical auditing terms: unqualified, qualified, adverse and disclaimer. An unqualified opinion by the OAGK suggests that the financial statements present a true and fair view of activities or are presented fairly, and public funds have been applied lawfully and effectively, while a qualified opinion means the OAGK has picked up a misstatement or limitation which needs an 'except for' opinion. Moreover, an adverse opinion occurs when audit matters on the financial statements are so material and pervasive that the OAGK concludes that the financial statements are misleading or incomplete. Finally, a disclaimer of opinion occurs where the possible effects of limitations are so material and pervasive that the OAGK is unable to obtain sufficient appropriate audit evidence and accordingly unable to express any meaningful audit opinion on the financial statements.

Sections 99–103 of the Constitution of Kenya stipulates that the Ministry of Finance should properly budget and manage public sector financial resources. The Ministry of Finance formulates and develops fiscal, monetary and financial policies. It regulates the financial sector, manages government revenue, expenditure and borrowing; it organises bilateral and multilateral development financing and technical assistance; it plans for donor support; it coordinates government ministries/departments for the preparation of the annual national budget; and it ensures ministerial budgets are carried out.

Table 9.2 Kenya's ministries and departments

Ministry of Devolution and Planning	Ministry of Forestry and Wildlife; Ministry of Nairobi Metropolitan Development; Kenya National Commission of Human Rights	Witness Protection Agency; Transition Authority
National Treasury	National Police Service Commission	Kenyan National Human Rights & Equality Commission
Ministry of Defence	Ministry of Interior and National Government; Ministry of Foreign Affairs; Ministry of Home Affairs; Office of Vice President; Medical Services; Ministry of Labour & HRD	Independent Electoral & Boundaries Commission; Parliamentary Service Commission
Ministry of Finance	Deputy Prime Minister's Office	Salaries and Remuneration Committee
State House	Ministry of Livestock Development	Teachers Services Commission
Ministry of State for Public Service	Ministry of Water & Irrigation; State Law Office; Judicial Department	National Police Services Commission
Ministry of Planning and National Development and Vision 2030	Ministry of Energy	Auditor General
Ministry of Agriculture	Ministry of Education; Ministry of Information; Ethics & Anti-Corruption Commission	Controller of the Budget; Commission of Administrative Justice
Ministry of Medical Services	Ministry of State for Special Programmes	National Gender & Equality Commission

(*continued*)

Table 9.2 (Continued)

Ministry of Local Government	Ministry of Youth Affairs & Sports	Independent Police Oversight Authority
Ministry of Labour	Ministry of Tourism	
Ministry of Justice	Office of the Prime Minister; Ministry of Forestry & Wildlife	
National Cohesion and Constitutional Affairs; Ministry of Gender, Children and Social Development	Ministry of Fisheries Development	
Ministry of Livestock Development	National Security Intelligence Service	
Ministry of Environment and Mineral Resources	Ministry of Public Works; Ministry of Industrialization; Directorate of Public Prosecutor	
Ministry of Co-operative Development and Marketing	Commission for the Implementation of the Constitution	
Cabinet Office	Registrar of Political Parties	
Ministry of East Africa Community		
Ministry of Immigration and Communication; Ethics and Anti-Corruption Commission		
Ministry of Lands; Ministry of State for Immigration and Registration of Persons; Ministry of State for National Heritage and Culture		
Ministry of Higher Education, Science and Technology		
Ministry of Housing		
National Security Intelligence Service; Ministry of Tourism; Office of the Prime Minister; Ministry of Public Health and Sanitation		

Table 9.3 County governments of Kenya

Baringo	Meru
Bomet	Migori
Bungoma	Mombasa
Busia	Muranga
Elgeyo-Marakwet	Nairobi
Embu, Garissa	Nakuru
Homa Bay	Nandi
Isiolo	Narok
Kajiado	Nyamira
Kakamega	Nyandurua
Kericho	Nyeri
Kiambu	Sambubu
Kilifi	Siaya
Kirinyaga	Taita
Kisumu	Taveta
Kitui	Tana River
Kwale	Tharaka Nithi
Laikipia	Tansa-Nzoia
Lamu	Turkana
Machakos	Uasin Gishu
Makueni	Vihiga
Mandera	Wajir and West Pokot.
Marsabit	

> The Ministry also provides Accounting, Auditing, IT, Insurance, Pensions, Procurement, Clearing and Forwarding services, and Divestiture services among others to other government ministries/departments (Ministry of Finance 2015, p. 1).

The National Treasury of the Ministry of Finance is responsible for strengthening the fiscal and financial relations between the national government and county governments.

Results

The audit of the financial statements for the year ending 2013 indicates that out of the 343 audited statements only 41 statements (or 12 %) had a clean (unqualified) audit opinion, while 172 (or 50 %) had qualified audit opinions. Forty-five statements (or 13 %) had an adverse opinion, while 85 statements (or 25 %) had a disclaimer of opinion reports. Details for the ratios of audit opinions for year ending 2011 to 2013 are provided in Table 9.4.

For year ending 2012, only 6 % of public sector entities were able to present financial statements that were deemed unqualified (clean) by the OAGK. Although this percentage increased for the year ending 2013 (12 %), it is still relatively low. Of greatest concern was the relatively high percentage of disclaimers of opinion received by public sector entities for both years. Here, the financial statements were materially mis-stated that the OAGK 'could not establish whether expenditure was incurred lawfully and in an effective manner' (OAGK 2014, p. 9).

The OAGK also scrutinised the revenue collected by the government of Kenya through an analysis of 23 revenue statements. For year ending 2013, only one revenue statement (Sales of Good and Services, which collected KES0.5 billion) received an unqualified opinion.

Qualified and adverse opinions on the remaining revenue statements arose because there were differences between the balances recorded by the Ministry of Finance and the Kenya Revenue Authority. The OAGK was also unable to confirm that expenditure of KES337,902,304,501 was legal. Recurrent and development expenditures were also qualified because of excessive expenditure, lack of adequate disclosures, misallocation of expenditure items, non-surrender of imprests, unauthorised expenditure, uncleared balances of the Statement of Assets and Liabilities and unsupported expenditure.

Table 9.4 Audit Opinions by OAGK

	Financial Year					
	Year ending 2013 (one year after PFM Act)		Year ending 2012		Year ending 2011 (one year before PFM Act)	
Audit Opinions	No. of Statements	%	No. of Statements	%	No. of Statements	%
Unqualified	41	12	15	6	0	0
Qualified	172	50	130	51	60	33
Adverse	45	13	24	10	0	0
Disclaimer	85	25	83	33	121	67
Total	343	100	252	100	181	100

Source: Adapted from OAGK (2014, p. 6; OAGK 2013a, b, p. IX)
Note: PFM Act refers to Public Finance Management Act, 2012

The OAGK also provided an adverse opinion because there were differences between year-ending 2012 closing balances and year-ending opening balances, discrepancies between the appropriation accounts and ledger accounts, lack of financial statement compliance with Treasury instructions and unsupported balances in the financial statements.

Disclaimers of opinion were expressed because of bookkeeping errors, failure to produce a trial balance for year ending 2013, lack of expenditure items in the appropriation accounts, unexplained balances in the financial statements and unsupported and unreconciled balances. In summary, the OAGK noted that accounts were characterised by excessive expenditure, mismanagement of imprests, non-maintenance of cash and bank accounts, non-maintenance of accounting records, pending bills, unsupported expenditure imprest balances shown in the statements of assets and liabilities did not agree with the amounts shown in the imprest registers and ledgers. There were also no reconciliations conducted. Further, there was a lack of supporting documentation for the imprest balances.

The OAGK also criticised departments and ministries, as instructed by National Treasury, for using the cash basis of accounting to prepare financial statements. Capital assets were expensed which meant that the Statements of Assets and Liabilities undervalued year-ending assets and liabilities. Thus, it was not possible to ascertain by year-ending 2013 what each ministry and department owned and owed. Nor was it possible to calculate the net worth of the whole of the Government of Kenya. The OAGK suggested that the Kenyan Government adopted either an accrual or modified accrual basis of accounting based on International Public Sector Accounting Standards.

Case Study of the Ministry of Finance

As stated earlier, there is a high level of expectation placed on the Ministry of Finance to budget and manage public sector financial resources.

However, the OAGK appears to have major concerns about the Ministry of Finance's reporting. The Ministry of Finance's *Statement of Receipts into and Issues from the Exchequer Account* for year ending 2012 received a qualified audit opinion from the OAGK (OAGK 2013b). This was because the Ministry of Finance over-issued KES6 billion from the Exchequer Account without parliamentary approval. It also received a qualified audit opinion for its *Financial Statements for Vote R.07* because of KES85.58 million worth of non-clarified expenditure, KES224 million mis-allocated expenditure, KES50 million unbudgeted expenditure, KES35.91 million over-expenditure and KES33 million unreconciled disbursements. *Financial Statements for Vote R.07*'s Statement of Assets and Liabilities was weakened by an unreconciled amount of KES115.2 billion and a lack of preparation of recurrent cashbook bank reconciliation. This compromised the accuracy of the cashbook with a balance of KES442.2 million. There was also no supporting documentation supporting movements in accounts related to standing imprest, special imprest, temporary imprest, advance of salary, items awaiting clearance, provincial/district suspense, Paymaster General and stale cheques worth in total KES695.3 million.

In contrast, the Ministry of Finance's *Financial Statements for Vote D.07* received a disclaimer of opinion from the OAGK (OAGK 2013b). Here, *Financial Statements for Vote D.07* contained discrepancies between the appropriation account and the ledger of KES48.77 million, discrepancies between the appropriation account and payment vouchers of KES967.6 million, under-expenditure in the appropriation account of KES5.8 billion and under-collection of appropriations-in-aid of KES3.7 b. 496.4 m. *Financial Statements for Vote D.07*'s Statement of Assets and Liabilities also had long outstanding debit and credit balances of KES47.6 billion and KES31.9 billion respectively. Further, debit balances of accounts totalling KES16.4 billion and credit balances of KES20 million had not been analysed and ascertained, thus further weakening governance.

The Ministry of Finance also received a qualified opinion for its *Statement of Assets and Liabilities for the Consolidated Fund Services*, which contained a Paymaster General Account balance of KES104.2 billion which was unsupported by documentation. The difficulty of constructing an account balance without documentation is that it is difficult to verify the balance stated. In relation to *The Financial Statements to Subscriptions* it was noted that KES107.2 billion subscriptions allegedly received by the government could not be confirmed by the international organizations. The *Statement of Expenditure for Public Debt* was also qualified with a matter of concern raised about expenditure of KES690 million 'on a project which did not take off and against which no value for money was realized' (OAGK 2013b, p. 12). Moreover, an emphasis of matter was made by the OAGK to stress the fact that the public debt balance has risen to KES1382.3 billion.

An adverse opinion was expressed by the OAGK on the Ministry of Finance's Statement of Assets and Liabilities of the Government Clearing Agency Fund which had a balance of KES284.8 million unverified by documentation. The Statement of Expenditure for the Consolidated Fund Services—Salaries, Allowances and Miscellaneous Services received a qualified opinion for under-colleting KES25.5 billion, suggesting 'persistent underlying weaknesses in the budgeting' (OAGK 2013b, p. 13).

In the Ministry of Finance's Statement of Outstanding Loans, the OAGK noted that KES87 billion was outstanding. In addition its Statement of the Provident Fund, Statement of the Asian Officers Family Pension Fund, Statement of Assets and Liabilities for Pensions and Gratuities Funds, Statements of the European Widows and Orphans Pension Scheme, Financial Statements of the District Cash Fund Account, Financial Statements of the Civil Contingencies Fund, Financial Statements of the Rural Enterprise Fund, Financial Statements of the Kenya Local Loan Support Fund, Financial Statements of the Asiatic Widows and Orphans Pension Fund and Statements of the Petroleum Development Levy Fund were all qualified.

An adverse opinion was also expressed by the OAGK for the Ministry's Financial Statements of the Treasury Main Clearance Fund with concerns that many of the debts amounting to KES3.7 billion were outstanding for a long time and that there had been an 'inordinate delay in recovery of the debts' (OAGK 2013b, p. 45). The accuracy of the sundry creditor's balance of KES3.4 billion could also not be assured. An adverse opinion was also levelled at the Statement of Assets and Liabilities for Deposits. Here, an unreconciled amount of KES15.5 billion was linked to the Paymaster General Account. Cash balances of KES445 billion had not been remitted to the Exchequer.

Discussion

The results of the study are informed by the chapter's theoretical constructs. Despite the very high numbers of unqualified, adverse and disclaimer audit opinions received by Kenyan public sector entities from the OAGK, the OAGK itself appears to have met the demands of what Ossewaarde, Nijhof and Heyse (2008) term regulatory (abiding rules and laws), normative (collective accounting of responsibility), cognitive (conformity of mission through knowledge and expertise) and output (transparent accounts and evidence) legitimacy.

In terms of regulatory legitimacy the OAGK has carefully cited local legislation to show how many ministries and departments do not meet national expectations of governance. The Ministry of Finance in particular is charged with wide-ranging governance expectations, which from the public audit perspectives, it appears unable or unwilling to meet. For years ending 2012 and 2013 the OAGK explained how it audits through the guidance of the Constitution and Public Audit Act (2003), the International Standards on Auditing, Government Financial Regulations and Procedures and Public Finance Management Act, 2012 so that it can obtain reasonable assurance about whether financial statements of public sector entities are free from material misstatements. It might be said that the timeliness of reporting is open to question as the publication of the year ending 2014 report is still pending but, in contrast to the difficulties of auditing reporting faced in other jurisdictions (Brown 2011), it has attempted to display its regulatory legitimacy.

Its expressions of collective accounting of responsibility are somewhat underplayed. It seldom frames its legitimacy through overt ethical statements. It might be argued that this responsibility rests with the parliamentary watchdogs of Kenya—the PAC and PIC—but given the very low number of the qualified financial statements prepared by Kenyan public sector entities there appears room for the OAGK to consider how it might improve its display of normative legitimacy to win over a key stakeholder base.

The OAGK's cognitive legitimacy is well demonstrated in the audit reports. The OAGK frames its audit by way of analysis of revenue statements and appropriation accounts. It hones in on unsupported and excessive expenditure. It comments on the management of imprests. It summarises the state of the whole of the Kenyan government's accounting records. It dwells on the statement of the whole of the government's assets and liabilities, and it probes the maintenance of bank and cash accounts. The OAGK's conformity of mission and purpose suggests that it provides a holistic picture of the state of accountability of the public sector of Kenya.

There appears scope for the Permanent Secretary, Treasury, Accounting Officers and Management to consider indigenous alternatives to improve the corporate governance of ministries and departments. Development practice might pay attention to placed-based conceptions of economy and community and identity. Arguably its keenest form of legitimacy is its output legitimacy. Figurations and tabulations are presented throughout the audit reports. There appears, however, room for expansion of normative legitimacy. Here the OAGK may open up the possibilities of using the theory of indigenous alternatives to generate an enhanced form of collective accounting of responsibility as follows.

First, there is scope for the OAGK to provide feedback by indigenous parliamentary watchdogs such as the Parliamentary Accounts Committee in the audits reports of the OAGK. Odhiambo-Mbai (2003) notes that parliament has taken little action to prosecute ministers or department heads for weak governance practices. It is timely, however, to use parliamentary commentaries in the audit reports to showcase the level of parliamentary criticism of the governance issues. It would also be instructive if the OAGK commented on the depth of scrutiny by Kenyan parliamentary committees of its audit reports. In this way, readers of the OAGK audit reports may gather a sense of the milieu of accountability of parliamentary accountability in Kenya.

Second, there is also an opportunity for the OAGK to record indigenous management responses to past audits of ministries and departments. There are a considerable number of qualified and disclaimed opinions expressed by the OAGK on compliance issues. It would be instructive to know how management responds to each of these observations on compliance. In this way, the reader of an audit report may get a sense of the difficulties management faces in complying with reporting governance. Lack of compliance may result, for example, by a lack of accounting resources or lack of accounting expertise. This could be easily rectified at a local level.

Third, in accordance with the tenets of the theory of indigenous alternatives, there appears scope for the OAGK to use oral forms of accountability for Kenya's taxpayers. Here, the OAGK might use different mediums of oral communication (e.g. radio and broadcasting media) to summarise the main audit findings to an interested community that may not have the time to read a detailed written audit report. Work by the Office of the Auditor General of Western Australia, for example, regularly presents oral summarised audit reports to the media that may be understood by literate and non-literate listeners.

Fourth, the theory of indigenous alternatives embraces the idea of local peoples' capacity to shape the development of governance. The OAGK may consider how to include local indigenous Kenyan feedback of the results of audit. In this way a seemingly indifferent ministry or department may take notice of a groundswell of opinion at grassroots level. Local level feedback on audit findings might consider an appropriate form of punishment for non-compliance given that billions of Kenyan shillings worth of inefficiencies in governance are occurring in Kenya on a yearly basis.

Fifth, it appears that one of the largest and most influential ministries on financial governance—the Ministry of Finance—owes local indigenous Kenyans an explanation of why it is not fulfilling its governance remit. It might be prudent for the OAGK to make space for these explanations in the annual OAGK audit. This will provide balanced perspectives for the public to understand not only the OAGK audit by the National Treasury which plays a critical role in public financial management. In the absence of any counter response to explain and in a simplified language glaring and alarming audit reports, Kenyans might argue that if the Ministry of Finance with its vast pool of resources is not able to govern properly, then it sets a poor example for the rest of the nation to abide by governance principles.

Sixth, given the enormous size of Kenya's public sector, there appears room for greater resources to be made available to the OAGK. The OAGK's record of fulfilling four levels of legitimacy appears to be consistent with the theory of indigenous alternatives in empowering local institutions to further the voices of indigenous people. Public understanding of audit reports is critical in eliciting public participation in this quintessential governance debate. This is also consistent with the Kenyan Constitution which has emphasised public participation in governance at both levels of governments—National and County.

Conclusion

Through the theory of indigenous alternatives, this chapter has considered corporate governance principles over a period of time (2011–2013) by using critical textual analysis of annual reports of the Office of the Auditor General on issues of governance and ethics. We found that the state auditor's framing of governance and ethical issues was based on introduced functionalist forms of development. Over a three-year period the percentage of qualified financial statements of ministries and departments had increased from 0 to 12 %. We have recommended six forms of local governance initiatives that may help ministries and departments of Kenya improve financial statement reporting. It appears that if corporate governance is to thrive in Kenya, then the public sector needs to set an example for all other sectors in the economy to follow.

References

Andon, P., Free, C., & Sivabalan, P. (2014). The legitimacy of new assurance providers: Making the cap fit. *Accounting, Organizations and Society, 39*, 75–96.

Barako, D. G. (2014). *Financial accountability in Africa*. Paper presented at fórum of African Association for Public Administrators and Management (AAPAM) titled; Enhancing Governance and Financial Administration in Africa, Gaborene, 15th–17th July.

Barako, D. G., & Brown, A. M. (2008). Corporate social reporting and board representation: Evidence from the Kenyan banking sector. *Journal of Management and Governance, 12*, 309–324 (Springer Netherlands, Netherlands).

Barako, D. G., & Brown, A. M. (2009). Evaluating anti-money laundering initiatives: A country perspective. *Evaluation Journal of Australasia, 9*(2), 16–23.

Barako, D. G., Taplin, R. H., & Brown, A. M. (2010). HIV/AIDS information by African companies: An empirical analysis. *Journal of Asian and African Studies, 45*(4), 387–405.

Brass, J. N. (2012). Blurring boundaries: The integration of NGOs into Governance in Kenya. *Governance: An International Journal of Policy, Administration, and Institutions, 25*(2), 209–235.

Brown, A. M. (2011). The milieu of government reporting in Vanuatu. *Pacific Accounting Review, 23*(2), 165–184.

Brown, A. M. (2013). Auditing Solomon Islands' health and medical governance. *Clinical Governance: An International Journal, 18*(3), 200–209.

Brown, A. M. (2014). The challenges of accountability in a national museum. *Museum Management and Curatorship, 29*(4), 311–326.

Curry, G. N. (2003). Moving beyond post development: facilitating indigenous alternatives for development. *Economic Geography, 79*(3), 405–423.

Diamond, J. (2002). *The role of internal audit in Government financial management: An International Perspectives* (IMF Working Paper. WP/02/94).

Goodson, S. G., Mary, K. J., Lapointe, J. R. (2012). Supplemental Guidance: The role of auditing in Public Sector Governance, The Institute of Internal Auditors, http\\na.theiia.org/standardsguidance/Public%20Documents/Public_Sector_Governance1_1_pdf

Hassid, J., & Brass, J. (2015). Scandals, media and good governance in China and Kenya. *Journal of Asian and African Studies, 50*(3), 325–342.

Hope, K. R. (2012). Managing the public sector in Kenya: Reform and transformation for improved performance. *Journal of Public Administration and Governance, 2*(4), 128–143.

Hoque, Z., & Thiagarajah, T. (2015). Public accountability and the role of the Auditor General in legislative oversight. In Z. Hoque (Ed.), *Making governments accountable: The role of public accounts and the national audit office* (pp. 3–23). Abingdon, Oxon: Routledge.

Hynes, N. (2010, February). Governance & ethics in Kenya. *Accountancy Ireland*, 42(1), 56–58.

Jacobs, K., & Jones, K. (2009). Legitimacy and parliamentary oversight in Australia: The rise and fall of two public accounts committees. *Accounting, Auditing & Accountability Journal, 22*(1), 13–34.

Jones, K. (2006). Exactly on all-fours with the English precedent – Establishing a public accounts committee in the antipodes. *Victorian Historical Journal, 77*(2), 194–211.

Jones, K., & Jacobs, K. (2006). Governing the government: The paradoxical place of the public accounts committee. *Australian Parliamentary Review, 21*(1), 63–79.

Jones, K., & Jacobs, K. (2009). Public accounts committees, new public management, and institutionalism: A case study. *Politics & Policy, 37*(5), 1023–1046.

K'akumu, O. A. (2004). Privatization of the urban water supply in Kenya: Policy options for the poor. *Environment and Urbanization, 16*(2), 213–222.

Katumanaga, M. (2013). Multi-partism and the political economy of exclusion in Kenya. In K. Njogu (Ed.), *Citizen participation in decision making: Towards inclusive development in Kenya*. Nairobi, Kenya: Twaweza Communication.

Kobia, M., & Mohamed, N. (2006). *The Kenyan experience with performance contracting*. Paper presented at the 28th African Association of Public Administrators and Management (AAPAM) Round Table Conference, Arusha, Tanzania, 4th–8th December.

Lienert, I., & Modi, J. (1997). *A decade of civil service reforms in sub-Saharan Africa* (IMF Working Paper. WP/97.179).

Ministry of Finance. (2015). National Treasury, http://www.treasury.go.ke/index.php/aboutus1/background-information

Montano, D. (2009). Financial accountability: Enhancing the functions of the public accounts committees in Trinidad and Tobago. *The Parliamentarian, 3*, 232–235.

Muthaura, F. K. (2010). *The role of Kenya's public service in a changing global environment: Opportunities and challenges*. Paper presented at Kenya Association of Public Administrators and Management (KAPAM) Annual Meeting, Nairobi, Kenya, 9th December.

Nolte, K., & Väth, S. (2015). Interplay of land governance and large-scale agricultural investment: Evidence from Ghana and Kenya. *The Journal of Modern African Studies, 53*(1), 69–92.

Nyamori, R. D., & Nyamori, B. (2015). Evolution and effectiveness of the Kenyan Public Accounts Committee. In Z. Hoque (Ed.), *Making governments accountable: The role of public accounts and the national audit office* (pp. 275–292). Abingdon, Oxon: Routledge.

Nyamori, R. D., and Gekara, V. O. (in press). Performance contracting and social capital (re)formation: A case study of Nairobi City Council in Kenya. *Critical Perspectives on Accounting*, http:\\dx.doi.org/10.1016/j.cpa.2015.06.004

OAGK. (2013a). Auditor-General on the Appropriation Accounts, Other Public Accounts and the Accounts of the Funds of the Republic of Kenya for the Year 2012/2013: Summary of the Report of Auditor-General for the Year 2011/2012, Office of the Auditor General, Nairobi.

OAGK. (2013b). Report of the Auditor General on the Appropriation Accounts, Other Public Accounts and the Accounts of the Funds for the Republic of Kenya for the Year 2011/2012, Office of the Auditor General, Nairobi.

OAGK. (2014). Auditor-General on the Appropriation Accounts, Other Public Accounts and the Accounts of the Funds of the Republic of Kenya for the

Year 2012/2013: Summary of the Report of Auditor-General for the Year 2012/2013, Office of the Auditor General, Nairobi.

Odhiambo-Mbai, C. (2003). Public service accountability and governance in Kenya since independence. *African Journal of Political Science, 8*(1), 113–145.

Osman, A. D., Lin, V., Robinson, P., & Jackson, D. (2011). Policy and governance issues in Kenya's border towns: The case of Wajir groundwater management. *The Australasian Review of African Studies, 32*(1), 32–58.

Ossewaarde, R., A. Nijhof and L. H. (2008). Dynamics of NGO Legitimacy: How organizing betrays core missions of Ingos. *Public Administration and Development, 28*(1), 42–53.

Ouma, S. (2010). Global standards, local realities: Private agrifood governance and the restructuring of the Kenyan horticulture industry. *Economic Geography, 86*(2), 197–222.

Parker, L. D. (2014). Corporate social accountability through action: Contemporary insights from British industrial pioneers. *Accounting, Organizations and Society, 38*, 632–659.

Pelizzo, R. (2010). Public Accounts Committees in the Pacific Region. *Politics & Policy, 38*(1), 117–137.

Porter, S., Brown, A. M., Purushothaman, M., & Scharl, A. (2006). The strategies of the IASB and its funders. *Journal of Strategic Change, 15*(6), 305–317.

Rahaman, A. S. (2010). Critical accounting research in Africa: Whence and whither. *Critical Perspectives on Accounting, 21*, 420–427.

Samsuddin, R. S., & Mohamed, N. (2009). The magnitude of public accounts committee's (PAC's) work in reviewing and reporting on state governments' financial statements. *Malaysian Accounting Review, 8*(2), 1–15.

Shore, C., & Wright, S. (1990). Audit culture and anthropology: Neo-liberalism in British higher education. *Journal of the Royal Anthropological Institute, 5*, 557–575.

Sian, S. (2006). Inclusion, exclusion and control: The case of the Kenyan accounting professionalisation project. *Accounting, Organizations and Society, 31*(3), 295–322.

Sian, S. (2007a). Reversing exclusion: The Africanisation of accountancy in Kenya, 1963–1970. *Critical Perspectives on Accounting, 18*(7), 831–872.

Sian, S. (2007b). Patterns of prejudice: Social exclusion and racial demarcation in professional accountancy in Kenya. *Accounting Historians Journal, 34*(2), 1–42.

Sian, S. (2010). Between the lines: The professionalisation of accountancy in Kenya. In C. Poullaos & S. Sian (Eds.), *Accountancy and empire: The British legacy of professional organisation*. Routledge New Works in Accounting History.

Taplin, R., Zhao, Y., & Brown, A. M. (2014). Failure of Auditors: The lack of compliance for business combinations in China. *Regulation & Governance, 8*, 310–331. doi:10.1111/rego.12011.

10

Conclusions

Kerry E. Howell

Continual inquiry in the search for understanding and truth identifies a central rationale for being and defines a continuing dialectical objective for human existence. However, as discussed in Chap. 2, the world we attempt to comprehend is opaque and our understandings of 'self is in many respects unknown and alien to itself' (Dillon 1997, p. 9). As we undertake inquiries we seek to 'overcome the world's otherness and our own self-estrangement', as both world and self 'transcend us' (ibid.). Given the shortcomings regarding our ability to comprehend the world and ourselves can we use the idea of progress in arts and culture, or the concept of an ideal society, against which the imperfections and shortcomings of actual social existence may be assessed? Ideas regarding the ideal social structure range from a golden age, the Platonic Republic and Utopia through to different models of existence identified by Enlightenment philosophers. 'Whatever the origins of such visions the conception itself

K.E. Howell (✉)
Graduate School of Management, Plymouth Business School, Plymouth University, Plymouth, UK
Newcastle Business School, Northumbria University, Newcastle Upon Tyne, UK

K.E. Howell, M.K. Sorour (eds.), *Corporate Governance in Africa*,
DOI 10.1057/978-1-137-56700-0_10

rests on the conviction that there exists true, immutable, universal, timeless objective values valid for all men, everywhere, at all times; that these values are at least in principle realisable, whether or not human beings are or have been, or ever will be, realising on earth' (Berlin 1979, p. 121). Such ideals provide a template against which imperfect existing modes of governance may be measured and assessed. The ideal corporate governance structure involves ethical, moral activity undertaken by human beings on the basis of developing a 'good' or 'just' environment. The ideal notion of corporate governance should involve an ethical approach which includes customs, rituals and values as well as organizational cultures: balanced objectives for all interested parties and the participation of key stakeholders in the company; open decision-making processes that provide equal access for the concerns of all stakeholders; that is, accountable and transparent procedures for all stakeholders (including shareholders). However, as this text has identified it is always difficult to define the concept of 'good', 'just' or ethical and the activities that best ensure such outcomes. We have identified means of achieving and measuring the idea of 'good' or 'just' in terms of social contact, self-interest (egoism) and common-interest (altruism) as well as problems regarding values and culture in relation to universal and relative principles. In addition, we have discussed and offered different philosophical approaches through paradigms of inquiry and methodologies for dealing with these difficult issues.

Even though an ideal structure may be posited this text perceives corporate governance as a socially constructed entity that varies in accordance with the historical and cultural values within which it is embedded. Case studies in African corporate governance have been undertaken to identify distinctions regarding cultural and ethical perspectives. Indeed, in Chap. 1 we identified the notion of social contract outlined by Hobbes, Locke, Rousseau and Kant and, based on these contractual arrangements, provided governance frameworks in relation to ethical perspectives. The emphasis on these thinkers/philosophers involved the development of the social contract as underpinning governance and ethics for social existence; issues such as egoism, altruism, relativism and universalism were outlined as were deontological and teleological ethical perspectives. Chapter 1 identified a framework through which analysis of governance and specifically corporate governance may be undertaken as well as developed relationships between general ethical perspectives and values in relation to those in the individual African states. Chapter 2 provided the paradigms of inquiry as the basis for the methodological approaches that may be used for undertaking research from a phenomenological and relativist position. Critical theory and constructivism involve interpretive perspectives which emphasise understanding and elevate the relationship (epistemology) between interpretation and the phenomenon under investigation. Critical theory and constructivist paradigms of inquiry involve notions of empowerment, challenges to injustice in social relations and pursue improvement for individual existence. Both constructivism and critical theory have a close connection with everyday life (life-world) and the abolition of social injustice. Each is underpinned by a phenomenological philosophical position (understanding through experience) and operationalised through methodological approaches such as grounded theory, phenomenological hermeneutics and constructivist ethnography. The studies presented in this text identified either critical theory or constructivist paradigms of inquiry and in most instances grounded theory was the preferred methodological approach. Case studies supplied a critique of the existing state of affairs in relation to the universal perspectives identified by global forces as well as relativist positions and perceived deficiencies in specific African states. Critical theory and constructivism studies provide rich understandings of the corporate governance phenomenon in specific situations through qualitative, inductive procedures. Such paradigms are normally 'inductive qualitative (and) allow the researcher to identify the main concern of a group of subjects and the behaviours they use to resolve their main concern' (Artinian et al. 2009, p. 3). Underpinned with historical/relativist ontologies, critical theory and constructivist methodologies can offer a deep understanding of socially constructed phenomena (Guba and Lincoln 1994).

In Chap. 3 Nwanji provided an in depth understanding of ethical perspectives in relation to relative and universal positions identified by Howell in Chaps. 1 and 2. This chapter outlined deontological and teleological ethical perspectives regarding corporate governance in general as well as global and relativist perspectives. Chapter 3 discussed ethical issues and the conduct of those who manage the affairs of corporations (directors' duties and responsibilities towards their stakeholders). Boards of directors have many responsibilities, some statutory and others based on trust. Accountability of directors is a central issue in general contexts but explicitly in terms of profit and loss accounts, the balance sheet and shareholder interests. The world economy depends on the capitalist and shareholder systems, which requires trust and credibility. Good and effective corporate governance is needed to achieve long-term business objectives of the corporation as well as profitability for shareholders and stakeholders. There may also be the need to introduce a 'global corporate governance' system that comprised both the Anglo-Saxon system (the shareholder model, also known as Anglo-American) and the German stakeholder system (stakeholder model). Ethical perspectives underpin notions of 'good' corporate governance which can be developed through both shareholder and stakeholder models. Chapter 3 proposes that the integrity and commitment of the board rather than compliance is at the root of accountability and relationships between corporate ethics and corporate objectives both at board level and amongst other organisational members.

Chapter 4 dealt with North Africa where Sorour and El Sakhawy used constructivism and grounded theory to investigate whether weak corporate governance may be seen as a dominant reason behind bank failures in Egypt during the late 1990s and the associated current problems that the Egyptian Banking System (EBS) is currently experiencing. Corporate governance reform and culture change in EBS witnessed serious efforts over the last decade to introduce ethical reform and 'good' governance. This drive for reform has arisen through pressures from universal and relative positions in terms of the CBE, international organisations such as the World Bank, the Basel Committee and the Egyptian government. The bank governance reform process was seen as imperative to the enablement of 'good' corporate governance in a safe and healthy banking system. Two main developments can be seen as the building blocks of changes in corporate governance culture: the corporate governance code and the creation of a corporate governance unit at the EBI. However, results have illustrated that current compliance levels with the required disclosures is low, suggesting that awareness problems along with lax enforcement are challenges that need to be addressed. Even though recent political and economic turbulences have interrupted the reforms further emphasis is required regarding ethical variables in the corporate governance structure. Here, the CBE leadership should ensure stronger ethical enforcement of the corporate governance code and at the same time encourage banking leaders to engage with good corporate governance procedures.

In Chap. 5 Boadu undertook a constructivist study of Ghana and noted that the nature of the Ghanaian business environment allowed traditional cultural values to permeate the governance practice but pointed out that these practices can fall short of promoting ethical, responsible and transparent corporate governance. A grounded theory study identified eight categories: ethics, accountability, effectiveness, culture, government interference, regulations, training and education and weak institutions and limited leadership. Through further analysis the study identified the influence of culture on governance practices as the core category. In a relativist context Ghanaian culture, values and norms influence corporate governance practices. However, through a universal perspective, corporate governance regulations and guidelines are expected to adhere to Western perspectives that do not reflect the Ghanaian culture. Indeed, because of a synthesis of these domains (universal and relativist) major elements of Ghanaian corporate governance practice that emerged from the study differed from the occidental model which included weak institutions, government interventions, political interference, gift giving/receiving, and deference to authority. Boadu argued that the extent to which gift giving or receiving is ethical or unethical involved four factors, which included: the intent, amount, the context, and the timing. Indeed the chapter concluded that the act of gift giving and gift receiving was a cultural phenomenon and not an unethical governance practice in itself. Gift giving and receiving was not negative because it assisted in establishing or enhancing all types of business relationships. The current state of corporate governance in Ghana could be improved. However, in attempting to do so, we need to look at how the positive aspects of Ghanaian culture together with best universal practices could be utilised to strengthen and develop good corporate governance.

In Chap. 6 Ibrahim continues the West African theme and explores non-economic variables to provide an understanding of corporate governance activities in banks in Nigeria and identify why these banks continue to fail despite continued government regulatory reform initiatives, such as privatisation and consolidation by different regimes (including international organisations). Through a constructivist grounded theory approach the study identified the need for greater altruism when applying corporate governance procedures and the utilisation of social contractual mechanisms to enable common-interest and trust. Human agency and leadership were the main factors in the corporate governance process and findings were identified through a substantive theoretical framework that emphasised leadership and culture variables. In addition, the chapter posited that effective corporate governance could not be addressed through codes or government regulations alone, other variables relating to human nature and behaviour were required as well as accountability and trust. In other words, to implement corporate governance procedures there was the need to employ the principles of social contract arrangements and develop notions of trust. This moral reasoning and motivation collectively strengthens the leadership and other stakeholders to overcome the embedded self-interests of decision-makers and lack of transparency in the activities of banks in Nigeria.

Chapter 7 deals with another West African country where Faye investigated corporate governance in The Gambia and identified that codes and regulations were not currently part of the regulatory framework for the banking industry. Through constructivist grounded theory Faye developed a substantive theory regarding the Gambian banking system and outlined a proposed ethical code of conduct. The combination of grounded theory and social constructivist paradigms enabled a strategy for exploring corporate governance regulation within context of the Gambian banking system. The bank corporate governance regulatory framework that currently existed was inconsistent and seen as a 'fractured … corporate governance regulatory framework'. Most banks have developed voluntary corporate governance codes and frameworks for internal use. Indeed, in certain instances these practices have been imposed on them by the main (international, and external) company which was reflected within the formation of internal control mechanisms. As a consequence of these strategies, banks are likely to be accountable and ethical, thereby enhancing supervision, compliance and trust. These will ultimately protect the interest of shareholders. However, the level of relativist values in relation to universal perspectives is unclear but through a synthesis of these positions distinct cultural values may be observed. Indeed, corporate governance regulation of countries and organisations are uniquely affected by a number of factors, including legal, regulatory, human, organisational and cultural factors. The study was aimed at assisting key stakeholders—such as investors, management and regulators—to address challenges, including obstacles that are impeding the development of and improving the corporate governance framework.

In Chap. 8 Dube concentrated on South Africa and analysed corporate governance and the King Reports from an African socio-economic and cultural perspective. Dube used the critical theorist paradigm of inquiry which enabled the dialogic interpretation of the changes in the corporate governance reports through an application of *ubuntu*. South Africa found itself on the road to democracy in 1994 and the sweeping reforms meant radical changes. The concept of *ubuntu* was more pronounced in King (ii) which considered that 'governance in any context reflects the value system of the society in which it operates … (consequently) it would be pertinent to observe and to take account of the African worldview and culture in the context of governance of companies in South Africa' (p. 17). However, it should be noted that the King Reports are Anglo-Saxon in nature and South African corporate governance largely based on the shareholder approach and the Reports seek to harmonise different perspectives through the spirit of inclusivity. The interpretation of the key changes in the King Reports through *ubuntu* sought to capture an 'African worldview and culture in the context of the governance of companies in South Africa' (p. 17). Indeed, in relation to the distinction between relative and universal perspectives in South Africa Okari et al. (2012) argued that 'corporate governance systems are culturally influenced and … existing theories in the realm of contemporary corporate governance systems are alien to the African culture and therefore might not offer sufficient solutions to challenges facing organizations operating in the African environment' (p. 24). Finally, through a critical theory approach Chap. 9 identified issues in East Africa where Barako and Brown develop a comprehension of constructions by the Office of the Auditor General of Kenya on corporate governance. Through the theory of indigenous alternatives, this chapter considered corporate governance principles over a period of time (2011–2013) by using critical textual analysis of the annual reports of the Office of the Auditor General on issues of Governance and Ethics. This chapter identified that the state auditor's framing of governance and ethical issues were based on functionalist forms of development. Fundamentally, corporate governance in Kenya needed to take the public sector as an example for other sectors in the economy to follow.

Many of the studies undertaken for this text used grounded theory methodology or an ethnographic approach based on phenomenology as well as critical theory and constructivist paradigms of inquiry. This enabled in-depth analysis, understanding and experiential validity of the individual cases. 'Experiential validity incorporates the level to which the research … reflects real life experience (and) … questions the level that the research captures or reflects people's everyday lives' (Howell 2013, p. 189). Reliability is more problematic and generalisation difficult. Consequently, we consider that the cases outlined in this text provide examples of transferability to similar situations and that each can inform an understanding of African corporate governance in general. Regional differences exist between the cases but similarities may be identified. Where this is most explicit is in the studies undertaken regarding West Africa (Ghana, Nigeria and The Gambia).

'Transferability reflects aspects of external validity and the extent findings can be generalised to other settings and/or situations. Phenomenological research entails in-depth study of groups and pursues depth of understanding regarding unique situations' (Howell 2013, p. 190). 'Thick descriptions' (i.e. including context) are the objective of this type of research, which through interpretive methods become 'thick interpretations' which provide a database that facilitates judgements about transferability of cases to other situations (Vidich and Lyman 2000).

In general, each chapter provided ethical perspectives and emphasised relationships between relative and universal perspectives of values and culture and the impact these have on the formulation of corporate governance in individual African states. Each state has been influenced by global or international variables (in some instances through remnants of colonisation) as well as the culture and values of the specific situation in relation to historical development. As noted by Berlin (1979), the ideal exists but it is unlikely that this will be realised by humanity. A general perspective of what corporate governance should entail is an important yardstick; however, given local values, customs symbols and rituals the lessons relayed by Herodotus as well as Protagoras and others should be heeded and corporate governance in individual states explicitly incorporate local culture. In each African state or case ethical perspectives were implicitly apparent in terms of trust, accountability and responsibility as were the relationships with shareholder and stakeholder models. Relationships exist through generic expectations regarding governance procedures and relativist notions that further inform local development through individual cultural perspectives.

References

Artinian, B. M., Giske, T., & Cone, P. H. (2009). *Glaserian grounded theory in nursing research: Trusting emergence*. New York: Springer.

Berlin, I. (1979). Vico and the ideal of enlightenment. In H. Hardy (Ed.), *Against the current: Essays in the history of ideas* (pp. 120–129). Oxford: Oxford University Press.

Dillon, M. C. (1997). *Merleau-Ponty's Ontology*. Evanston Illinois: Northwestern University.

Guba, E. G., & Lincoln, Y. S. (1994). Competing paradigms in qualitative research. In N. Denzin & Y. S. Lincoln (Eds.), *Handbook of qualitative research* (pp. 105–117). Thousand Oaks: Sage.

Howell, K. E. (2013). *An introduction to the philosophy of methodology*. London: Sage Publications.

King Report on Corporate Governance in South Africa. (2002). Institute of Directors. Johannesburg, South Africa (March 2002). http://www.iodsa.co.za/?kingIII. Accessed 3 June 2015.

King Report ii. (2009). King code of governance for South Africa. (Online). Available from: http://www.ecgi.org/codes/documents/king3.pdf. Accessed 3 June 2015.

Okari, H., Keraro, V., & Kiambati, H. (2012). The principle of participation in corporate governance; An African perspective. *IJMBS, 2*(3), 24–28.

Vidich, A. S., & Lyman, S. M. (2000). Qualitative methods their history in sociology and anthropology. In Denzin, N. K., & Lincoln, Y. S. (Eds.), *Handbook of qualitative research* (pp. 37–84). Thousand Oaks, CA: Sage Publications.

Index

A

accountability, 49, 62, 117, 140, 165, 167, 185, 187, 204, 205, 224–30
Accounting and Auditing Organisation for Islamic Finance Institutions (AAOIFI), 180
Africa, 2–3, 69–93
African Development Bank (ADB), 163–168, 171
Agu, C.C., 165
Akinboade, O.A., 203
altruism, 2, 19, 250, 254
Amel, D., 138
Anglo-American model, 21
Anscombe, G.E.M., 56–7
Arab Gambia Islamic Bank, 180
Artigas, M., 179
axiology, 34

B

Bank of Ghana (BoG), 100
Barako, D.G., 223–43
Barsade, S.G., 109
Basu, K., 107
Berlin, I., 256
Boadu, M., 97–126
board evaluation, 103–4
Bourdieu, P., 148
Brass, J.N., 228
Brown, A., 22
Brown, A.M., 223–43

K.E. Howell, M.K. Sorour (eds.), *Corporate Governance in Africa*,
DOI 10.1057/978-1-137-56700-0

Bryant, A., 182
Bryman, A., 182
Bulmer, M., 183

C

Cadbury Report, 49, 201
capitalism, 36
categorical imperative, 13
Cavana, R.Y., 61
Central Bank of Egypt (CBE), 70, 72–92
Central Bank of Nigeria (CBN), 134, 140, 141
Central Bank of The Gambia (CBG), 173
Charkham, P.J., 137
Charmaz, K., 145, 174, 175, 178, 183
Choo, J., 2
citizenship, 181, 217
Code of Corporate Governance for Banks, 138–9
code of ethics, 114–15
Collis, 101
commitment, 206
community governance, 19
Company and Allied Matters Act (CAMA), 137–9
competence, 206
compliance level, 90–2
Conger, J.A., 147
conscience, 206
constructivism, 33–7, 42–4
Corbin, J., 182, 186
Corbin, J.M., 73
corporate governance, 1–4, 250–7
  analytical approach, 60–3
  business ethics, 60–1
  constructivism, 33–7, 42–4
  critical theory, 33–41
  definition, 49–51
  deontological *vs.* teleological, 57–8
  ethical perspectives, 11–17, 19–23
  ethics, 55–7
  global debate, 51–5
  levels, 17–19
  shareholder theory, 59–60
  social contracts, 4–11
  teleology, 57–9
  theoretical frameworks, 19–23
corporate social responsibility (CSR), 50, 116
courage, 206
critical theory, 33–41
Crosse, H.D., 165

D

Daily, C., 201
Darty-Baah, K., 200
Davies, H., 179
Davis, S.M., 148
deontology, 54–5
Dey, B.L., 71, 88
Diamond, J., 226
Donaldson, T., 62
Dube, Z.L., 199–220

E

ecological fallacy ethics, 164
egoism, 2, 6, 19, 250
Egyptian Banking Institute (EBI), 74–5, 79

Egyptian banking sector (EBS), 69–2
compliance level, 90–2
content, 79–80
efficiency and effectiveness, 83–4
enforcement, 79–80
governmental entities pressure, 77
Hawkamat Al-Sharikat, 84–5
independent entities pressure, 73–6
laws and regulations, 81
protection of interests, 78–9
public governance, 87
reform and culture, 72–5
reformers, 85–7
supervision processes, 82–3
Egyptian Codes of Corporate Governance, 80
Egyptian Institute of Directors (EIOD), 71, 77
Electronic Longman Dictionary, 81
Elias, A.A., 61, 62
enforcement, 83–4
epistemology, 33, 3640–3, 73, 200, 211–251
European Union, 51
Evan, W.M., 22

F

fairness, 205
family systems, 111–12
Faye, S., 159–89
Fligstein, N., 2
Flinstead, N., 23
Forster, W., 22
Freeland, R., 23
Freeman, E., 60, 61
Freeman, R.E., 22
free market, 18, 20, 60, 118
Friedman, M., 21, 48

G

Gambia, 159–62
constructivism, 171–4
corporate governance, 164–69
ethical codes, 179–84
grounded theory, 174–9
legislative and regulatory, 170–1
paucity of literature, 162–4
substantive theory, 185–7
Gergen, K.J., 40
Ghana, 99–101
accountability, 117
board evaluation, 103–4
board issues, 104–6
code of ethics 114–15
compliance and enforcement, 121–2
content, 120
corporate governance, 99–101
corporate social responsibility, 116
family systems, 111–12
gift giving/receiving, 107–10
government influence, 118–19
government interference, 118–20
methodology, 101–2
minority shareholder education, 117–18
respect for authority, 112–13
responsiveness, 114
training and minority shareholder awareness, 122–3
weak institutions and poor leadership, 124–5

Ghana Institute of Directors (GIoD), 102–3, 122–5
Ghana Stock Exchange (GSE), 99, 100
Gibson, 109
Glaser, B.G., 176
globalization, 18, 39, 53
goodwill, 12–13
Goulding, C., 144
governance. *See* corporate governance
government interference, 118–19
Greene, J.C., 172
Gregory, C.A., 107
grounded theory, 44, 101–2, 145, 171, 176–81
Gstrauntlhaler, T., 204, 217
Guba, E.G., 211
Guha, K., 171

H

Habermas, J., 18, 37, 38
Hampel Committee Report, 49, 62
Hampel, G.H., 165
Happiness Principle, 14
Hawkamat Al-Sharikat culture, 84–5
Haynes, C., 165
Heffernan, S.A., 165
Hegel, G.W.F., 30
Herodotus, 16
Heyse, L., 230
historical realism, 38
Hobbes, T., 6, 7, 151
Hofstede, G.H., 148
Honneth, A., 38
Horkheimer, M., 37
Howard, M., 165
Howell, K.E., 1–24, 29–44, 142, 143, 173, 177, 202, 249–57
human factor model, 184
humanity, 8, 9, 20
Hume, D., 8
Hussey, R., 101
hybridisation, 231

I

Ibrahim, U.A., 131–54
inclusivity of stakeholders, 206
indigenisation policy, 133n1
Institute of Certified Public Accountants of Kenya (ICPAK), 230
Integrated Financial Management Information System (IFMIS), 226
internal governance mechanisms, 139
Internal Revenue Service Act, 109
International Accounting Standards Board (IASB), 225
International Monetary Fund (IMF), 18

J

Johannesburg Stock Exchange, 203
Jolis, A., 181
Jones, R., 174, 181

K

Kalhoefer, C., 72
Kant, I., 10, 12, 13, 17, 214
Kaptein, M., 57, 58

Kelsall, T., 168, 169
Kenya, 223–7
  accountability, 228–30
  corporate governance, 227–8
  county governments, 235
  critical theory, 231
  ethical issues, 227–8
  hybridisation, 231–2
  ministries and departments, 233–4
  Ministry of Finance, 237–43
  OAGK, audit, 236–7
Khomba, J.K., 201
King Codes of Corporate Governance, 204
King Report, 199–201
  analysis, 213–19
  corporate governance, 201–6
  critical theory, 211–12
  methodology, 212–13
  ubuntu, 206–10

L

Lanoo, K., 202
legitimacy, 224, 240
Letza, S., 202, 218
Lienert, I., 226
Lincoln, Y.S., 211
Locke, J., 7, 8–9, 151
Longino, H., 41

M

Machiavelli, N., 56
market governance, 18
Martin, P.Y., 174
Mauss, M., 107
McAllister, P., 209
Metcalfe, C.E., 62
Mhlanga, D., 208
Ministry of Finance, 237–43
Modi, J., 226
Money Laundering Act, 171
morality, 11
Muhammad, Y., 181
Myers, M.D., 175

N

national culture influence, 98, 107
Ndondo, S., 208
Nigeria, 133–4
  corporate governance, banks, 132–6
  culture and leadership, 142, 147
  data analysis and substantive theory, 143–4
  information disclosure, 140–1
  internal control mechanisms, 139–40
  methodological approach, 142–3
  profile of banks, 133–4
  regulation and code of governance, 136–9
  selective coding, 144–6
  social contract theory, 151–2
  strategic approach, 151
  substantive theory, 147–51
  trust, 152–3
Nigerian Deposit Insurance Corporation (NDIC), 135
Nijhof, A., 230
Noble, G., 175, 181
North, D.C., 17
NPL problem, 72

Nussbaum, B., 207, 209, 210
Nwanji, T.I., 47–64
Nyamori, R.D., 228

O

Odhiambo-Mbai, C., 228
Office of the Auditor General of Kenya (OAGK), 223–4, 226–7, 232, 236–43
Okeahalam, C., 203
Okike, E.N.M., 132, 137
ontology, 15, 33, 38, 40, 41, 211, 212, 219
open coding analysis, 102, 143–4
Organisation for Economic Co-operation and Development (OECD), 51, 52, 86, 117, 120, 123, 201
Osborn, N.R., 149
Ouma, S., 227

P

Parkinson, J.E., 49
paucity of literature, 162–4
phenomenology, 29–30
Phillips, R., 63
Popper, K.R., 212
Prempeh, H.K., 101
Preston, L., 62

R

relativism, 14–16, 19
Report on the Observance of Standards and Codes (ROSC), 98, 114–15, 135
responsibility, 205
Robinson, A., 202
Rousseau, J.J., 9, 151
Roussouw, G.J., 2–3

S

Sakhawy, A.E., 69–92
Salem, R., 72
Sanusi, L.S., 140, 141
Sarbanes-Oxley Act (SOX), 52
Schein, E., 142
Schein, E.H., 85
Schwartz, H., 148
Schwartz, M.S., 181
Securities and Exchange Commission (SEC), 97, 100–1
Securities Industry Law, 99, 100
self-interest, 2, 6, 10, 17–22, 34, 116, 145, 146, 148, 149, 201
shareholdership, 23, 52, 64
shareholder theory, 59–60
Shleifer, A., 203
short-termism, 202
Sian, S., 230
Sibanda, P., 207
Smith, A., 19–20
social constructivism, 173, 174
social contract theory, 4–11, 151–2
Soludo, C., 135
Sorour, M.K., 69–92
South Africa, 199–201
  analysis, 213–19
  corporate governance, 201–6
  critical theory, 211–12
  methodology, 212–13
  ubuntu, 206–10

stakeholder model, 22
stakeholdership, 52, 63, 141, 219
State Enterprises Commission, 123
Steinberg, E., 202, 203
Stigler, G., 21
Strauss, A., 174, 182, 186
Strauss, A.L., 73
substantive theory, 147–8, 185–7
  cultural process, 148
  leadership process, 149
  substantive GT, 149–51
Sun, X., 218
supervision process, 82–3

T

Takatera, S., 106
Tawiah, K.A., 200, 217
teleological theory, 55–7
Ticker, R.I., 49
transparency, 205
Transparency Corruption Index (CPI), 87
Tricker, B., 203
Tricker, R.I., 140–1
trust, 152–3
Truth and Reconciliation Commission (TRC), 207
Turner, B.A., 174
Turyahikayo, E., 201, 208

U

ubuntu, 200, 201, 206–10, 213, 215, 218
UK, 51
universalism, 15, 250
unsocial sociability, 10
USA, 52
utilitarianism, 13, 55

V

Vishny, R.W., 203
Vittas, D., 165

W

Wasserman, J.A., 182
weak institutions and poor leadership, 102, 124–5
welfarism, 13–14
Wempe, J., 55, 57, 58
West, A., 216
Westminster parliamentary system, 228–9
Worrell, D., 165

Y

Yakasai, A.G.A., 132, 140
Yamamoto, M., 106